RETHINK

Gordon Rattray Taylor

RETHINK
A Paraprimitive Solution

The optimist proclaims that we live in the
best of all possible worlds; and the pessimist
fears this is true.

James Branch Cabell

BOOK CLUB ASSOCIATES
LONDON

This edition published 1972 by
Book Club Associates
By arrangement with Martin Secker & Warburg Limited
Copyright © Gordon Rattray Taylor 1972

Printed in Great Britain by
Richard Clay (The Chaucer Press) Limited
Bungay, Suffolk

For Denys and Susan

Contents

III. PROSPECTS FOR THE FUTURE

Foreword

A DAY or two after the war ended in 1945 I began to write a book in which I put forward a group of ideas about how Western society should be reorganized so as to give its members the greatest chance of attaining a measure of happiness. This was published in 1949 in England by the Bodley Head, and in 1950 in the USA by Houghton Mifflin under the title *Conditions of Happiness*. As it turned out, nobody wanted to reorganize Western society at that time: they just wanted to get rid of food and fuel rationing and pick up where they left off—except that in England a measure of socialism was favoured. So, though *Conditions of Happiness* received glowingly favourable notices and evoked letters from some prominent and perceptive people it made singularly little impact.

Today, many of the frustrations examined in that book have become of urgent interest. People are no longer so convinced that the familiar political approaches can solve these problems. So, twenty-five years later, I have returned to the subject. Though the presentation is completely different, many of the ideas put forward in *Conditions of Happiness* reappear in this book: there has been no need to alter them, for the passage of time has endorsed their validity. Some are even becoming quite fashionable, such as job enrichment, decentralization and the obsession with economic growth. The present book goes further, however, in the direction of practical solutions and contains less academic discussion of principles. It is the fifth in a group of books which I am trying to write dealing with the way our society is developing and the problems with which we are in consequence faced. I call the series 'The Social Imperative'.

My sincere thanks are due to all those who kindly gave permission to quote passages from their works (such quotations are credited individually in the notes), and to my secretary, Caroline Ingle, who coped with the complexities of the notes and the bibliography, as well as with all the other problems associated with working for an author.

Prologue

JUST before Cromwell came to power in England, the Puritans became much exercised about the appearance of groups of people who held very un-Puritan views. They were known as 'Libertines' and maintained that property should be abolished and all things held in common; that authority should vanish, for all men were equal, and that by the same token all class distinctions should be abolished. Worse still, they thought that sex was to be enjoyed, and that people should share their wives or commit adultery if they felt like it. In fact, they welcomed pleasure in all its forms, and are depicted in prints of the period as drinking and smoking tobacco, both of which the Puritans objected to.

As the Puritan divine, Richard Baxter, bitterly complained: 'They taught . . . that to the Pure all things are Pure (even things forbidden): and so as allowed by God they spoke most hideous words of blasphemy, and many of them committed Whoredoms commonly; Insomuch that a Matron of great Note for Godliness and Sobriety, being perverted by them, turned so shameless a Whore, that she was Carted in the streets of London.'

The absolute rejection of Puritan standards by these seventeenth-century hippies was summarized in a tract of 1650 about the women of the sect, in these appealing words: '. . . she speaks highly in commendation of those husbands that give liberty to their wives, and will freely give consent that she should associate herself with any other of her fellow-creatures, which she shall make choice of; she commends the Organ, Viol, Symbal and Tonges in Charterhouse-Lane to be heavenly musick; she tosseth her glasses freely, and concludeth there is no heaven but the pleasures she injoyeth on earth, she is very familiar at the first sight [i.e. friendly on first acquaintance] and danceth the Canaries at the sound of a hornpipe.'

But this was not mere hedonism, for many of this persuasion left their homes, or sold all their possessions and embraced a life of poverty. Moreover, they felt that theirs was, in some profound moral sense, the right way to live and sought to convert others to their point of view, despite persecution and physical attack by the Puritans.

Strange as the Libertines seemed, they were only the latest wave of a tide which swelled again and again, in many parts of Europe, for five hundred years. Again and again popular movements arose marked by a fierce rejection of conventional attitudes and beliefs. Typically, their supporters were a 'mobile, restless intelligentsia' to which unemployed and unemployable members of the working class would attach themselves. They rejected the bourgeois life of the merchant with its luxuries and deliberately chose poverty, sometimes living together in communes, sometimes as individuals begging in the streets and 'sleeping rough', sometimes living at home on their parents. They grew their hair long, did not trouble about personal cleanliness and wore unusual clothes, sometimes ragged, but sometimes costly. 'Every kind of dress was permissible,' says one historian; they would sew on patches or split their robe from the waist down. Of one young man, the illiterate young Antwerp artisan Loy Pruystinck, who had a considerable following about 1525, we are told that his robes were cut like rags but also sewn with jewels.

They maintained that there was no such thing as sin for them, and lived in complete sexual freedom. This served partly as a sign of their emancipation from convention. Indeed, many of them held that the sexual act was a means of mystical experience. Women were much attracted to the movement, and over them the leaders exerted a powerful sway, even though the women held that they owed no natural obedience to men. They 'knew nothing of conscience or remorse'. 'The free man was quite right to do whatever gives him pleasure.' The Catholic mystic, Heinrich Suso said: 'It would be better that the whole world should be destroyed and perish utterly than that a "free man" should refrain from one act to which his nature moves him.'

It was not only a right, but almost a duty to rob the rich. Professor Norman Cohn in *The Pursuit of the Millennium* (1957), speaks of the 'blithe dishonesty', which, century after century, was noted as being peculiarly characteristic of these above all other sectarians. (He is referring to the Brethren of the Free Spirit, as they called themselves.) 'An adept of the Free Spirit was free to eat in a tavern and then refuse to pay; if the tavern keeper asked for money he should be beaten.' 'Whatever the eye sees and covets, let the hand grasp it,' was one of their sayings.

All things were to be held in common among them, and all men were equal, so that none was entitled to more than another. Some of these movements, of which we begin to hear from the end of the eleventh century, were primarily movements of political protest—as we should say now, left-wing organizations: they arose among the poor, and especially among the landless urban proletariat which came into existence with the rise of the weaving industry, Europe's first mass industry. If their protest was directed mainly at the Church, it was because so many priests and prelates lived in luxury, while preaching poverty and abstinence to their flock. In contrast, the Brethren of the Free Spirit was predominantly a movement of the educated classes: its members were famed for the subtlety of their philosophical arguments and it is known that it received support from merchants and even nobles. Moreover, women played a large part in it.

We first hear of this movement about 1200: by the end of the century it was cropping up in many parts of Germany and Northern France and spreading into the Low Countries. It was well established in North Italy, and later we hear of something similar in Spain. Later still it was reported from Switzerland and from Bohemia. In the middle of the fourteenth century, the Pope appointed an Inquisitor to suppress it, earlier attempts to push the members into closed communities having failed. In the sixteenth century, Calvin was inveighing against it, claiming there were 10,000 Brethren in Cambrai and Valenciennes alone.

Since the Brethren embraced voluntary poverty and supported themselves by begging, they received the name Beghards ('. . . ard' is a derogatory ending, as in coward or drunkard), and they were known by their peculiar and brightly coloured clothes, which were noticeably different from the conventional browns, greys and blacks. In the Middle Ages, clothing, even more than now, indicated status, and to affect unconventional attire made it clear to everyone that the wearer was in revolt.

Of course, not everyone who begged was a Brother of the Free Spirit. To be a Brother entailed holding certain social and personal beliefs: the movement had its special literature, which the Church sought strenuously to destroy, but three of its books have come down to us. And since the philosophy of subordination to authority and the wickedness of pleasure, especially sexual pleasure, was preached by the Church as being part of religion, naturally the opposing philosophy had to be cast in a religious form and expressed in religious language. Thus it was seen by the Church as a heresy, and its leaders, when captured, were burned, not beheaded—burning being the fate appropriate to heretics.

According to their opponents, the Brethren believed that they had actually become God, and that, accordingly, everything was permitted to them; some went so far as to say that even murder was no sin, though they do not seem, in general, to have committed murder: the point was one of principle, and Suso's remark anticipates Blake's dictum: 'Sooner murder a child in its cradle than nurse unacted desires.' When asked by their enemies why, if they were God, they were not omnipotent and all-knowing, they explained that they were not *the* God, but they were simply expressions of the deity, and at death would be reabsorbed into the divine ground. Thus their religious views were derived from pantheism. (We shall see later how the views of the hippies fall into the same category.) Psychologically, we may say, they got rid of the severe father-figure which the Church offered them, by identifying with him.

In some variants of the movement, the candidate had to take a vow of absolute obedience to the adept who initiated him: if he then was ordered to follow his impulses, he had transferred the whole responsibility for his actions to the adept. The vow was a shrewd psychological device for abolishing guilt at one stroke.

In 1393, a man named Martin of Mainz was burnt at Cologne. He was a disciple of one Nicholas of Basle, a guru who had a following all along the Rhine valley, and who was himself later burnt by the Inquisition at Vienna. Martin maintained that his followers must make an act of absolute submission to Nicholas—after which, to obey his orders was no sin, whatever they might be. 'One could commit fornication or murder without a qualm if he ordered it . . .' At the moment when one made the act of submission to him one 'entered into a state of primal innocence'. The parallel with Charles Manson, who ordered the Sharon Tate murders, is obvious.

The sexual act (in the absence of drugs the only available method of dissolving personality) was in fact seen as a sacrament, and was called 'the delight of Paradise' or (by a group known as the Blood Friends) as 'Christerie'. In many cases, the members indulged in ritual nakedness— which was naturally seen by the orthodox as lascivious and shocking, and was perhaps sometimes meant to shock them—but which was, in the eyes of the Adamites, as they were called, a demonstration of primitive simplicity, and unself-consciousness, akin to the nudist movements today.

Parallel with this dispersed and unorganized movement, which Cohn describes as 'mystical anarchism', went other more definitely political movements, which aimed to overthrow the existing system and establish a classless society and a Golden Age on earth. What has been called the most influential political system known to Europe before Marxism was devised by Joachim of Fiore about 1200 and still existed, influencing Lessing, Schelling and Fichte, and perhaps also Hegel, in the nineteenth century. The three stages of primitive communism postulated by Marx himself echo the three stages postulated by Joachim. The Peasants' Revolt of 1381 in England was distinctly egalitarian: according to the preacher John Ball: 'Good folk, things cannot go well in England, nor ever shall until all things are in common and there is neither villein nor noble, but all of us are one condition.' But it was in Bohemia that the idea of a communist society first achieved a practical expression. In 1419, groups, mainly artisans but including clergy, left Prague, where King Wenceslas was suppressing the Hussite rebellion, and set up communes in various parts of the country. The first of these was at a place which they renamed Mount Tabor, which led to the sobriquet 'Taborites'. Subsequently, communes were established within towns also. The Taborites preached a class war. 'All nobles, lords and knights shall be cut down and exterminated in the forests like outlaws.' Wealthy merchants and town-dwellers were especially disliked. Politically, they were anarcho-communists. Taxes and rents were to be abolished, and private property of all kinds. There was to be no authority of any sort. However, many of the Taborites refused to work, and the communes began to prey upon the surrounding communities.

This activist movement, which spread to France and Germany, took an increasingly violent form. At Würzburg, a few years later, the leader of the movement declared it was a meritorious act to kill a priest, and at Mühlhausen, parties of Taborites actually destroyed monasteries and nunneries before their group was crushed. By 1510, a gentleman known as the Revolutionary of the Upper Rhine, whose *Book of 100 Chapters* became a bible of revolt, was urging: 'Go on hitting them, from the Pope right down to the little students! Kill every one of them!' He forecasts that 2,300 clerics will be killed every day—he is particularly against clerics—and those priests who break their vow of chastity should be strangled or burned alive. He too hopes for the abolition of all property and all taxes—and those who do not conform are to be executed forthwith by secret messengers of unquestionable piety, i.e. a secret police.

In short, there were two favoured responses to the situation: the one, communist, directed to establishing an ideal society on earth; the other, one of personal fulfilment, religious in a pantheistic sense, but apolitical, or, in some cases, anarchist.

Cohn, from whose book I have taken many of these facts, declares that these movements arise when the traditional life is becoming impossible in a period of rapid socio-economic change, and especially when a threat is felt. Today is certainly such a period, but it lacks the obvious features of the past—extreme poverty and a fanatically rigid moral code imposed by the Church. But though today does not see the widespread poverty of the past, the contrast between the rich and the poor is even greater and is certainly better understood, so that envy is a powerful factor.

It does not call for much imagination to see a parallel between this uninhibited, egalitarian outlook and that of the youth movements of today. Indeed, the parallel goes further, and is worth exploring for the light it casts on the situation today. It is a first step towards understanding the contemporary youth protest to realize that it is not a unique phenomenon, but something the world has often had to cope with before. And study of its earlier forms provides us with clues to the mechanism which impels people to such behaviour.

Again, we have the extremely permissive attitude to sex and other pleasures, with the rejection of the normal forms of marriage and monogamy. We see the wandering life of poverty, based on begging, coupled with the reluctance to work. We see also the preoccupation with the self, the readiness to respond to impulse and the feeling that impulse should be obeyed, whatever it may suggest. Furthermore, the hippie movement is strongly egalitarian, rejects property and, in the extreme cases, regards theft as justifiable, since property is theft. Women take part as often as men, and bizarre clothing and nudity are features. Finally, the movement has a political wing, committed to violent methods, and aiming to overthrow the system and establish a Golden Age on earth.

One of the most striking features of the contemporary youth movement is, as everyone knows, its preoccupation with drugs and particularly with drugs which induce subjective reveries or visions, the psychedelic drugs. Since the seventeenth-century hippies did not have access to such drugs, it is all the more impressive to find that they nevertheless had the visions. As a playwright of the period wrote:

> All lie down, as in a swown [faint]
> To have a pleasing vision.
> And then rise with bared thighs,
> Who'd fear such sweet incision?

Contemporary youth's protest, which seems to many people so inexplicable and unprecedented, is neither: it is just a modern variant on a familiar theme. To be sure, the situation contains an important new element: the effects of modern technology. These enable the movement to cohere better, to spread faster. It also provides them with the drugs which they use to enhance their supposedly mystical experience, and with the weapons of destruction which the activist groups employ. But the phenomenon itself is far from new. What is new is that today we know enough anthropology and psychology to divine the reasons for it, and perhaps even to infer what we ought to be doing about it.

The Receding Utopia

I. *Where Did We Go Wrong?*

WHEN the new railway from Islington to Camberwell was opened nearly a century ago, amid much self-congratulation, Matthew Arnold enquired what was the value of a railway which enabled one to pass 'from a dismal and illiberal life in Islington to a dismal and illiberal life in Camberwell?' His question was naturally ignored. Today, we begin to see that he may have had a point.

At least in the developed countries of the world the suspicion seems to be crystallizing that somewhere down the line we took a wrong turning. While the marvels of technology bestow on almost everyone gifts and opportunities denied even to kings in the past, people in general seem more dissatisfied, more frustrated than ever before. So much so, that many young people are now turning their backs on our society altogether, and are attempting to set up communities run on an entirely different basis from that of industrial society, in which they reckon to be happier and more satisfied than they ever could be in society as they find it. Others take to a wandering life, based on begging or on theft, not unlike the Beghards of the fourteenth century. Others turn to mysticism and contemplation, life-styles which have not been in favour in the West for centuries. Others turn to political action based on violence. Some turn to crime. The search for new ways of living has brought the word 'life-style' into fashion.

Recently, this awareness of the need for a reconsideration of our values has become more marked among the older generation. A significant indication of this was given by the Nobel Foundation when it called a special conference in 1970 on 'The Place of Values in a World of Facts'. The Nobelist, Professor Arne Tiselius, in his opening speech, spoke of 'a growing awareness among people of all nations that something is wrong with the world and that there is an urgent need to come together to see what should be done'.

Christopher Mayhew, the chairman of Britain's National Association for Mental Health, has specified the 'something wrong' in vivid terms: 'We are better fed, better clothed, better housed, and better educated, our young are taller and stronger, and our old live longer. Yet we are more troubled in mind, less well-behaved and less happy. There is probably more rootlessness, more loneliness, more stress and certainly more suicide attempts and use of drugs.'

Or, as an American Congressman, Allard Lowenstein, succinctly put it at an international conference in Princeton in 1968: 'We've discovered that even after we've removed the exterior causes of unhappiness we don't produce a happy society at all.'

Dissatisfaction with the world-as-it-is is felt especially strongly by the young, encountering reality for the first time, and finding that life falls so far behind one's most generous ideals.

Margaret Mead quotes an essay by a fifteen-year-old Texan boy, Shannon Dixon: 'We see the world as a huge rumble as it swiftly goes by with wars, poverty, prejudice, and the lack of understanding among people and nations. Then we stop and think: there must be a better way and we have to find it.' He feels that the present generation is 'being used almost like a machine', in the sense that it is being trained to follow in the footsteps of the older generation. 'But why? If we are to be a generation of repetition, the situation will be worse. But how shall we change? We need a great deal of love for everyone, we need a universal understanding among people, we need to think of ourselves and express our feelings, but that is not all. I have yet to discover what else we need . . .' And he adds: 'The answer is out there somewhere. We need to search for it.'

Dixon sees, and Margaret Mead emphasizes, that the future cannot be, must not be, simply an extension of the past: a radical rethinking of the whole system is needed.

In his book *Beyond Economics*, Professor Kenneth Boulding, a President of the American Economic Association, argues that there are historical discontinuities which he calls 'system breaks'—moments when the bag is shaken up and the contents settle down in a new configuration. The end of the Middle Ages was obviously one such moment, the birth of the industrial revolution another. We are undoubtedly in such a phase today, world-wide, and by the year 2000 will probably have settled down securely into the new pattern. My object in this book is to identify the forces which are causing the 'system break' and to speed up the process of readjustment by defining the pattern we are moving towards.

Reconsideration of basic assumptions is under way in many spheres—domestic, economic, industrial, political and religious. The Western world is engaged in a massive rethink which cannot fail to prove a turning point in its development. (The third world is also engaged in a mighty readjustment, though its problems are the converse of the West's.) But the nature of the total problem remains ill-defined. The field is full of woolly cliché. What do people mean when they ask for 'a change of values', for instance?

One way of looking at the process we are living through is in terms of a change of social objectives. What I shall call the Old Line stressed hard work and self-control and offered material satisfaction as its reward. This, often known as the Protestant work-ethic, was probably more strongly and widely held in America than anywhere else, except perhaps Japan, and accounts for the material prosperity of those countries. What I shall call the New Line is gradually being clarified, but seems to be based on a vision of man fulfilling all of his potentialities. Material plenty is taken for granted; and instead of hard work, agreeable and challenging tasks are expected; instead of self-control, self-fulfilment. There is also a perversion of the New Line which one might call the Side Line, in which self-fulfilment becomes continuous self-indulgence, and dissatisfaction with the world-as-it-is is vented in destructive action and cynicism, rather than in self-development and the meeting of challenges.

On the whole it is the young who espouse the New Line and the Side Line, the old who stick to the Old Line. But there are also 'oldsters' who see the light, so I shall not speak of the young and the old, but of the New Liners and the Old Liners.

Unsurprisingly, the new 'morality of abundance' has developed first in the well-heeled middle-class, among those who have always had a sufficiency of material comforts. There are still plenty of people who do not have such a sufficiency, but their number is steadily declining, especially in countries which are partly or fully socialist. It is striking that even in the less-privileged (though not the very under-privileged) sectors, signs of a change of attitude are occurring. When a miner stays in bed on Monday morning, losing the pay for the shift, he has clearly chosen leisure in place of goods. And even in the USA there have been strikes, not about money but for easier or more interesting ways of doing the job. Dr Arnold Mitchell, of the Stanford Research Institute in Palo Alto, California, is typical of those young sociologists who have grasped the trend: 'The point is simple,' he says. 'So many of us have "made it" in material terms that we are ready for change . . . We are beginning to sense that our old goals of plenty are but a waypost on the highway to a higher view of men.' The same point is made more elegantly by Bertrand de Jouvenel, the French economist and diplomat, when he says: 'I take it that our concern is to place our descendants in circumstances conducive to the flowering of *la pianta uomo*, according to the expression of the poet Alfieri, which strongly suggest the dual aims of prosperity and quality . . .'

While the younger generation expresses its dissatisfaction by revolt or by dropping out, the older generation, too deeply committed to traditional life-styles to react in this relatively unfrustrating way, seem to suffer acute frustration and feelings of anxiety. When the US Public

Health Service conducted a survey of 6,672 adults not long ago, nearly 60 per cent said that they were 'fidgety, tense at times to the point of being bothered'. Furthermore, 4·9 per cent had had nervous break-downs and 12·8 per cent felt that a breakdown was impending. Thus some 20 million adults, roughly one in six of the population, were suffering 'severe psychological stress'. (In a moment, I shall look at some other signs of stress in our society, such as alcoholism and suicide.)

Even those who remain calm are not necessarily relaxed about the situation. Many of them feel that, as a direct result of the stream of technological advances which are occurring, certain ill-defined human values are being lost, and are deeply concerned about the direction Western civilization is taking. Books by the score are published lament-ing the trend; novelists depict the unlovely future to which we are remorselessly advancing. But such protests have little effect. Indeed, many people feel themselves helpless in the grip of nameless forces. Like a spaceship which has failed to enter orbit, the world seems to be trapped in a course from which it cannot escape—and perhaps, like the spaceship, is doomed to perish.

All this is quite contrary to the expectations which ruled about the beginning of the century and which persisted, at least in the USA, until the beginning of the Second World War. (Europe began to have doubts rather earlier.) In the visions of H. G. Wells, sensible, moderate people, sensibly clad, lead sensible, moderate, civilized lives. Crime is almost unknown. In the pamphlets of the Fabian socialists, people only steal because they are desperate for food or other necessities: secured from poverty, people will steal no more. Today, however, we have learned that it is generally the comfortably-off middle-classes which produce the wildest, most anti-social characters and that theft is commoner among the well-fed than the hungry.

We are therefore faced with a double problem: on the one hand, what was the flaw in the arguments which linked material advance to advances in satisfaction?* On the other hand, if existing society is un-satisfactory, is there any form of society which would be more satisfy-ing? Could we modify or reconstruct society on some other plan which —even if not perfect—would be better than the present one?

Obviously this is a question of outstanding importance, so it is strange that in the present century it has not been much debated and certainly forms no part of education, so that rebels are left with nothing to build on but the conclusions of nineteenth-century social theorists, such as Proudhon, Kropotkin, Landauer and, of course, the Marx–Engels–Lenin trinity. These amateurish early speculations, like the speculations of nineteenth-century anthropologists, served a purpose in

* Strangely enough, we have no comprehensive term for non-material satisfac-tions, except the rather debatable word 'happiness'.

opening the subject up and represented the best that could be done at that time: but since then we have nearly a century of work in the social and life-sciences to go on, and can expect something more reliable. Though these sciences are still in an early stage of development compared with the physical sciences, enough has been learned to make most nineteenth-century political philosophy obsolete.

So, in this book, I intend to draw on the findings of the social sciences to arrive at some conclusions about the kind of society we ought to be aiming at, and this will lead us into considering the complex problems of how a new kind of society could be brought about.

In this respect, we stand at an extraordinary point in man's social development. Really, for the first time, we are beginning to be in a position to devise, intentionally, the style of life in which we believe we should live, instead of having to accept society as we find it.* This is why people are beginning to speak of the communes and experimental patterns of living as 'intentional societies'—in contrast with the un-intentionally-arrived-at societies the world has seen in the past. Actually, it must be noted, the devising of intentional societies is not quite so novel as many of those concerned (in their ignorance of history) think. In the Prologue I mentioned a number of permissive and communalist groups set up in the late Middle Ages and in the seventeenth century. The nineteenth century saw a rash of such experiments, most of which failed, like the co-operatives started by Robert Owen in Scotland and Indiana, or the Icaria community of Cabet. But only where a strong religious conviction motivated the group, as with the Hutterites, do such communities seem to have endured; later, we shall see the reasons for these failures.

My plan of action will be, first to look at existing and previously existing societies in order to determine what the possible patterns of social behaviour are—and also to discover how social change actually takes place—for society has a dynamic of its own, and it may well be useless for us to yearn after one life-pattern if society is remorselessly carrying us towards another. Unless we can understand the dynamics of social change, unless we can discover the pressure points which enable us to control it, we are likely to waste our efforts.

Secondly, I propose to look at our own society in the light of these findings, to define what adjustments it seems to need. (I call the pattern which seems desirable a paraprimitive society.) Finally, I shall consider

---

* To be sure, socialists aim to modify society, but they have been no more successful than conservatives in avoiding the frustrations and deep-lying dis-satisfactions which assail capitalist societies, and in some respects even less success-ful. Their analysis of the problem was too narrowly economic, and flouted the psychological realities: they treated man as an economic unit, rather than as a human being. I discuss this point further in Chapter 11.

how the needed changes could be brought about. I shall argue that it is only by changing people that it is possible; that political solutions, unless based on personal preferences and needs, always fail. This is not to say that our political institutions are adequate: they are at least a century out of date.

At least part of the frustration people feel today comes from their being forced into life-styles which are uncongenial. The would-be mystic who is forced to become a bank clerk is as frustrated as would be the born bank clerk compelled to become a mystic. But though there is much vague talk about life-styles, few have stopped to analyse the notion. I would like to make it more precise.

II. *What are Life-styles?*

What we are really talking about are dominant human preferences, and of these there are only a dozen or so, though, since many different admixtures are possible, it could be said that there are countless life-styles. Let us take as examples the life of service to others, the life based on manipulating materials and the intellectual life.* Practical instances of these are the nurse, the craftsman and the scholar. But mixtures of these occur—for example, the doctor, whose life combines service with a considerable intellectual component, while the surgeon combines service with manipulative ability. Each preference is dictated by the possession of a particular human capacity, thanks to the fact that most people prefer to do what they are good at. The scholar exploits his intellectual capacities, the craftsman his adeptness, the hedonist his senses. For some people the dominant need is to remain in contact with nature, so that they become farmers or foresters: this too, as we shall see, is a basic human characteristic.

If it is asked whether any one of these life-patterns is better than any other, the final answer must be, I think, that the ideal life-style involves a balance of all the components. The scholar who has a fine brain but is emotionally frozen, or even physically clumsy, loses something in consequence. The man of action who never creates anything must finally begin to wonder if his actions are worth while. However, people are what they are, and must, by and large, accept their built-in limitations. From the social viewpoint, such specialization of function may even be desirable. Society needs contributions in all possible spheres.

Problems arise when society offers a range of choice which differs from the range which its members demand—and that is what is happen-

---

* Others are the life of action, of social contacts, of intrigue (manipulation of people) of creation (poets, artists) of contemplation (the mystic or monk) and the gipsy, the adventurer and the entertainer. There are also hedonists and those with neurotic demands.

ing today. Western society fails to offer slots in the same numerical proportion as the number of people in each group. Thus it offers more slots
for manipulation of people and materials than there are people to fill
them—since these are capacities needed by commerce and industry. It
offers too few opportunities in the emotional and creative spheres. It
offers too few opportunities for service, too few for contemplation. On
the other hand, it has begun to offer too many slots calling for high
intelligence combined with practicality.

There are even slots which it fails to offer at all: the gipsy and the
adventurer for instance. Those who prefer a nomadic life do not fit
easily into a society in which there are tabs on everybody, taxes to pay,
a social security system based on assumptions of fixed residence and
known income, and so on—which is why the gipsy constitutes a social
problem in European countries. The man who needs the stimulus of
danger, who wishes to brave the unknown, can find less and less unknown to brave. War apart, the only dangerous adventure for which
society requires volunteers, on a whole-time basis, is probably space-
travel, and this opening is obviously available to very few people. If the
adventure-seeker gets into trouble, society feels obliged to try to get
him out of it, and so is led to protect him from danger. Mountain trails
are signposted, precipices fenced, refuges provided, rescue teams established, until the danger vanishes and the fun has gone. To the un-
adventurous individual, especially the bureaucrat, these unwanted
precautions seem only common sense, so little do the two types understand one another.

Why is it, then, that our society fails to offer the range of opportunities that people desire? I think three factors are involved. First, there is
no natural balance between what society requires and what individuals
want. Many people like to consume goods, but not everyone likes to
make goods. More people want to become actors than the theatre-going
and film-going public want to watch. (This lack of balance is upset still
further when a technical invention, in this case the motion-picture,
enables a smaller number of actors to present themselves to a much
larger public.) Despite this, society seeks to adjust itself to the needs of
its members: if people become more interested in dancing, say, then
occasions and places will be created for this purpose. Trouble arises
when people's interests shift—and this is what has happened today.
Fewer people are interested in the opportunities offered by commerce
and industry: more people want to be fashion photographers,
mystics, etc. More people want to farm, at a time when technology has
reduced the number of people required to grow a given amount of
food.

So the question becomes: why have people's interests shifted? The
answer is that there has been a change in the norm of personality—what

is known to anthropologists as the modal personality structure. Societies exhibit a certain style or ethos which reflects the preferences of most of their members. Thus Victorian society was biased in favour of self-control and against spontaneity, because most of the members of Victorian society felt that way. Application and industriousness were rewarded, orgiastic behaviour was penalized. It was a good place for a soldier or a businessman, a bad place for an artist or a sun-worshipper. Today the norm of personality structure has shifted, but society has not yet adapted to the change. It is trying to do so, but the process is a slow one. Institutions are difficult to change. People continue to pay lip-service to certain values and behaviour patterns long after they have ceased to matter to them. It is this time-lag which is the prime source of our present unrest.

Additionally, in a society like ours, power tends to rest in the hands of people of a restricted number of personality-types, and they naturally tend to preserve the institutions and patterns which *they* value. The political and economic systems are ineffective mechanisms for expressing the preferences of people of completely different persuasions. Economists tell us that the price mechanism enables people to express their preference for particular goods or services, but fail to see that it cannot express their desire to be a mystic, or adapt agriculture to meet their desire to be a farmer. Political scientists suppose that a voting system enables people to express preferences which the economic system fails to respond to—but how can one vote for more adventure or for a contemplative life?

Thus, while economics and politics are certainly faulty, the real problem lies elsewhere. The change which our society is trying to make necessitates adjustments not simply in our political and economic institutions, but in the behaviour of individuals generally and in the ideas which animate them. If we wish to establish new life-styles, we have to ask: why do societies adopt particular value systems, and how can they be changed? We shall have to go into the psychology of personality, rather than into politics and economics, and in the next two chapters I shall be pursuing this line. I shall ask what people are, what they could be, what they should be. Above all, I shall try to show *why* the basic personality structure of our society has recently changed.

If you reflect on this analysis of the situation, you will perceive that the character of the problem is somewhat different from what it appeared to be when first stated. We must not think simply in terms of fitting society to people, which might leave important functions understaffed, nor in terms of fitting people to society, which would lead to many people being frustrated. We have to compromise. So we are led to the idea that the distribution of personality-types in a society may be pathological, or at least abnormal. How far can we, in the course of time, shift the modal personality structure to a more normal pattern, which can then more readily find satisfaction?

If a society contains sadists, there will be a demand for institutions which indulge sadism. It is self-evident, surely, that in such a situation, our proper course is not to create such institutions but to prevent the formation of sadistic personalities. In short, we must not think simply in terms of matching society to the demands people put upon it—and this is how most people do think today—we must think in terms of improving mental health, creating sound basic personalities and then matching social institutions to them. A sound society is the reflection of a sound personality. At the same time it is perfectly true that sadists and other types of personality distortion are produced (largely or wholly) by social experiences, so that we must work to prevent such experiences occurring. The crucial thing is to identify these constitutive experiences. This interplay of personality and society is the central theme of my book, and I call it the *psychosocial nexus*. (Jargon, I agree, but so is 'downdraught carburettor'—technical matters necessitate technical descriptions.)

In the past, it has been customary to blame the faults of society on the faults of individuals. Today, we have swung to the other extreme and tend to blame society for corrupting or distorting individuals. Each of these views is incomplete: the truth is a synthesis of the two.

III. *Dimensions of Misery*

Books are bought mainly by the more comfortably placed members of society, so the readers of this book may find it difficult to imagine the degree of frustration, boredom, loneliness and despair which tortures many members of society. It is hard to put oneself in the place of a friendless woman living in a bed-sitting-room, a repetition worker wrapping boxes, the inhabitant of an old people's home or even of a young man in the throes of puberty and the transition to manhood. It is therefore worth looking closely at some of the statistics, because to recognize the existence of these states of mind is a first step to understanding the situation.

In Britain, for instance, an estimated 50,000 people attempt suicide every year: that is, about three million attempts have occurred in the course of my lifetime. And the figure is rising, perhaps by 10 per cent per annum. Professor E. Stengel has estimated that half a million people now living in Britain have tried to kill themselves. Studying a series of 167 attempted suicides admitted to a general hospital, A. W. Stearns found that two-thirds were financially well-off and only 14 per cent were economically dependant. In the USA, however, the great industrial society with its 'high standard of living', the rate is about three times as high as in the UK. This suggests that about 1,500 people attempt suicide every day in the USA.* That bears thinking about.

When people are bored and miserable, when life is empty, they take to drink to dull their sorrows. In the USA the existence of alcohol-addiction is well recognized; in Britain the problem has been largely ignored until recently. It is now realized that it is far more serious than was thought: the World Health Organization estimates that there are 350,000 alcoholics in Britain—say, one in every 100 adults. In the USA the rate is more than four times this, and in France, five times. Convictions for drunkenness provide some clue, though not all drunks are alcoholics, by any means. In Britain, they have risen from 20,000 in 1946 to over 68,000 in 1960—an increase of 250 per cent in fourteen years. It is true that the alcohol addict is a person with definite personality defects (as Howard Jones has shown in his *Alcohol Addiction*, 1963) but equally they are people who have been under stress. I am not at this point concerned to examine the causes of alcoholism: I only wish to establish the existence of misery.

Perhaps the most exhaustive study of mental ill-health, outside the mental hospital, was the 'Midtown' Study, in which 2,000 people, aged from twenty to fifty-nine, living in part of Manhattan, were exhaustively interviewed and tested over a period of ten years. Two psychiatrists made independent estimates of the mental health of all these people, and their findings turned out to be in close agreement with the test results. By both systems they found that fewer than 19 per cent of those examined could be regarded as mentally healthy. Roughly 40 per cent of the total were mildly affected, 20 per cent moderately and another 20 per cent so severely that their functioning was impaired. The rates increased with advancing age, and were higher at the lower end of the socio-economic scale. Furthermore, over 70 per cent were classified as suffering from 'mixed anxiety' and 4·6 per cent were alcoholics.

The rising rates of crime and violence also indicate some degree of social pathology.† Attempts are made to dismiss the figures as being due to changes in the method of reporting. But that some increase has occurred in the past quarter-century cannot be denied, while on conventional arguments a decrease might have been expected. Juvenile crime, particularly, suggests that something is amiss. In the USA one child in six is likely to find itself before the courts. That is hardly something to be complacent about.

* While I was writing this an American doctor went on record as saying that the USA had little to worry about as its suicide rate was no worse than any other nation's!

† In the first nine months of 1971 murders were 30 per cent up in New York—1,067. Crimes of violence in the USA as a whole were up 10 per cent on the same period last year, which was 101 up on the year before. (Dept. of Justice figures.) Britain's prison population has doubled in twenty years, despite increased use of probation and the so-called intermediate system.

These statistics are staggering. Nothing like it is found in primitive societies—nor do we find murder, alcoholism or suicide on anything like the same scale in primitive societies, except where they are disintegrating under the impact of Western culture. Yet we treat them with amazing calm. Far less money is devoted to mental health than to physical health. Any society in which one-third of the population is mentally disturbed is in a desperate state, and should be devoting a major effort to finding out why and doing something about it.

Is all this misery simply unavoidable, the psychological cost of living, so to speak? No: the fact that the rates of suicide, alcoholism and mental disease, to say nothing of crime, vary widely in different countries, prove that social forces are at work, and, while we could never eliminate all such misery, there is a considerable range of possibilities open to us. The complex ways in which social conditions impose more or less stress on individuals are what we now have to explore. Furthermore, the fact that primitive societies in general do not exhibit such signs of stress suggests that such stresses are the product of an unsuitable way of life.

Another explanation which has been put forward is that we have 'run out of motivation'. There is some truth in this. When a man is often cold and hungry, he is highly motivated to build himself a shelter, make clothes and grow food. He does not ask what is the purpose of life, but presses on with urgent necessities. As more and more of his demands are met, each new enterprise brings less and less satisfaction and sense of achievement, and he begins to look for some further purpose. Today, many people are asking: 'What is it all in aid of?' And if they find no answer, they are apt to sink into apathy or despair.

This sense of lack of purpose is especially strong in those for whom everything is provided—today, notably the young, meaning those who have not yet reached the point of earning their own living. When they start to do so, some of their *Angst* vanishes. But adults, too, if and when they have managed to assure that their material needs and more obvious psychological needs are covered, begin to ask for more. Some find the answer in service to others; some in 'excitement' or intensifying the stimulus they receive; others take refuge from boredom by means of drink, sex or drugs.

George E. Brown, Jr, a former Congressman from California, also an engineer, physicist and banker, writing in *Physics Today* (October 1971) regards this as the primary problem. He quotes Robert Redfield, who spent much of his life studying the impact of civilization on primitive societies, as saying in his book *Peasant Society*: 'People develop wants whose satisfaction brings no satisfaction.' Brown's suggestion is that we should make the attempt to understand the universe our motive— and hence that instead of cutting back on science budgets we should expand them. This is just the suggestion that one would expect from someone who started out to be a physicist. Naturally, scientists are strongly motivated by curiosity: that is why they become scientists. The majority of people lack this persistent kind of curiosity, or are more curious about people than things. As a general motive for the whole of society, curiosity doesn't stand a chance, I fear; only a scientist would imagine it to be right, which shows the danger of leaving things to scientists.

However, the need for a sense of purpose is only part of the problem, as we shall see.

Another scientist–engineer–administrator, Jerome Wiesner, Provost of MIT, offered the House Committee on Science and Astronautics a different analysis: '. . . at the same time that technology emancipates man, freeing him from the necessity to slave at manual labor for a bare subsistence and promising him the opportunity for fulfilment as a truly human being, it threatens to dehumanize him more completely than the often uneven struggle of earlier times. This is why so many of our fellow-citizens feel so cheated, so alienated.'

There, I think, Wiesner has identified the problem correctly, while leaving very vague what is really meant by the word 'dehumanization'. In the following chapters I mean to explore the very complex system of elements which go to make up being human.

I have made it plain, I hope, that I think that the younger generation is right in maintaining that there is something radically wrong with our society. So now I want to make it equally clear that I think that, speaking generally, they have done so for the wrong reasons and their conception of what would be right is in its way just as undesirable as what they complain of.

IV. *The Turnover Point*

When Ulysses and his men were shipwrecked, they first lit a fire of driftwood and cooked a meal. After they had eaten, they remembered their drowned companions and wept.

Homer's account rings true. Our physical needs take priority over our emotional demands, but, once the former have been satisfied, the profounder requirements of our humanity reassert themselves. And what happens on the personal scale can also happen on the world scale. The industrialized nations have now managed, broadly speaking, to provide their citizens with food, shelter and clothing. As a result, those citizens are becoming more aware of other and subtler needs. But a society geared to the production of goods is precisely a society which is poorly adapted to satisfying psychological needs. The very processes by which we manufacture goods so effectively actually *reduce* psychological satisfactions. Hence the further we push technological advance, the worse the psychological environment becomes. We have scrambled out of physical poverty only to fall into psychological poverty. Indeed our condition is worse than poverty; we live in a psychological slum.

In short, in the technological growth of any social organism, there is a turnover point at which effort needs to be transferred from material to non-material needs. This point we have now reached, or passed. This is why we have to rethink our entire social technique. How can we satisfy our psychological needs, in a technologically advanced society? That is the central question.

When psychological needs are not met, people can be said to be frustrated. Their efforts to attain some kind of psychological satisfaction are in vain. (The word frustration comes from the Latin *frustra*, in vain.) Now, as the American psychologists Dollard and Miller showed a quarter of a century ago, frustration leads to aggression. When we cannot repair our car, we feel like giving it a kick. (There is more to be said about the origins of aggression, of course, and I shall say it later on: this is just a preliminary sketch.) In short, it is the existence of widespread frustration which is the prime cause of the mounting toll of violence which the world is now witnessing. So, if that frustration can be shown to be caused by industrial society and the conditions it imposes, then the violence must be regarded as a cost of production. Frustration is the price of material affluence.

It also follows that alcoholism, suicide, mental disturbance, etc., will not be abolished by voting large sums of money for psychiatric care. They will only be reduced by altering the structure and values of society.

It is against this background that arguments about the desirability of economic growth must be set. It is not enough to point to the merits of a computer, a supersonic aircraft or a plastic wrap. It is a question of weighing their advantages against the psychological costs of producing them. It is very nice to have a kitchen mixer, to be sure: but if the price includes being mugged while you are walking home, it may seem too high. Unfortunately, the chain of cause and effect is rather long, and many people fail to see the connection between the goods and the bads. In a later chapter, I shall try to demonstrate that it exists, by defining man's psychological needs in some detail, in order to show how modern society frustrates them, and what to do about it.

Unfortunately, there is some feedback in this system. We can make use of goods in order to satisfy not only physical but also psychological needs—as happens for instance when we acquire things we do not want in themselves because they confer status. Industry has been ingenious in catering for such demands, with the result that a vicious circle has been established. The more frustrated industry makes us, the more goods we buy in an attempt to relieve our frustration. Such pointless persistence is known to psychologists as perseveration. A rat which has been rewarded for jumping at one window will continue to jump at it even when it receives an electric shock for doing so, even when food is obtainable at a different window. Like the rat, man perseverates. Hence the consumer society. But the power of goods to satisfy psychological needs is quite limited, as we shall see.

The proposition that industrial society frustrates many of its members to the point of breakdown may seem implausible to the fortunate exceptions: those are mainly professional men and women, working at a job which challenges their ability, is not monotonous, and allows them some personal freedom and the opportunity to plan their own time. Since this includes almost all those who are, in a broad sense, intellectual leaders—politicians, journalists, scientists, doctors, architects, musicians, dons, senior civil servants and leaders of industry, to name no others—the frustrating nature of modern society has been generally ignored. For them, modern society is, by and large, rather satisfactory. Told that it drives many of the population to distraction, they find the assertion hard to take seriously.

Again, when anyone speaks against a policy of maximizing the supply of goods, there are always those who misinterpret this as an attempt to preserve privilege. Why should not those who are now poor have the same privileges—cars, cocktail cabinets and foreign holidays—as the rich?

Of course, it is true that, even in the Western world, there are areas of poverty in which the supply of goods has not reached the turn-over point—this is due to inequalities of distribution rather than to inability to manufacture enough, as has long been recognized. There is no need to go into the various reasons for such a situation here. Nothing that I say should be taken as implying that the problems of the slums, of malnutrition, of equal educational opportunity, etc., should be neglected. If any limitation or cut-back of industrial output is necessary —and later, I shall debate this point—clearly it should not fall upon the supply of necessities.*

V. *The Search for Happiness*

When anyone raises the idea of improving society there are always some who cry: 'This is Utopianism!' Today, we are disillusioned about the possibility of doing so. In part, this is simple cynicism: if the world is to be improved at all, they say, it will be by *ad hoc* efforts towards improv-

---

* As Professor Galbraith has pointed out, poverty in Western societies is due to educational, racial and family background and is not eliminated by raising the level of incomes. See *The Affluent Society*, Chapter 22.

ing specific institutions. Attempts to design whole societies are futile because no one knows enough about society to do so. And it is true that the Utopias of the past, including that of Sir Thomas More himself, are obviously unworkable and would probably be unsatisfactory to live in, in any case. Today, I believe, we can approach the subject with more confidence, because we know much more about the nature of society.

Some people, however, are less cynical than despairing. They doubt that any improvement in the situation is possible, in actual practice. They feel that the forces maintaining the present system are too strong, its inertia too great for a minority to shift, unless indeed by violent revolution. This feeling of despair arises, I believe, because they feel the mechanisms of society are unanalysed and unanalysable. Hence to control them seems impossible. I hope to show that this is a mistaken view. Social control can be achieved, and that without enslavement to a dictatorship or some subtler 'thought control' system. I must add that we shall find that such changes cannot be effected rapidly, in relation to the human life-span. It takes a generation or two, at the speediest. To the young, who want Utopia tomorrow, or the day after, at latest, this will not seem fast enough, but I believe it is the best we can do. You cannot bring an ocean liner to a stop within its own length.

It can also be objected that society is always changing, so that any given solution to the problem of designing society could at best be effective only for a while. This, I think, is true: it is useless to look for a static solution or to try to design a social system. But if we understand the mechanisms of social change we can chart a course, even if we cannot promise a landfall. We can see in what direction we ought to move from where we are. If, in the course of time, our position alters, so will the course we have to set. And we can usefully discuss how to trim our sails to make that course. In short we can discuss ends and means.

But the cry of Utopianism comes in many cases from the Marxists who have a different objection in mind. According to Marx, history is evolving inevitably towards a socialist Utopia, so that all the ordinary man needs to do is to help the process on a little. To design futures is a waste of time, because we have no choice. The socialist Utopia will come sooner or later, whether we design it or not. To ensure that it is sooner, all we have to do is to concentrate on the revolution.

This is the historical origin of the claim made by activists today that all we need to do is to sweep away the existing system, and a new and better one will arise in its place. Unfortunately, history shows that this is a disastrous error. Violent revolutions bring to the top strong, authoritarian figures, who oust the original leaders and set about restoring order by oppressive means. Thus it was that the Russian revolution, which started out with the aim of establishing self-governing communes and which in so many words rejected the whole concept of

the centralist state, ended in establishing a completely centralized dictatorship. It follows that, if society is going to change, it is vital to work
out the path we want to follow. To leave it to the course of events to
decide will ensure a disaster; the activists constitute a serious threat to
our society not because they want to change it but because their
methods ensure that the change will be for the worse.

In talking about creating a better, more satisfactory society, we inevitably begin to think of a happier society. This is a controversial
word, and I must explain how I intend to use it. There are some for
whom happiness is actually undesirable: they visualize a world of total
euphoria, in which nothing would be achieved because no one would
have any motivation to do anything. But obviously a world in which
people did not maintain the necessary services would soon become an
unhappy one. In any case, we are unlikely to achieve total euphoria. At
present the situation is rather that many people function less effectively
than they might, because of their unhappiness—if we can use the word
to cover their frustration, boredom and despair.

Another group regards happiness as impossible, except as a brief
experience. When a much longed-for goal is achieved, for a while there
is a glow of pure pleasure, as when the mother receives back her long-
lost son, or the businessman consummates an intricate deal. But soon
the glow fades, and we begin to launch fresh plans, to set fresh goals.
And as we look back, we see that much of what now appears to us as
happiness lay in the struggle. The problem is how to make the most of
the struggle. It is unsatisfying to fight an opponent who is overwhelm-
ingly better than oneself, and tedious to play against a rabbit whom one
can defeat without effort. It is a struggle which tests one's capacities to
the full which is satisfying. It is for this reason that men sail boats,
climb mountains and take on other challenges, including intellectual
ones. Thus *the task of society is to offer a wide range of challenges* so that all its
members can find challenges suited to their capacities and tastes. Lacking challenges, we feel boredom; faced with impossible ones we feel
frustration and despair. In either case, we can be said to be unhappy. I
suggest accordingly that we might use the word 'joy' for the momen-
tary glow, and use the word happiness for the long-term state of mind
which is based on steady achievement.

It is easy to tell when people are happy: it shows in their walk and
posture, in the vitality and rhythm of their movements and facial
expression, in their whole 'style'. A look round any subway car or bus
must tell us how few people are happy in our society, and especially
urban society.

As Professor Abraham Maslow has cogently argued in his stimulating
book *Motivation and Personality*, the most basic of all needs is the need to
actualize one's potentialities. I believe that no one has ever tried to

measure how far people actually achieve such actualization or self-fulfilment. Drawing some numbers from the air, for purposes of illustration, Professor Maslow suggests that, in the West, while most of us are perhaps 85 per cent satisfied at the physiological level, and perhaps 50 per cent in our emotional needs, we may be only 10 per cent satisfied at the level of self-actualization. For my part, I shall argue that in many unindustrialized 'uncivilized' countries, the proportion may run in the opposite sense, with a higher degree of actualization despite a lower level of physiological gratification.

Obviously no social system can protect people from individual loss—a personal accident or illness, the death or loss of a loved one, or even the failure of a cherished plan. Nevertheless, when we survey the societies studied by anthropologists, we can see that some are certainly happier than others. In some the people are, on the whole, cheerful, productive, friendly and contented, as in Samoa. In others the reverse is true, as with the Dobu of the Western Pacific, who live in a state of perpetual suspicion and regard a friendly individual as weak in the head. Thus variations in the general level of happiness *are* possible. And even if we hold that this world is only the preparation for a better one, surely it must still be desirable that society should free people for such preparation, and not crush or frustrate them to the point where they commit suicide or take to drink, instead of preparing themselves for futurity.

However, the point I am chiefly trying to make is that the pursuit of happiness is not simply a task for the individual as has generally been assumed. For the fact is, that some societies make the attainment of fulfilment much harder than do others: they provide structures which are well adapted to facilitate human ambitions or others which frustrate them. They impose conditions and obligations which make fulfilment difficult or easy. In the West, I believe, we have created a social pattern in which the attainment of happiness is, for most people, very difficult and for some impossible. Our society does not provide the conditions for happiness to a growing number of people, despite our convictions to the contrary.

Anyone who ventures to write a book suggesting that society can be ameliorated is likely to be labelled an optimist and to be told that Utopias are impossible. Perfect societies are, true enough, impossible, but if we use the word Eutopia to mean a reasonably satisfactory society, then I am optimistic enough to believe that Eutopias are possible. On the other hand, whether politicians or the voters on whom they depend will adopt the kind of thinking I am putting forward is quite another question. As to this, I am a pessimist. Nevertheless, it is urgently necessary to define the processes involved and to work out a logical solution.

To summarize: Western society is beginning to face up to several fundamental questions. The first which has emerged clearly is: must we limit our demand for goods in order to protect the environment? But this is only the entering edge of a larger question: to what extent do we want goods if this means sacrificing personal satisfactions and fulfilment? We have created a marvellous industrial machine, but it necessitates crowding people into cities. Cities have high crime rates, high suicide rates, high disease rates and loneliness. Is this too high a price to pay? Is it necessary? Is it not possible to get the goods we need at a lower social and personal cost? Is our economic system capable of solving this choice-problem? Then again, is the small family really as rewarding a social pattern as the more communal type of living common in the past? Some people are beginning to say that the family is dead.

Do we really want a permissive society? Personally, I would prefer the man who drives the train or aircraft in which I travel to be a teetotal Puritan rather than a carefree *bon viveur*. And, as we have seen, people are querying whether society offers the range of life-styles needed to fulfil human potentialities.

What people have not cottoned on to is that all these questions are interconnected. Frustration in one area is the price of fulfilment in another.

Finally, how are social changes brought about? The eighteenth century was a permissive society; the nineteenth century a restrictive one. Now we are in a permissive phase again. Will the twenty-first century be restrictive once more? It is quite on the cards. Unless we understand the reasons for such changes, it is useless to plan social reforms for society will simply carry us somewhere else. So it is with social change that I open the discussion.

I. Patterns of the Past

The Sexual Swings

I. *Spontaneity/Control*

IN the long perspective of history many societies can be seen to swing gently between two extremes. It is not a regular movement: sometimes a society will remain for centuries in a particular posture, without much change—then it may move quite rapidly to the other extreme. There it may remain for a while, or it may begin to swing back again almost immediately. Furthermore, these societies reach their highest achievements when they are near the mid-point between these extremes. But the trick of staying at this productive point of balance is one that has never been learned.

The one extreme is characterized by spontaneity, taking no thought for the morrow, 'doing one's own thing'. The other extreme is characterized by inhibition, self-control, conformity to custom. As we shall see, there are other differences, and they are important ones. But, at a quick glance, spontaneity and control are the striking features of the dichotomy.

The implications of these facts for our own society are obvious: a century or so ago we were at the 'self-control' end of the scale—today we are approaching the 'let yourself go' end of the scale. Very many of the social phenomena which people find puzzling can be explained by reference to this fact. The permissive society is just a name for the 'doing your own thing' philosophy, which is another way of saying: obey your impulses, be spontaneous! And when we look more closely we shall see that many other aspects—from long hair to Women's Lib—can be traced back to the same psychological mechanisms that account for the swing in sexual morality. Are we going to remain out on the spontaneity end of the scale indefinitely? Many young people imagine that the new morality is here to stay: that the Western world has broken out of an age-old strait-jacket and will never be put back into it.

But if we look back a century and a half, we can see, in England, another permissive age. The diaries of men like Horace Walpole and the reports of foreign visitors like Le Blanc from France or Zetzner from Germany depict a society hardly less permissive than our own. Zetzner, while much impressed by Englishwomen, wrote that 'the women of this country are much given to sensuality, to carnal inclinations, to gambling, to drink and to idleness'. Le Blanc noted that they did not suffer from false modesty: 'If a girl fancies a man and can't get to know him, she'll send him a message with her proposal, or advertise.' And in his book he reproduces one of these newspaper advertisements. Walpole describes how he had to wait half an hour while his girl-friend made her face up. There was even a Women's Lib movement, led by Mary Wollstonecraft, whose *Vindication of the Rights of Women* was a best-seller in 1792.*

Yet within little more than a generation, long before Victoria came to the throne, a period of strict morality had set in. Make-up was taboo, women no longer went for walks with men unknown to their husbands and, far from having admitted carnal inclinations, were hardly considered to exist below the waist.

Such changes have often occurred in history. Early Roman fortitude declined in a couple of centuries to the voluptuary self-indulgence of a Petronius or a Nero. Sparta remained locked in self-control—every schoolboy knows the story of the boy who remained silent when a fox was gnawing his vitals—when nearby Athens was in the productive middle stage. The permissiveness of early Semitic peoples was transformed into the strictness of classical Jewry. The pre-Christian Celts did not prize virginity. Thus Queen Medb boasted to her husband that she had always had a secret lover in addition to her official lover before she was married. (The records are full of such stories. For instance, when Princess Findabair mentioned to her mother that she rather fancied the messenger who had been sent from the enemy camp, the Queen replied: 'If you love him, then sleep with him tonight.' By the Middle Ages, of course, a severe morality had been established, with stringent bans on all kinds of sexual intercourse, which was even regulated closely within marriage, as I have described in *Sex in History*.

Who knows, therefore, whether within a generation or so, the Western world will not be herded back into a new Victorianism? It is an intriguing thought, but not much heeded by the futurologists and planners for tomorrow, who allow no space for crinolines in their egg-like environments-for-living.

II. *Matrism and Patrism*

The first steps towards an understanding of this very potent social process were taken more than half a century ago when anthropologists, at that time much preoccupied with primitive religion, noticed that many societies believed in a father-figure living in the sky as a supreme deity,

* For many further details of eighteenth-century morality, see *Sex in History* (1954), Chapter 9, and for the women's side of the story, *The Angel Makers* (1958), Chapter 14.

while others thought in terms of a mother-figure, identified as the earth. The identification was almost literal. Thus a nineteenth-century anthropologist reports how a Red Indian, Smohalla, refused to work the earth, saying: 'Shall I take a knife and tear my mother's bosom? . . . You ask me to dig for stone! Shall I dig under her skin for her bones? . . . You ask me to cut grass and make hay and sell it, and be rich like white men! But how dare I cut off my mother's hair?' In the Mediterranean world, at the time of Christ, there were earth-mothers in every direction: Cybele, Astarte, Ceres, Demeter, Ishtar, Magna Mater . . . they had many names, but all were conceived as female and as guardians of the earth's fruitfulness. As for sky-fathers, we have only to think of the Christian religion, or that of the Egyptians.

Some societies (such as the Greeks) had both sky-fathers and earth-mothers, and believed that the one fertilized the other, as the rain from the sky makes the earth fruitful.

What the anthropologists further observed was that, when a society believed primarily or exclusively in a sky-father, it tended to be restrictive in sexual matters, assign a low status to women and exhibit an authoritarian political structure; whereas, if it worshipped an earth-mother, it was likely to be permissive in sexual matters, assign a high status to women and to have an egalitarian or (as we would now say) a democratic political system. Thus the worship of the earth-mothers was attended by orgiastic behaviour, while the condemnation of sex by the early Christian fathers is well known.

Now it is something new to see three apparently quite separate features of society—religion, politics and the position of women, tied into a single pattern: it suggests that what goes on in society is not as random as it usually seems.

When I was thinking over the nature of society, shortly after the last war, it suddenly occurred to me that these two contrasting attitudes could well be explained in Freudian terms. Freud described how the child incorporates the behaviour it sees in its parents in its own character, and how it identifies itself with them. Normally the child identifies itself mainly with the parent of the same sex; sons with fathers, daughters with mothers. Identification begins to take place when the child first becomes aware of the fact that it does not monopolize the affection of its mother, but shares it with the father—the famous Oedipus situation. Normally, a child identifies to some extent with both of its parents. As Anthony Storr puts it, it says to itself in effect: 'I must be like them or they will be angry.' As the child develops, it normally reduces its identification and feels free to become itself. But what if the parents are not equally loving? In such cases the child may identify with one parent to secure the love of the other. Thus if the father seems unloving the child is likely to identify with the mother—by becoming the mother, so to speak, it makes itself into its father's love-object, and thus solves the Oedipal problem with its attendant guilt-feelings. To identify with a person is, to some extent, to annihilate them or swallow them up, at least to step into their shoes. If the mother is loving, the child obscurely feels that it can risk this aggressive act (for such it is at the unconscious psychological level) without the mother retaliating. In short, the combination of an unloving, or supposedly unloving, father with a loving mother is the basic situation tending to lead to mother-identification.*

These Freudian ideas are commonplaces of individual psychology. The thought which now struck me was: where the father is introjected, the deity will be visualized as a father; where the mother, as a mother. At once, anthropology was linked with psychology and the rest became clear. Where fathers are upgraded, women will be downgraded. Since fathers are figures of authority, this will seem the way to run society in a father-identifying culture. And since (as Freud explains at great length) the Oedipus situation leads to guilt feelings, the child's love for its mother (which, as Freud also explained, is inherently sexually toned) will seem to be wicked. Thus sex will be wicked: it is the fear of the father's anger at the child's rivalry (in the primitive non-rational thinking of the very small child) which makes sex a dangerous or forbidden act. Conversely, where the mother-figure is introjected, the deity will seem to be a mother, and will be seen as supportive and nourishing, rather than as disciplinary. Women, consequently, will have a high status. Authority will be at a discount, and, like a family of children, men will all be equally important in her eyes, however much they may squabble among one another.

It seemed necessary to invent labels for these two patterns, and I proposed to call them *patrist* and *matrist*.

Patrism combines two ideas: hierarchy and discipline. The individual fits into an organizational structure, in which orders come from above, and rules exist to cover almost every kind of situation. The Army is the classic example of a patrist structure; the Roman Catholic Church is another. Each is organized in ranks, or layers, individuals at one level being in charge of those immediately below, and responsible to someone immediately above. In contrast, matrism sees the individual as free from all external compulsions and hence obviously equal to all other individuals, in the sense of having no authority over them, nor recognizing any. The contrast is between Discipline and Spontaneity. The patrist may incorporate the rules he learns into his personality, where

* In all this I write with the male child in mind: the case for girls is slightly different since their first love-object—their mother—is of their own sex. But for the purpose of understanding the matrist trend in society we need not explore this variation here.

they become known as conscience (or super-ego), and the discipline becomes self-discipline. The matrist, in contrast, responds only to internal impulses, coming from the id rather than the super-ego.

A second consequence is that the patrist tends to wish to preserve the past, as being the work of his forefathers. It is unwise to tamper with anything our fathers have arranged. So the patrist is a conservative—one who wishes to conserve the past unchanged. Any change, he suspects, is for the worse. Thus his attitude is inherently pessimistic.

Also arising from the constraint and discipline of patrism, we find a constraint in movement, gesture and voice; while the matrist is typically free-and-easy, full of quick, uninhibited movements. The sober gait of the Puritan, who frowned on running and laughter, contrasts with the dancing movements and cheerful songs of the matrist. Indeed, dancing and impromptu music or song are specifically matrist activities, whereas marching (or better still, sitting still) and solid, highly organized achievements like architecture are to the patrist taste.

A feature of patrist periods, which derives from the Oedipal situation, is the presence of jealousy feelings, which are sanctioned by society. At such times, a husband whose wife has committed adultery is expected to kill her as well as the seducer, and normally this is excused. Even today French law treats the offender in a *crime passionel* much more lightly than an ordinary murderer. The plays of such periods are preoccupied with jealousy situations, especially in countries like Italy. It is therefore no coincidence that the patrist religion describes its deity as 'a jealous God'—this was the expected attitude of a father-figure.

In matrist periods such jealousy seems to vanish. Irritation may be felt by the betrayed husband, even strong disappointment and a sense of rejection, but not jealousy. Next, simplified divorce enables a man (or woman) to have a succession of mates—a situation which has been termed 'serial polygamy'. This appears as an intermediate stage in the development of sexual promiscuity. Taken further, we find wife-swapping, 'swinging' and so on, indicating a total absence of possessive feelings in the sexual sphere. While wife-swapping is the resort of the married, for the unmarried young simple promiscuity suffices: and to the existence of this the rise in the number of illegitimate pregnancies is sufficient witness, as is the rising abortion rate.

Thus, as anthropologists have noted, matrist societies tend to regard offences against the food supply as more serious than offences against property, while patrist societies take the reverse view. Again, it is noticeable that patrist societies are much shocked by homosexuality, whereas matrist societies are tolerant of homosexuality but alarmed by incest. This too follows from psychoanalytic theory. (For instance, the easy-going Trobrianders, whom Malinowski studied, were quite concerned about incest and had elaborate exogamic regulations.)

Furthermore, I argued that societies do not necessarily remain patrist or matrist indefinitely, but move from one position to another, or remain for considerable periods in an intermediate position: this in fact is the commonest situation.

Before we start to assess the contemporary situation, let us summarize the points made so far, in tabular form.

Patrism	*Matrism*
Restrictive, especially sex.	Permissive, especially sex
Authoritarian	Democratic
Hierarchic	Egalitarian
Women: low status	Women: high status
Conservative	Adaptable
Looks to past	Looks to present or future
Pessimistic, depressive	Optimistic, euphoric
Self-control valued	Spontaneity valued
Homosexuality taboo	Incest taboo
Sexual jealousy	Lack of jealousy
Sky-father religion	Earth-mother or pantheist religion

As we shall see later, yet other distinctions can be found, notably in the field of arts, but this list is sufficient for present purposes.

III. *Our Matrist Age*

When we look at the contemporary scene, we can see very easily that *all* these criteria, without exception, indicate a marked shift towards matrism, and of course most noticeably in the young, who are the coming generation.

It is hardly necessary to produce detailed evidence to prove the existence of a more permissive attitude to sex, and to behaviour generally. The fact that clothes are bright and informal is equally obvious. The increase in tolerance for homosexuality (but not for incest) is attested by changes in the law. It does not need the existence of women's liberation movements to prove rising status for women, interpreted in the sense of identity with men rather than simply admiration for their qualities: the movement started in the last century with Amelia Bloomer and the suffragettes. Above all, the demand for equality and the utter rejection of class or hierarchic differences is widespread: the young simply carry it further when they reject even the right of their teachers to teach and wish to organize their own instruction themselves. The desire for euphoria can be seen in the passion for rock music, which blocks intellectual activity and opens the mind to impulse and euphoric sensations. Drugs also do this, though here other factors are also present, including the desire to defy authority. (It does not seem to have occurred to the 'authorities' as they so accurately describe themselves, that, in a matrist age, to prohibit something is the best way to ensure that people do it.)

We now worry much more about destitution and about nutrition generally than was the case a century ago, whereas crimes against property, which used to be visited with transportation, or in some cases with the death penalty, now receive, as a rule, remarkably light sentences.*

The only item about which some doubt might be expressed is the exchange of a severe sky-father religion for a supportive earth-mother religion. It is certainly true that the sky-father is in disrepute. The 'jealous God' of the Old Testament has been watered down to a supportive form, hell has been put aside and the 'gentle Jesus' forms the centre of religion for those who subscribe to the old forms. Many people, however, have abandoned traditional Christianity for a vague humanism, or for atheism. Others believe in some ill-defined force for good. But out on the wing, we find an orgiastic attitude reminiscent of fertility religion.

The earth-mother religions of the Mediterranean, to which I have referred, were of course fertility religions, marked by periodic orgies—but these orgies were not mere sensuality. The sexual act was seen as a manifestation of life and of the deity identified with life: to perform it ritually was thus a sacrament and at the same time a magical act ensuring fertility in general. The God fertilized through the man, and the man partook in some measure of godhood as a result. Thus it was not far removed from pantheism.

At the same time, the woman who was fertilized was assimilated to the earth. As Shakespeare said: 'An if she were a thornier piece of ground than she is, she shall be ploughed.'

The ecstatic element in sex is certainly stressed by some of the more extreme proponents of the new doctrine. Thus Timothy Leary declares in *The Politics of Ecstasy*: 'The three inevitable goals of the LSD session are to discover and make love with God, to discover and make love with yourself, and to discover and make love with a woman . . . One of the great purposes of an LSD session is sexual union,' and: 'Remember, your body is the kingdom of heaven.'

No doubt about it, we are certainly living in an age of growing matrism.

* 'A Brisbane man aged 20 was convicted for the 96th time and sentenced to 140 years in prison on 20 charges in Australia yesterday. The charges included breaking and entering and theft. The judge recommended that he be released on probation after 3½ years' (*Guardian*, 18 January 1972).

Speaking loosely, one can say that a century is at a given time some-what matrist or somewhat patrist. Of course when we look closely at any particular country, especially if it is a large one, we see that it is made up of groups which may differ considerably among one another in their position on the patrist–matrist scale. This is notably the case in the United States, today. Some of the young are at the very extreme of the matrist scale, others much less so, and a few are quite conservative, especially in states like Utah and Idaho where Mormon influence is strong. At the patrist end of the scale we find the John Birch Society and the Ku Klux Klan, as well as the 'hard-hat' workers and many of the rich, especially on the west coast. Others have adopted the sexual and verbal permissiveness, and the neglect of convention—especially in the semi-wealthy suburbs of big cities—without the element of protest and active rejection of authority.

However, despite these variations, we can still say with truth that the average or norm has shifted towards the matrist in America and Europe. It is not merely a question of private behaviour. Half a century ago, factories and firms were run in a markedly authoritarian way. The employee did just what he was told to do, or was fired. Today, there is much more consultation with employees, more explaining of the reasons for orders and in a few cases the whole arrangement of the work is planned jointly. If the trend goes further, however, and employees consult their personal convenience rather than the needs of the group, the situation will begin to worsen for all. We see the warning signs of this in the taking of time off without notice, which upsets the pro-duction schedule and wastes the time of those who do attend but cannot work in consequence. (If the man who operates the cage, or mineshaft lift, in a coal mine fails to report for work, the entire mine, or that section of it, is brought to a standstill.) Strikes by key workers or groups of workers have a similar effect. Similarly in schools, which were once run on wholly authoritarian lines, a much more permissive and democratic atmosphere reigns and pupils' preferences are consulted.

While the bulk of the population has certainly moved in the matrist direction during the past half century or so, the existence in the USA of unrepentantly patrist and determinedly matrist groups numbering several millions each constitutes a social division which is potentially quite dangerous.

In Europe, I think, there is still rather more homogeneity. Perhaps least in France, where the entire administrative and educational machine is a century out of date in its whole conception. (Though it is hard for an American or a Briton to believe, in every French school on a given day at a given hour, every pupil in a given class is opening the same textbook at the same page.) Holland, too, with its strong Protestant tradition, seems sharply split. In England, on the other hand (except for the judiciary, which has remained patrist in the extreme), there has been a considerable modification of attitude even in the army and police forces, and still more in education. England has a long tradition of absorbing new elements into the ruling class: this has been made possible by its pragmatic 'common-sense' tendency and distaste for being governed by abstract principles. England has, to be sure, its Mosley and its Powell and a small group of Conservatives of the extreme right: interestingly enough, their support comes largely from women. And while the trade unions remain largely patrist, they are less militantly so than the 'hard hats' of America. (English Unions *are* militant about money of course, if not about manners and customs generally.)

It would be interesting to know more about the situation in Russia, where a patrist administration is in conflict with matrist youth. But where naked force is freely available, organized patrists can always crush the disorganized matrists, since matrists are by their nature incapable of order (cf. the crushing of millenarian movements in European history).

To identify today's trend towards license as a familiar historical phenomenon is a small step forward: it holds out the possibility that we may be able to assess it better. Moreover, it enables us to see the likely future, for history suggests that when society becomes too anarchic, a swing-back automatically results. Alarmed, people turn to a strong ruler, or a dictator, to restore order and purpose to society. Society gets out of the fire, only to find itself back in the frying-pan. This is a real danger today.

The crucial question then is: will the trend towards matrism continue, or will some sudden swing-back develop? To answer this we need to examine the causes which bring about movements of this type.

The foregoing analysis also explains convincingly a number of other features of the contemporary scene which people often find puzzling.

IV. *Further Aspects*

Inspection of patrist and matrist phases in society shows the rather unexpected fact that in patrist phases there is a wide difference between the clothes and general appearance of men and those of women, while in matrist periods the appearance of the two sexes becomes very similar. Even seen in silhouette against the sky, no one could mistake the outline of a Victorian man for that of his wife. But in the more matrist age of Charles II, the clothes of the two sexes (though not in the patrist Puritan groups, of course) became amazingly similar. Both men and women wore elaborate lace collars, broad-brimmed hats with feathers and buckled shoes. To be sure, the man's breeches, though bulky, were noticeably different from the skirts of his spouse, but the materials used

and the colours were the same. Today, as everyone knows, the assimilation between the appearance of the two sexes is very striking. Both in
clothes and hair-styles, the two are often indistinguishable. Odd as some
people find it, it was entirely predictable, and as a matter of fact I did
predict it in 1954 in my *Sex in History*.

Patrist clothes, because of the fear of spontaneity, are formal in
appearance, restrained in colour. Matrist clothes are extravagant in
colour and cut, highly personal and the style changes frequently. We
have only to think of the Puritans with their greys and browns, or the
sober habits of the monks and friars (the word 'sober' is significant)
contrasted with the fantastic shapes and colours of a matrist period,
such as our own. The patrist also likes to formalize clothing, prescrib-
ing just what shall be worn; the army does this explicitly, as does the
Church. The Victorians formalized men's clothing so much that a
difference in the number of buttons on the cuff or the style of securing
a boot became matters of attention and censure.

In 1954, although the clothes of women had become assimilated to
those of men, surprisingly men had not shown a parallel movement
towards femininity. That movement has now occurred. The psychological explanation is sufficiently obvious. Men seek to meet female
standards when they have incorporated a feminine model, but fear to
be thought unmasculine when they have identified with a male figure.

Clothes, however, are only the outward and visible sign of the desire
of the two sexes to approximate: more significant is the behavioural
trend: the desire to approach life in the same way, to make jobs open
to both sexes (whereas under patrism some jobs are decisively men's,
others ineluctably women's) and in general to bring the sexes into what
is called equality, but is perhaps more accurately identity—as the word
'unisex' so well expresses.

A minor but intriguing distinction between matrist and patrist is the
matrist preference for shagginess, the patrist preference for smoothness
—preferences which appear not only in respect of hair but in terms of
tidiness and formality generally. Mary Douglas, noting this contrast,
interprets it simply in terms of rejecting a norm: matrists are shaggy, she
would say, because they reject patrist norms. But there is more to it than
that. For example, we find that the patrist admires rather peaceful,
tidied-up scenery, where the matrist admires wildness, roughness, brilliant colours and even ruin and decay. The beetling cliff topped by a
blasted pine and fringed with a thundering waterfall appeals to them
more than a peaceful meadow or ships at anchor. Thus we see the
formal parterres and neat topiary of the seventeenth century giving way
to the natural, assymetrical concept of landscape in the eighteenth.
Addison argued as early as 1712 for the 'beautiful wildness of nature' as
against 'the nicer Elegancies of Art'. He liked 'trees and shrubs growing

freely' and a stream that runs 'as it would do in an open field'. By the end of the century Uvedale Price, in his classic statement *On the Picturesque* was admiring the 'animation of windblown trees'; he preferred dead and decaying trees to live ones, since they exhibit 'a variety of tints, of mellow and brilliant lights, with deep and peculiar shades, which healthy trees cannot exhibit'.* Patrists, of course, with function in view, root out dead and decaying trees and replant. In fine, the matrist feeling for shagginess goes back to his basic preference for spontaneity and movement, as against discipline and planning. Wild and untamed scenery reflects his own uninhibited impulses. Indeed, he comes to regard impulse as a positive good, and to seek within himself for new experience—hence the appeal of mind-changing drugs. The wild and savage act begins to have a certain beauty of its own, for much the same reason that wild and savage scenery has: it proves the power and freedom from constraint of his personal impulses.

Another distinction I owe to Piers and Singer, whose important book *Shame and Guilt* is too little known. These writers, one a sociologist the other a psychologist, noticed that societies tend to be regulated either by shame or by guilt. Shame may be defined as a reaction to a loss of social approval, in contrast with guilt which arises from failure to live up to an internalized standard, i.e. the demands of conscience. Where the person motivated only by a sense of shame is prepared to perform any act which is socially approved, the guilt-ridden person is ready to defy public opinion to preserve his private conception of what is right. We can see these distinctions clearly in history: the guilt-ridden Puritan defying social codes and indeed attacking them, while in the eighteenth century the concept of 'honour' reflects a preoccupation with the opinion of others.

Today we often hear some minor misdemeanour defended by the argument 'Well, everybody does it.' Small-scale theft, bribery, deception, lack of consideration, etc., which a conscientious person would eschew, have become all too common. We are in a shame-society, not a guilt-society. When the New Liners boast that we have got rid of guilt, they do not realize that they have made the Good Society harder to attain, not easier. Once again, the explanation is in terms of internalizing a stern father-figure.†

My third point brings together two areas of human activity which are constantly in conflict, and never more so than today: art and morality.

---

* For a much fuller treatment of this topic, see *The Angel Makers*, Chapter 11, where other Romantic preferences are also linked to this one.

† Strictly speaking, the sense of guilt is laid down on top of the sense of shame, so that the patrist does respond to public opinion when no guilt-feelings are involved, or if they reinforce public opinion. 'What will Mrs Grundy say?' (from *Speed the Plough*, 1796) became a tag-line in the nineteenth century because it encapsulated this awareness of public censure.

The conflict becomes intelligible when we come to realize that the patrist judges art by moral standards, where the matrist judges human behaviour by aesthetic standards. When a French schoolboy and a middle-aged schoolteacher developed a mad passion for each other and began to live together, despite disastrous consequences for the education of the one and career of the other, many young people thought it 'beautiful' and the film dramatization drew crowds. Conversely, phrases like 'that's not very pretty' are often used to describe unethical behaviour. And the literal way in which the patrist applies moral standards to art is amusingly shown by Dr Johnson's objection to the fashion for serpentine (i.e. curving) paths, which, he thought, sought to make the distance between two points seem longer than it really was. 'A lie, Sir, is a lie,' he said, 'whether it be a lie to the eye or a lie to the ear.'

Because the patrist's preoccupation is moral, when he finds it necessary to produce something which could be regarded as art, he uses it for a moral purpose. Thus pictures and novels must be 'improving to the mind'. Patrists do not have to paint pictures, but they need buildings, so that the point is shown especially clearly in architecture. The early Christian churches were built to meet certain needs—they were functional—and at the same time they used symbolism to preach a message. They were shaped like a cross and they pointed towards Jerusalem. Paintings and carvings did not attempt naturalism: they were simply pictographs or strip cartoons conveying a moral message. As the great age of Gothic churches developed, decoration for decoration's sake became general. By the eighteenth century churches were rarely cross-shaped and often faced in the direction required by the aesthetics of their siting.

In contrast, the matrist sacrifices morality and even functional effectiveness to aesthetic standards. In Vanbrugh's great palace of Blenheim, the kitchens are a quarter of a mile from the dining-room!

When we appreciate this distinction, many things become clear: for instance, we see why the functional architecture of the Bauhaus school arose in the more patrist country of Germany, in reaction to the matrist excesses of the French surrealists. Much as I should like to explore these artistic implications further, my purpose here is to cast light on our own society. So I need only observe that the modern tendency to judge behaviour by aesthetic standards is as dangerous as the habit of judging art by moral standards. Indeed, it may be more so, if it leads to the motiveless murders of a Manson or the 'murder for thrills' of Leopold and Loeb. The truth is that we must always keep both aspects in view. Buildings and machines should be both functional *and* aesthetic. A film may be morally degrading even though beautiful, and the one does not excuse the other.

Quite a number of further inferences from the patrist–matrist theory can be made, but I will limit myself to only one more, since it is relevant to our main purpose, the devising of a better society. This I will call, rather sonorously, the Doctrine of the Fall and the Belief in a Golden Age.

The patrist, at least in Western society, believes that once there was a Golden Age, a Paradise, in which everything was perfect: plants grew without effort, there was no aggression, the climate was mild, and so on. He feels that things 'are not what they were', that the country is going to the dogs. This depressive attitude can be traced in part to the sexual frustration which he creates by his restrictive morality—Freud taught us that repression causes depression. And psychoanalysts would say that the vision of a peaceful, effortless age is a memory of infancy, or even of life in the womb.

In contrast, the matrist has little respect for the past—as witness our students with their rejection of history as 'irrelevant' and their conviction that even the immediately preceding generation has little to teach them. The matrist lives for the present, and tends to optimism about the future. Thus the orientation of the two types towards time is quite different. The patrist does not only look back to the past, to the precedents established by his forefathers, but by virtue of his self-control, he is able to postpone satisfaction: and so can undertake great works which take many years to come to fruition, or even, like the medieval cathedrals, consume many lifetimes, so that the initiators never see the fruits of their work. I am reminded of the great garden at Inver-ewe on the stormy north-western coast of Scotland, which took three generations to establish. The founder, Osgood Mackenzie, simply planted shelter belts of trees, without which no garden was possible. His son planted the shrubs and decorative trees; his grandson completed the task. (Who is there in this matrist age who would take on such a project?)

The matrist prefers to express himself in spontaneous forms, which require a minimum of preparation, such as informal dancing, where there are no set manoeuvres, or extempore music. In pictorial art, he would rather roll a naked woman daubed with printing ink over a sheet of paper than elaborately plot perspective like a Leonardo, or chip with infinite care like a Michelangelo.

The short time-perspective of the matrist makes it impossible for him to build Utopias. He may imagine them, and demand them, but patrists take the revolution over and see it through—to a patrist conclusion.

The matrist, therefore, one could say, concentrates on Being, whereas the patrist concentrates on Doing. Quite recently, many New Liners have become conscious of this distinction and claim with satisfaction they are 'be' people and not 'do' people. However, as we shall see, this is no cause for pride, for there is a third possibility which is more constructive.

V. *Middle Positions*

In the first enthusiasm generated by breaking free of rigid and probably obsolete patrist controls, many people fall into the error of regarding matrism as an ideal, a state to be aimed at. Freedom is intoxicating and we tend to feel we cannot have enough of it: but one can easily have too much of an intoxicant. The lesson of history—and history does have lessons for us if we look at it correctly—is that society functions best and most creatively when there is a balance of father and mother introjections. Middle positions are best.

When Europe burst free of the patrist restrictions of the Middle Ages there was a creative outburst, and it was especially strong in England which rejected the rule of the Catholic Church without falling into the fire of a Calvinistic puritanism. An 'Elizabethan age' has become a synonym for a period of bold endeavour. And it is entirely consonant with my theory that the creative outburst appeared first and reached its highest artistic peaks in Italy, a country which has long tended to display a matrist element, as we can deduce from the development of a cult of the Virgin Mary from the eleventh century onward. In the popular mind, as Robert Briffault has shown, she shed her specifically Christian attributes and became a succouring mother-figure, whose interventions even included, reputedly, taking the place in bed of an unfaithful wife so that her husband should not suspect that his wife was really with her lover! She was accorded the same worship as Ceres, the presentation of cakes symbolic of fertility, and was reputed to be able to cure impotence.

Similarly, when Victorian restrictions broke down at the end of the nineteenth century, as when Roman patrism began to crumble in the first century, we find a period of novel developments, bold projects and artistic achievement.

The reason is not hard to find. Extreme patrism clamps down on the creative urge, at the individual level, and, at the social level, dislikes and discourages innovation. On the other hand, extreme matrism develops creative impulses, but lacks the self-discipline to carry them to fulfilment. If men always give way to the impulses of the moment, no one will plant the corn for next year, or learn the techniques which make society civilized. If you are having your car serviced, it is desirable that the mechanic should check the oil and brake-fluid with a puritanical attention to detail. (Perhaps that is why the engineers of British steamships were so often Scotsmen!) On the other hand, a society in which all behaviour is prescribed becomes rigid: when circumstances change its customs are inappropriate to the new situation but it cannot adapt. It is liable to perish from ossification, just as the spontaneous society will perish from too casual an attitude to its problems.

Fathers and mothers each have something to contribute to the human psyche, and it is in the integration of these contributions that greatness is born. Genius is based on such a synthesis, as we see in a man like Wolfgang von Goethe. As the psychoanalyst Eduard Hitschmann has shown in some detail, Goethe's personality combined elements from his earnest, strict and industrious father and his cheerful and loving mother.* His supreme self-confidence was based on his mother's un-wavering support and admiration, but his drive and his many-sided interests were directly derived from his father, Kaspar. The latter, despite his industry and curiosity, lacked the energy and spontaneity to achieve creative results and was obliged to fulfil himself through his gifted son.

If mid-positions are best, then we must conclude that the current worship of spontaneity in certain sections of society is greatly overdone and represents a threat to society. I am resigned to the fact that anyone who opposes the gospel of 'doing one's own thing' will be labelled a reactionary and accused of wishing to return to strict puritanism. And no doubt it is the case that many of those who are most outspoken about matrist behaviour are patrists and would like to see a much stricter code than I am advocating. That is the difficulty: the moderates find them-selves in uneasy alliance with the extremists, and see that, if they are not careful, the pendulum may swing too far. So I must emphasize that in criticizing current extremes of spontaneity I am simply advocating a balanced, middle position.

It is a depressing feature of human nature that extremists frequently wish to impose their own conception of how to live on those who feel differently. The history of the Christian Church is one long series of attempts by patrists to impose severe, inhibited and guilt-ridden be-haviour on the rest of society. Matrists, since they are more concerned with being than doing, tend to let other people go their own way. They do not normally insist on puritans throwing off their inhibitions and having orgies. They may mock them, call them 'square', even attempt to embarrass them a little, but they do not set up a machinery of control. However, this may be too flattering a view, for recently we have seen signs of matrists consciously working for the overthrow of 'bourgeois morality'. (Thus when the young editors of *Oz* were on trial in Britain for attempting to subvert schoolchildren, they insisted that they were doing so as part of a social mission to change society. In the USA,

* 'Psychoanalytisches zur Personlichkeit Goethes' (1932), reprinted in *Neurose und Genialität* (ed. Johannes Cremerius) (S. Fischer Verlag, 1971).

Timothy Leary has consciously made propaganda for his orgiastic views. No doubt it is this wish to go to extremes which makes the pendulum swing, and hinders maintaining mid-positions.)

VI. *Reasons for the Swing*

Since we know that society has moved, on the whole, from father- to mother-identification we may expect to find evidence of fathers who appear to be unloving.

It hardly needs saying that the father who is most likely to seem unloving is the one who is absent. And even if one were sure of his love, it would still be difficult to introject (incorporate in oneself) his attitudes and personality: to model oneself on him, in plainer words. It is parents' behaviour, rather than their views, which we emulate as children: we cannot emulate a parent we never see. The case-books of psychiatrists are full of instances of mother-identifying adults who report: 'Father left home when I was five.'

Now in modern society, it is quite common for fathers to return from work after the child has gone to bed. When the child is very young, and goes to bed perhaps at 6 p.m., many a father, commuting to and from work, comes home after it is asleep. In other cases, the father travels during the week, or is away for months at a time: he may be an oil geologist, a seaman, a commercial traveller or an anthropologist. Modern travel facilities make it easy for people who a century ago would rarely have left their home town—university teachers, say—to go abroad to conferences, to work in other laboratories and so on. As far as I know, no research has been done into the number of hours of weekly exposure to the father experienced by children at various ages in all the various groups and sections of society; it is badly needed. There are businessmen who, when they do come home, retire to the study with documents and see little of their families; there are men who spend Sunday fishing or in some group of adult friends, and see little of their children. This is especially true when the children are very small, the crucial period. Later, the father may enjoy taking his son with him to golf, fish or whatever; but when he is two or three years old contact depends on father devoting his weekend to his family.

Modern society has separated the mother from young children to a much less dramatic extent, partly because of their obvious need. Where it separates both parents from the child, a total failure of its capacity for affection and delinquency or severe emotional troubles in adult life commonly follow, but this is another story.

Naturally, it is not only absent fathers who are not introjected. It is difficult to introject a father who is harsh, violent, drunken, psychotic or highly inconsistent; and if he is schizoid and unable to display affection, it is evident that an affectionate relationship cannot be developed. In all such cases, identification may occur.

Thus the development of social pathology in the form of drunkenness, schizophrenia, etc., may be expected to favour mother-identification. Later, we shall see why such social pathology is so severe and probably increasing.

To some, the idea of an identification with the mother, however logically argued, will seem strange. The facts, however, speak for themselves. Thus Dr Anthony Storr says: 'In adult life it is not rare to meet neurotics who still cannot distinguish between what they feel and what their mother feels, and who attribute to their mothers thoughts and even bodily sensations which, to an outside observer, have nothing to do with anyone else.' And he goes on to make the comment: 'It is my impression that the children who are most identified with their parents are those whose upbringing has been most fraught with anxiety; and, if they become parents in adult life, one can observe with what irrational fear even the smallest departure from parental standards is attended.'

History has many examples of authoritarian fathers being followed by authoritarian sons, as well as of sons who rebound to the other extreme. This suggests that severity (as distinct from sadistic harshness, bullying, neglect and so on) does not of itself prevent introjection occurring. The child has a great readiness to accept what it finds as normal, and can accept harshness as normal, provided it senses an underlying affection and support. Indeed, a father who displays no aggression leaves his children insecure because they have no evidence that he will effectively defend them against outside attack. A certain roughness is expected of a father. A child who has been threatened with punishment if it pursues a certain course, and then does so, is left in uncertainty if the punishment it invited does not materialize. As Madame Montessori pointed out seventy years ago, children seek to establish the limits society sets to their activity. They accept that if these limits are overstepped, something drastic will happen, just as they accept that if they touch the fire they will be burned. They hold no grudge, if the punishment is just. (As Kipling's schoolboys said of their housemaster, not without affection: 'He is a beast, but a just beast.') On the other hand, failure of the expected punishment to materialize leaves them uncertain and insecure.

Today, many parents are very reluctant to punish, even when punishment has been promised. And by some misunderstanding of Freud's teaching, they believe that a child should be frustrated as little as possible, so that they set few limits in any case, but tend to throw on the child the responsibility for deciding how to behave long before it is ready to carry such a burden.

Thus even the boy who introjects his father is today likely to introject a very weak or indulgent father, deprived of the authoritarian and conservative attributes we associate with fathers in principle. This therefore contributes to the matrist trend, for it weakens the father-figure at a time when the mother-figure is being strengthened.

When identification with the mother is carried to the extreme it may lead to homosexuality: the attempt to become one's father's wife is made a literal one. However, there are other quite different mechanisms leading to homosexuality, one of them being fear of the mother, who has to be annihilated. There is no need to pursue this complex subject here: I mention the point simply to make clear why, in matrist periods, homosexuality is condemned much less, if at all, than in patrist ages. By the same token the incest of a son and a mother continues to arouse repugnance.

The account I have just given is a highly simplified one. But nothing in life is simple, least of all human personality and behaviour. It is sufficient for the present purpose, but I should perhaps add one or two points.

The abdicating father evidently provides little material for the achievement of a classic father introjection. As we shall see in Chapter 10, the most obvious consequence of this is failure to form an adequate superego, and it is to this, in conjunction with other supporting factors, that we can attribute the rise in dishonesty, pilfering, misrepresentation and the like, which is a depressingly common feature of contemporary life.

We have considered only the simple case of one loving and one unloving parent: but in life much more complex situations may develop. First one parent may be absent, then the other, for instance. Both parents may be very affectionate, but both may die. And so on.

There is a further aspect of this intriguing constellation of ideas which the reader will soon recognize. One might call it 'father-rejection'. The father-rejector is more than a rebel, he wants to destroy father and his authority altogether.

When a boy-infant identifies with his mother he may, if the relationship is satisfying enough, be simply indifferent about his father and authority. But often he feels bitterly angry and resentful of him for his neglect. The poet Shelley is a classic example of the father-rejector. At Oxford, for instance, he was in trouble for proposing the toast: 'To the confusion of my father and the King!' Mother-identification explains his lack of sexual jealousy—he invited his best friend to share the favours of his wife, Harriet, at a time when he was happily married to her; and later, when he ran off to Switzerland with Mary Godwin, he wrote to Harriet suggesting that she join them. Blake is another matrist figure who had mixed feelings about fathers: his poem 'To Nobodaddy' looks like an attempt to annihilate the father.

The father-rejector is not only opposed to all authority but takes pleasure in flouting the conventions and behaviour approved by the authority—examples are all around us. The students who invade the dean's office, sit in his chair and smoke his cigars, are obviously doing more than protest. The poor unfledged things are trying to take Daddy's place!

I am inclined to think that the father-rejector is one who has failed to get from his mother the kind of support which would compensate for his loss of the father. Such a thing can happen even when the mother is normally affectionate if she has to transfer much of her attention to a younger or an ailing child, for instance. And if the mother denigrates her husband to her child, this seems to have a damaging effect.

In short, father-rejection and mother-identification tend to go hand in hand, but sometimes the accent falls more heavily on one element than on the other. It follows that the father-rejector who is not greatly mother-identified will lack many of the specifically matrist attitudes which I have described—the interest in the arts, and so on. His motives are different; if he espouses Women's Lib, let us say, it is more because he wishes to annoy men than to gratify women. All in all, the pure father-rejector is a much more anti-social figure than the uncomplicated mother-identifier. And today the woods are full of them.

I have the impression that father-rejectors often revert to patrism later in life, and more particularly after their fathers are dead. Revenge becomes a dead issue, and he now feels free to step into his father's shoes: he may then become as intolerable a conservative as he once was a radical.

VII. *Reversing the Trend*

By the same token, a comprehensive policy for reversing the trend would also have to include factors which we have not yet considered, yet it may be interesting even at this early stage to indicate the sort of measures which seem required to bring about a swing back towards the centre as far as the matrist/patrist elements are concerned.

Clearly they include a firmer attitude on the part of parents towards children, and in particular the restoration of the father as a mildly authoritative figure, both in the sense of one who reinforces the mother's authority in punishing serious misbehaviour, and in the more general sense of one who sets aims and standards and supports the reasonable conventions of civilized living. More specifically, parents should not consult the whims and preferences of the child to the extreme now common. It is difficult to write such prescriptions without seeming to advocate a return to real Victorianism and I must emphasize that it is only a moderate tightening-up that I am proposing on the basis of the known facts. Obviously a child must be allowed to have some preferences and they must be respected, but there is a difference between preferences and whims. Thus, children often have a rooted dislike of certain foods—dislikes which may pass away later—and these dislikes may have real physiological or psychological bases. It would be cruel and unnecessary to compel it to eat such foods. It is quite another thing for a child to refuse acceptable food from whim, desire for something more luxurious or the wish to be difficult.

Not only must the father resume his natural role, but, of course, he must be present often enough to exert it. Apart from the need to make introjections, small children need the emotional link with both parents, and absences of more than a few hours are harmful in the first years of life; absences of a week or two are acceptable by the age of six or seven, of a month or more a little later.

The extreme confidence shown by most young people today suggests that the link with the mother is strong enough, though of course there are many individual exceptions.

Eventually other figures, schoolteachers or admired heroes in sport or adventure become models too, and so there is some obligation on them too to set standards of behaviour.*

However, it is too early in my story to explore the question of child upbringing and education in much detail. Here I am mainly concerned to show the nature and origins of two opposing 'life-styles' which seem to have alternate innings in Western culture. At the same time, I am trying to convince you that the decisions we take, and the values on which we base them, which seem to us so natural as to be almost beyond discussion, are in fact quite arbitrary. Until you recognize that society is a psychological machine which moulds you without your being aware of it, you are wearing blinkers which make it impossible for you to assess where society is or where it should go in any rational manner.

But matrism and patrism are not the only possible life-styles: there is at least one other two-pronged choice which offers contrasting value

---

* At this point, we come up against the much-debated question of the influence of films and television. The fact that the public continues to worry about this, despite the frequent disclaimers issued, suggests that they have strong intuitive suspicions that the media are influential. And, as has been pointed out, if they do *not* influence behaviour, there would be no reason for advertisers to spend large sums on advertising designed to influence behaviour through the media. From a sociological viewpoint, I believe it can be safely said that the media are at fault if, taking the output as a whole, they present an incorrect picture of what life is like and of what behaviour is acceptable. It is not that bad behaviour should not be shown, but that it should not be shown disproportionately to good behaviour.

systems and ways of behaving. It has been called by many names, and its origins in the psyche are less well understood than those of matrism and patrism. It has to do with sympathy and ruthlessness, with individuality and group-allegiance, with pantheism and with retributive deities. But we are already in the next chapter . . .

The Success Society

I. *Tough and Tender*

LOOKING back over human history, one observes astonishing extremes of human behaviour. On the one hand, the Tartar hordes making pyramids of human skulls from their victims; on the other, the tender love of uncounted mothers, the self-transcendence of a Florence Nightingale or a Captain Oates. On the one hand, Genghis Khan and the Spanish Inquisition. On the other, Saint Francis de Sales and Oxfam. Familiarity blinds us to the strangeness of this fact. How can some human beings be so insensitive to the suffering of others, while others feel physically sick at the sight? In fourteenth-century Provence, the favourite amusement of Raymond de Turenne was to compel his prisoners to jump to their death from the walls of his cliff-hung castle. We are told that he laughed until the tears ran down his face as he watched their hesitation and anguish. I can imagine a tyrant feeling sadistic satisfaction at such a spectacle, but my imagination boggles at simple-hearted mirth.

The great American psychologist William James considered that the range from tough-mindedness to tender-mindedness was one of the most fundamental parameters in personality. In recent years, Professor H. J. Eysenck of the London Institute of Psychiatry has explored this tough–tender scale in some detail, showing that it corresponds closely to the extroversion–introversion scale proposed by the Swiss psychoanalyst Carl Jung. The extrovert is practical, materialistic and deals with the environment by force (e.g. the soldier) or by manipulation (e.g. the scientist). That is, he is tough, whereas the introvert is idealistic, theoretical and deals with problems by thinking (e.g. the philosopher) or by belief (e.g. the priest). He is tender-minded. The one is pessimistic and sceptical, the other optimistic and dogmatic.

Incidentally, Eysenck places great emphasis on another even more fundamental parameter, the range from conservative to radical, and shows how many political attitudes can be regarded as a combination of these two factors. Thus the fascist is conservative and tough, the communist radical and tough. The tender conservative is religiously minded—often a cleric—the tender radical is a humanitarian, maybe a humanist. When people are questioned concerning their attitudes on specific issues such as birth-control or the death penalty, these fit in with their personality in a logical manner: for instance, tough conservatives favour the death penalty and think children should be brought up strictly; tender radicals are pacifist, and so forth.*

It will be obvious that Eysenck's conservative–radical scale corresponds closely to my patrist–matrist distinction, though it is conceived in much narrower terms. Eysenck is a bitter critic of psychoanalysis, which seems to drive him to such extremes of exasperation that a psychoanalyst could not help but suspect that Eysenck is influenced by some unconscious motive. This blind spot cuts Eysenck off from recognizing the link between patrism and such factors as jealousy or the wish to distinguish the sexes clearly, which otherwise he might have explored with his statistical techniques and which would undoubtedly have confirmed and extended his very useful investigations. But, within its limits, Eysenck's very different approach strikingly confirms my earlier predictions. (Eysenck, I must make clear, is only concerned with understanding the personality of individuals and does not extrapolate from the individual to the pattern of society as a whole, as I am doing.)

In order to understand where our own society is going, we need to take notice of the tough–tender element, as well as the patrist–matrist one. It is clear that there has been a considerable change from toughness to tenderness in the past hundred years: we now undertake all sorts of aid for poor, sick and disadvantaged people, both at home and in other countries, on a scale undreamed of a century ago. We concern ourselves more with the misfortunes of those persecuted by dictatorial régimes and of the victims of foreign wars. Many people could now be described as idealist and anti-materialist, whereas a century ago the see-saw would have been down at the other end.

But in my view the tough–tender parameter is much too narrowly conceived, and to understand the psychological forces of which it is the index, we need to approach the subject from a fresh angle.

Long before psychologists revived the tough–tender scale, anthropologists were busy making a distinction in the study of societies which I believe is related to it. The story starts with the late Ruth Benedict's bombshell of a book, *Patterns of Culture*, first published in 1938. In it she presented studies of three societies: the Pueblo Indians of Mexico, and specifically the Zuñi tribe among them; the Dobu of south-west New Guinea, and the Kwakiutl of the north-west American coast. These names have become almost hackneyed in anthropological literature, thanks to the immense interest her book aroused.

What had struck Benedict so forcibly was the fantastic individualism

* See Eysenck's excellent *The Psychology of Politics* (Routledge and Kegan Paul, 1954).

and aggressiveness of the Dobu and the Kwakiutl, contrasted with the extreme peacefulness and group-mindedness of the Zuñi. The Dobu think only in terms of personal success and doing the other man down. Trading is a mania with them; their marriages are more like duels than partnerships. The Zuñi could not be more different: a man who has built a house or raised a crop and who, for some reason is obliged to leave the pueblo, has no feeling of loss—he worked for the group, not for himself. When a Zuñi is asked to take on the post of *kachina* (a kind of elder in the tribe) he refuses, and strong pressure is needed to obtain acceptance. A death is mourned because the group has lost a member, not because of a personal loss.

Later, the anthropologist Mary Douglas christened the society of individualists a 'success society' and I have borrowed the term for the heading of this chapter, though unfortunately there is no equally graphic term for the group-minded society. The reader will see at once that the nineteenth-century United States was unequivocally a success society. The formation of communes today, and the rejection of the 'rat race' by many young people, and some not so young, is just as evidently a revolt from the concept of personal success and a manifestation of 'groupiness'—a horrible word which I first heard at the National Laboratory for Group Development, at Bethel, Maine in 1949 and which has become part of the jargon. The current fashion for 'grope-groups' and sensitivity training is palpably another manifestation of the same social swing.

I named the United States as a classic example of the success society, for in European countries the position was more complex. In Europe, a rising 'middle class' devoted to success gradually submerged a hierarchically ordered society, in which each person accepted the station in life to which it had pleased God to call him, and did not presume to mount the social scale. Thus patrism gave way to individualism more obviously than in the United States, where hierarchy had gone out when the father-rejectors expelled the British. These are generalizations, to be sure; the French revolution modified the picture in France; the moulding of Germany from the dukedoms gave the German story its special character; and even in England dukes sometimes married actresses. But the broad picture remains valid: we are witnessing a swing in social ethos or preferred life-style from individualism to group-ism. And just as in the case of matrism and patrism, we are justified in suspecting that a mid-position of some kind is more desirable than either extreme.

But why should this really rather curious change in attitude take place? What is the underlying mechanism? When we have identified it, we shall see that the distinction is a good deal more far-reaching than either the behaviourist psychologists or the anthropologists suppose.

II. *Pantheist and Puritan*

Religious beliefs take their form from unconscious preoccupations and, like dreams, are the royal road to understanding the unconscious level of the mind. It was the contrast between sky-fathers and earth-mothers which first demonstrated the matrist–patrist distinction; there should then be some religious contrast which reflects the individualist–group-minded distinction.

And when I ask myself where in Western history have I seen intense self-preoccupation contrasted with a loss of sense of self I am immediately struck by the sense of isolation of the protestant–puritan and the pantheistic sense of one-ness with others and with nature in the poems of Lord Shaftesbury and much later, the Lake Poets. (There were also, as a matter of fact, religious groups of a pantheistic character, though not much is known about them.)

The sense of unity with all nature seems to burst on people as a sudden, blinding experience and one of the most vivid descriptions of this is given by Dr P. M. Bucke, who was so struck by it that he collected many other accounts and published them under the title *Cosmic Consciousness* in 1901. He writes: 'I had spent the evening in a great city, with two friends, reading and discussing poetry and philosophy. We parted at midnight. I had a long drive in my hansom to my lodging. My mind, deeply under the influence of the ideas, images and emotions called up by the reading and talk, was calm and peaceful. I was in a state of quiet, almost passive enjoyment, not actually thinking but letting ideas, images and emotions flow of themselves, as it were, through my mind. All at once, without warning of any kind, I found myself wrapped in a flame-coloured cloud. For an instant I thought of fire, an immense conflagration somewhere close by in that great city; the next, I knew that the fire was within myself. Directly afterwards there came upon me a sense of exultation, of immense joyousness accompanied or immediately followed by an intellectual illumination impossible to describe. Among other things, I did not merely come to believe, but I saw that the universe is not composed of dead matter but is, on the contrary, a living Presence; and I became conscious in myself of eternal life. I saw that all men are immortal; that the cosmic order is such that without any peradventure all things work together for the good of each and all. The vision lasted a few seconds and was gone; but the memory of it and the sense of reality of what it taught has remained during the quarter of a century which has since elapsed.'*

---

* I give this passage in the version cited by Don Cuthbert Butler in his *Western Mysticism* (1922), which differs from the version in the US edition of *Cosmic Consciousness*, available to me, in being in direct speech. The indirect form reads awkwardly today.

It was clear enough to Dr Bucke that his experience was religious in nature, for among the other instances he lists are the conversion of St Paul and the visions of several of the Christian mystics. Freud also recognized this experience, which he termed 'the oceanic feeling'. People generally find it hard to describe, but poets are trained in using language to convey feelings and so Tennyson's account in his reminiscences is particularly valuable. 'I have never had any revelations through anaesthetics,' he writes, 'but a kind of waking trance—this for lack of a better word—I have frequently had, quite up from boyhood, when I have been alone. This has come upon me from repeating my own name two or three times to myself silently, till all at once, as it were out of the intensity of the consciousness of individuality, individuality itself seemed to dissolve and fade away into boundless being, and this is not a confused state, but the clearest of the clearest, and the surest of the surest, the weirdest of the weirdest, utterly beyond words, where death was an almost laughable impossibility, the loss of personality (if so it were) seeming no extinction, but the only true life. I am ashamed of my feeble description. Have I not said the state is utterly beyond words?'

Where Tennyson stresses the dissolution of self, Wordsworth puts forward the idea (also mentioned by Bucke) of feeling a divine presence. In the *Lines Written above Tintern Abbey*, he describes how in his youth, though he had a passion for nature, he experienced no special mystical insight. But later he learned 'to look on nature, not as in the hour of thoughtless youth, but hearing oftentimes the still, sad music of humanity.'

> And I have felt
> A *presence* that disturbs me with the joy
> Of elevated thoughts; a sense sublime
> Of something far more deeply interfused
> Whose dwelling is the light of setting suns,
> And the round ocean and the living air,
> And the blue sky, and in the mind of man:
> A motion and a spirit that impels
> All thinking things, all objects of all thought,
> And rolls through all things. Therefore am I still
> A lover of the meadows and the woods
> And mountains: and of all that we behold
> From this green earth; of all the mighty world
> Of eye, and ear—both what they half create,
> And what perceive; well pleased to recognize
> In nature and the language of the sense
> The anchor of my purest thoughts, the nurse,
> The guide, the guardian of my heart and soul,
> Of all my moral being.

Thus Nature is a sustaining power, a nurse. It is also 'a living presence' and a moral force.

> One impulse from a vernal wood
> May teach you more of man,
> Of moral evil, and of good,
> Than all the sages can.

Byron was another who expressed similar feelings:

> I live not in myself, but I become
> Portion of that around me; and to me
> High mountains are a feeling.

Wordsworth, moreover, speaks of a kind of trance, in which he has a special sight into nature; he too records the moral aspect:

> We are laid asleep
> In body and become a living soul:
> While with an eye made quiet by the power
> Of harmony, and the deep power of joy,
> We see into the life of things . . .

> To every natural form, rock, fruit and flower
> Even the loose stones that cover the highway,
> I gave a moral life; I saw them feel,
> Or linked them to some feeling: the great mass
> Lay bedded in a quickening soul, and all
> That I beheld transpired with inward meaning.

These passages of nature mysticism are not explicitly linked with the divine, but in the same poem we find the following passage, surely remarkable for one nominally a member of the Church of England:

> O'er the wide earth, on mountain and on plain
> Dwells in the affections and the soul of man
> A Godhead, like the universal PAN;
> But more exalted.

(It is, of course, no accident that the deity is called 'Pan': the Greek for everything'. Hence the word 'pantheism'.)

Let me now contrast with this joyful experience the dreadful sense of isolation of the Puritan.

The Puritan was preoccupied with the idea of a severe father-deity who was likely to punish one savagely—hardly surprising in view of the severity of real parents. Many Puritans describe powerful aggressive feelings: 'I took a diabolical pleasure in hanging dogs and worrying cats, and killing birds and insects, mangling and cutting them to pieces,' records Christopher Hopper, a Durham farmer's son. He particularly remembered smashing up a large number of frogs with stones, and afterwards having a nightmare in which frogs were eating the flesh off his bones. He awoke, 'sweating and trembling, and half dead with fear'.

God was conceived, not as loving man but almost as hating him. Thus Jonathan Edwards, the great American preacher, in a sermon entitled 'Sinners in the Hands of an Angry God', tells his listeners: 'You would have gone to hell last night had he not held you like a loathsome spider over the flames by a thread. Every moment of delay accumulates wrath.' In another sermon he returned to the image of the spider suspended over the flames. 'No wonder they are ready to expect every moment when this angry God will let them drop, and no wonder they cry out at their misery, and no wonder that the wrath of God, when manifested but a little to the soul, overbears human strength.' Christianity being, nominally, a religion based on love, one might have thought it impossible for a Christian minister so to corrupt its intentions.

Evidently Puritanism is, in part, an attempt to cope with the aggression evoked by a severe father; and the conversions of many of these Puritans to Methodism caused a sudden reversal of the sense of abandonment and rejection, curiously like the experiences of the pantheists. Peter Jaco, a Cornishman, after being driven 'to the brink of despair' by convictions of guilt, suddenly thought that Christ had died to save him. 'In that moment it seemed to me as though a new creation had taken place. I felt no guilt, no distress of any kind. My soul was filled with light and love.' 'My peace flowed like a river,' said Duncan Wright of Perthshire.

The contrast between pantheistic euphoria and Puritan despair is identical with the contrast between mania and depression and, as is well known, some people suffer both manic and depressive episodes. The poet Cowper was one such: he had many depressive attacks, and one or two joyous manic ones. 'I was struck, not long after my settlement in the Temple, with such a dejection of spirits as none but they who have felt the same, can have the least conception of. Day and night I was upon the rack, lying down in horror and rising up in despair. In this state of mind I continued near a twelvemonth . . .' But later, having gone to live in beautiful country near Southampton, he climbed a hill and sat down. 'It was, on a sudden, as if another sun had been kindled that instant in the heavens . . . I felt the weight of all my misery taken off; my heart became light and joyful in a moment; I could have wept with transport had I been alone.'

But more relevant to my theme is the Puritan's preoccupation with the idea of 'self'. As has been said, the Puritan's god is concerned only with individuals, not with mankind. Significantly, Puritan writers constantly use phrases beginning with 'self'—self-indulgence, self-will and especially self-control. (Others have spoken of their self-satisfaction.) The very word 'selfish' is a Puritan introduction. The Puritan spends a great deal of time brooding over himself and his own personality, the state of his soul and his prospects for the future. This led the German historian Schuecking to speak of the Puritan's 'moral hypochondria'.

Because the Puritan is so concerned about his own affairs (which incidentally tends to make him successful in business) he is strikingly neglectful of the needs and wishes of others. Often he seems to have inhibited his power of feeling for others completely. Sewall, for instance, briefly records in his diary, for 26 May 1720: 'About midnight my dear wife expired to our great astonishment, especially mine.'

This, I think, enables us to identify the origins of the tough–tender dichotomy: the Puritan is tough because he is only interested in himself: information about the sufferings of others carries little emotional weight for him. The pantheist, in contrast, feels the sufferings of others almost as if they were his own, and even feels identified with animals, plants and inanimate nature itself, so that the rape of the earth is like a wound to himself.

How shall we interpret this phenomenon in psychological terms? It seems to me that we are concerned with the ego—that part of our psyche which we learn to recognize as 'I'. When the poet feels himself identified with stones, plants, and so on, it seems clear that the bounds of his ego have been dissolved—as Tennyson specifically states. If in the brain there is a mechanism which tags certain sensations, beliefs, etc., with the label 'part of me', then this mechanism is evidently in abeyance during such an experience. Conversely, in the experience of being cast out, the walls of the ego become, as it were, inordinately thick: the sense of relatedness is in abeyance. I propose therefore to refer to these two remarkable conditions as 'hard' ego and 'soft' ego, for lack of better, accepted terms.*

The experiences just described are, certainly, rather exceptional and extreme: I cite them because they demonstrate that individuals can differ greatly in ego-definition and some individuals undergo involuntary changes in definition. This entitles us to infer that more ordinary individuals differ in ego-definition, though they may never suffer the

---

* This is not to be confused with the terms 'strong' ego and 'weak' ego, as used by psychoanalysts. By these expressions they seem to mean, on the one hand, a well-integrated system of aims, abilities, etc., which enables the possessor to move in a coherent and efficient manner towards some end, and on the other, conflicting or uncertain aims, ill-supported by skills and knowledge, which leave the possessor in an incoherent and ineffective state. The decisiveness and effectiveness of some people, and the inconsistent, ineffective behaviour of others is a matter of experience, and integration of ego-functions is, it goes without saying, clinically important, but the point is a different one.

abrupt changes I have alluded to. Furthermore, we now know that similar changes can be temporarily induced by chemical substances such as LSD.

In addition, it would seem that the ego tends to harden with age as well as to become more patrist: Tennyson, for instance, ended up as rather querulous. Wordsworth, who made a plea for universal education in his youth, ended by complaining that the 'mechanics' institutes simply made 'discontented spirits and insubordinate and presumptuous workmen', and later asked even more conservatively: 'Can it, in a *general* view, be good that an infant can learn much which its parents do not know?' Similarly Coleridge, a pantheist in his youth, finally abandoned poetry and believed the Bible the only revelation needed. He himself spoke of the 'disease' of his mind, and said, 'I have been so forsaken by all the *forms* and *colourings* of existence, as if the organs of life had been dried up.' His self-centredness became a matter for comment.

III. *The Idea of the Holy*

The quotations I have made hint at an interesting difference between these two types of individuals: the individualist's sense of God as a clearly defined individual situated in a specific place, Heaven, a long way distant from the everyday world, and the pantheist's idea of God as omnipresent, a 'living Presence' everywhere. I cannot resist quoting a passage from Lord Shaftesbury's famous work, 'The Characteristicks', written more than a century earlier than the time of the Lake Poets, partly for the beauty of the language, but also because it dramatizes certain other aspects of the matter:

'But here mid-way the *Mountain*, a spacious Border of thick Wood harbours our weary'd Travellers: who now are come among the evergreen and lofty Pines, the Firs, the noble Cedars whose tow'ring Heads seem endless in the Sky; the rest of the Trees appearing only as Shrubs beside them. And here a different Horror seizes our shelter'd Travellers when they see the Day diminish'd by the deep Shades of the vast Wood; which closing thick above spreads Darkness and eternal Night below. The faint and gloomy Light looks horrid as the Shade itself: and the profound Stillness of these Places imposes Silence upon Men, struck with the hoarse echoings of every Sound within the spacious Caverns of the Wood. Here *Space* astonishes. *Silence* itself seems pregnant; whilst an unknown Force works upon the Mind, and dubious Objects move the wakeful Sense. Mysterious Voices are either heard or fancy'd, and various forms of *Deity* seem to present themselves, and appear more manifest in these sacred sylvan Scenes; such as of old gave rise to Temples, and favour'd the Religion of the antient World.'

The feeling which Professor Otto in a famous phrase called 'the sense of the numinous' could hardly be more clearly expressed. The Gothic cathedral, with its tree-like branching columns and its shafts of filtered light, likewise serves to evoke the sense of the numinous, which is the basis of religious feeling.

The above passage, while bringing out the importance of nature as the residence of deity, also shows the relation of all this to the idea of mystery and its physical counterpart, obscurity. This is in powerful contrast with the scientific, or indeed the business attitude; the scientist wishes to attain the utmost clarity, and finds mystery disturbing. If there is rumoured to be a monster in Loch Ness he is at once filled with the urge to find out whether this is so, and what kind of monster, if so. He cannot understand that there are others who prefer that the mystery should remain, who like to think it is possible that the moon is made of cheese or inhabited by little green men. He cannot see that his efforts actually make the world *less* agreeable for some people, that stripping away the veils of mystery can be viewed as a disaster, not as progress.

I believe that it is in an attempt to restore the needed element of mystery that people so tenaciously insist on the existence of flying saucers, piloted by people with arcane knowledge; that they wish to believe in the Yeti and the sea-serpent; and that they trust in astrology and are perpetually interested in ghosts, precognition and extra-sensory perception.

Many primitive peoples live in an atmosphere of this kind: spirits of many kinds surround them, magic and sorcery are commonplaces. It may be that man needs some mystery in his life. Perhaps here too we have to find a mid-position between blinding clarity and total obscurity.

People often find it surprising that psychological forces determine not only major political and religious attitudes but permeate, subtly, our feelings about quite everyday matters. Thus in the last chapter, I pointed out how the patrist and matrist conceptions of architecture and of gardening differed. We should, then, be able to see analogous differences arising from the soft/hard-ego distinction. Thus we might expect the individualist's garden to be divided by hedges into formal plots, and separated from the house—whereas the soft-ego garden should be laid out in a more natural way. Sure enough, we find the seventeenth-century garden formalized, with elaborate topiary work and geometrical parterres. By the middle of the eighteenth century, naturalism was all the rage. Streams, instead of being canalized in stone-lined ponds and channels, wander as if made by nature, and the ha-ha or sunken ditch replaces the hedge, so that the garden seems continuous with the landscape.* Addison, the essayist, had launched the new trend; he argued

* The first man to make a winding stream in a garden was Lord Bathurst at Ryskins. 'So unusual was the effect that his friend, Lord Stafford, could not believe

that the garden of his day failed to yield 'one of the keenest pleasures imaginable, the astonishment and thrilling sense of liberty derivable . . . when the eye is conscious of no boundary short of the horizon itself'. He urged that the whole estate be turned into a 'kind of garden' embracing even the meadows and 'fields of corn'. Soon walls and hedges were being torn down everywhere.

And in the tree forced into the likeness of a peacock or a sphere by the topiarist's shears we can see an analogy with the child forced into an approved social role. In the eighteenth century's preference for fine individual specimens of naturally grown trees we can see the opposing attitude.

In the nineteenth century, the swing was reversed. Formality came back. The open rooms of the eighteenth-century inn were replaced by the Victorian pub divided by panels into six or seven chambers where one could be private. Children were forced into a mould. Lace curtains formed a barrier between house and passer-by. Today the pendulum has swung back again: picture windows are replacing lace curtains. Children are encouraged to develop according to the dictates of their own natures.

IV. *From Success to Excess*

We can now see even more clearly that the New Line in our society is not only a move from patrism to matrism but a move from individualism to group-mindedness, from toughness to tenderness and from success to an abnegation of self which often verges on pantheism. Thus Paul McCartney, one of the Beatles, as quoted by Miss Alice Bacon in the British House of Commons, has declared: 'God is in everything. God is in the space between us. God is in that table in front of you. God is everything and everywhere and everyone.' You can't put it plainer than that.

Nor do I need to spend much time demonstrating that the New Liners are against 'success'. They reject the 'rat race' precisely because it is a race for success. Instead, they drop out. They favour communal living, they minimize personal possessions, and feel free to borrow or steal the property of others since they feel all things are held in common.

Furthermore, they are in favour of trance and pleased by mystery. Hence, they welcome drug experiences, which are chemically induced trances, and practise meditation. They reject science with its search for clarity, and prefer obscurity both in real life and in the field of ideas.

---

it had been done on purpose, and supposing it had been for economy asked him to own fairly how little more it would have cost to make the course of the brook in a straight direction.' See *The Angel Makers*, Chapter 11, for this and many other references.

And to complete the catalogue, they are, for the most part, in favour of preserving nature and natural ways of doing things: they reject the machine culture and many of them reject city life.

For many of them the supreme experience is the sense of comradeship which comes when thousands of them are gathered together at a pop festival. One day, I hope, they will throw up the poet who will immortalize this feeling; at present it appears in banal form in the lyrics of many pop-singers. Sometimes a New Liner will try to express how 'great' it felt in halting words.

It is natural enough that spontaneity, which means relinquishing the control of the cortex, implies irrationality of behaviour. Behaviour is dictated by emotion, not by reason. Beliefs are dictated by wishes rather than by facts. Such facts as are available are fitted into delusional systems, without the close scrutiny which would reveal their lack of coherence.

When the individuals concerned are deprived and downtrodden, they frequently develop myths of saviours who will lift them from misery to contentment, as in the 'cargo-cults' which sprang up in several South Sea islands after the Second World War. (Mysterious white men would arrive with cargoes of goodies.)

Exactly similar are the millenary cults which I described in the prologue. The informal, multi-coloured clothing, the shaggy appearance, the begging, the sexual permissiveness, the outbursts of aggression, the inability to plan ahead—all are there.

Today we have the irony of millenary cults for people of middle-class origin, who are far from deprived in a material sense, but which follow the classic pattern nevertheless. Thus theories of the origin of such movements which make economic problems the cause are clearly erroneous.

Nevertheless, our own society, while increasingly matrist, is still pretty much a hard-ego or success society. Society as a whole continues to run on a hard-ego philosophy and this philosophy is embedded in the economic system, inasmuch as it is based on the pursuit of profit with little regard for the effects either on employees, customers or the general public. Only when the effects become visibly harmful does the ordinary manufacturer respond to public pressure and modify his practices: this has been demonstrated especially clearly in the effects of polluting activities on the health of employees and the general environment. The revolt of the young is specifically a revolt against this attitude.

As one French student, aged twenty, put it after the student rising of 1968 in Paris: 'I think that the world of today is a world without values, without real values; that is to say, to use another term, a world without ideals. So the principal criticism that I would perhaps make of the régime is precisely that the régime supports this lack of values.'

The philosophy of the conservatives in Britain, as in America and elsewhere, is that undertakings should only be carried out if they can pay for themselves. Later we shall see how impossible this is and that they do not themselves really believe it. Here it is the mere fact that such a materialistic claim can seriously be made that is interesting. Human history is the story of attempts to impose spiritual or higher values on the simple pursuit of personal profit: it is the rejection of this whole programme which rightly alarms the young.

Admirable as such idealism may be, the fact remains that—just as in the case of matrism and patrism—the most desirable position lies mid-way between soft- and hard-ego. If the hard man is too selfish, so is the soft man too woolly and disorganized. The euphoric optimism of a Timothy Leary, who believes that if people simply heeded their inner selves and gave up all struggling, all would be well is, if anything, dottier than the merciless drive of the success-seeker.

A society which, like ours, contains a mixture of the two extremes is perhaps the worst case of all. And unfortunately we know much less about the psychological origins of soft- and hard-ego patterns, so that we do not know what we could do to bring about an integration of the two.

V. *The Two Axes*

If I am right, then, all individuals and hence, generally, all societies, can be assigned a position on two distinct scales: patrist/matrist and hard-ego/soft-ego. I hasten to repeat the qualification already made in respect of patrism/matrism. Of course this does not mean that every individual in a given society occupies the same position as every other individual, nor does it mean that each individual is himself a clear-cut example of one or the other. We are simply talking about a dominant ethos.

In principle, then, we could have four main types of person: patrist and hard-ego, or patrist and soft-ego; matrist and hard-ego, matrist and soft-ego. We could also have societies which were strong on one scale but in a mid-position on the other. Some of these combinations can readily be recognized. The Puritan is a patrist (of an unusually guilt-ridden type) combined with hard-ego. The hard-ego/patrist combination is also typified by many judges, who combine conservative-authoritarian views with severity (flogging, hanging, etc.) and, in an earlier age, by Puritans like Cromwell or Calvin (who put so many people to death even when he had promised them immunity), and of course the Inquisition. The businessman of today, however, is often no Puritan and may even tends towards matrism; it is his hard-ego or 'tough' aspect which makes him a businessman. Conversely, the soft-ego matrist is easy to recognize in the hippie group. The tough matrist appears as the Weatherman or violent revolutionary. The soft-ego individual who is at mid-point on the patrist/matrist scale could be Tennyson, or the administrator of a charitable foundation.*

We find, if rarely, people who display both patrist and soft-ego symptoms: such are many of the Christian mystics—men like Eckhart, Suso and Boehme, who seek union with God and absorption in him, yet who insist on the father-like relation, the subordination and so on. Christian mysticism has always been very narrowly regarded by the Roman church, and many of its manifestations have been declared heretical or at least undesirable. St John of the Cross spent twenty years in prison because his experiences did not conform to the approved doctrinal position. When we inspect these objectionable experiences, we note that the father-element has vanished: they have become pantheistic. The Church was always acutely aware of the danger of a non-paternalist mysticism, since its authority (and eventually its continued existence) depended on the paternal component, and hence on God conceived in some sense as a person, not a divine ground. Its objection to Neoplatonism was precisely this, and elsewhere I have argued that early Christianity itself was relatively pantheist and father-free. The best-known of the Oxyrinchus Logia of Jesus declares: 'Lift the stone and you will find me, cleave the wood and I am there,' a notable expression of the immanence of deity.

The Quakers, and some allied sects, also provide an example of soft-ego patrism. The taking of decisions by 'the sense of the meeting' is specifically soft-ego, as is the desire for illumination; yet the dislike of colours, activity, and spontaneity generally, for which Quakers are renowned, is clearly patrist.

Similarly, if we consider whole societies or social groups, we can see that they tend to fall into the same categories. The distribution is most easily indicated by a diagram, similar to the diagram of personality patterns used by Eysenck, in which patrism and matrism forms one axis, hard- and soft-ego the other:

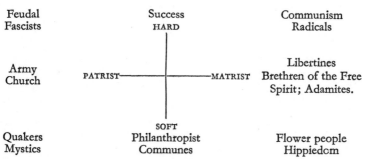

Feudal Fascists	Success HARD	Communism Radicals
Army Church	PATRIST————————MATRIST	Libertines Brethren of the Free Spirit; Adamites.
	SOFT	
Quakers Mystics	Philanthropist Communes	Flower people Hippiedom

* Although we do find hard-ego matrists, it seems that hard-ego is most usually associated with patrism, perhaps because the introjection of a father-figure is one of the processes which serves to form the ego.

Societies of these kinds are easily recognized among primitive peoples: thus the Mandari, a Nilotic tribe, are substantially patrist; the Nuer of the Sudan are substantially a success society; the Zuñi are group-centred, and so on.

The change which our society underwent in the pre-industrial period was one from patrism to success, or, as is often said, from status to contract. The relations between individuals, instead of being governed by ritual, convention and the social position of those concerned, came to be governed by negotiation, and embodied in contracts. Not only personal relationships but many other aspects of social life can be linked to this pattern.*

Today, we are seeing a switch from the success society to matrism, with elements of soft-ego. History suggests that all such swings reverse themselves eventually.

Once one has grasped the idea that the way in which personality elements are grouped can influence the whole pattern of society, the mind at once leaps to the idea that there may be other factors of importance, in addition to the two groups we have been discussing. There is, in fact, one other group which demands attention, though it is not distributed in quite the same way as those we have seen.

VI. *Power, Avarice and Dependency*

Acquisitiveness for goods and acquisitiveness for power are obviously forces of great social importance, and any society which harbours a considerable number of people with drives of this kind will take on a certain form. The kindly, co-operative Utopias of William Morris and H. G. Wells blithely assume that such characters will not be around to exploit the situation. Alas, it does not take many wolves to decimate a flock of sheep.

These two drives are not mutually exclusive opposites, like matrism and patrism. Though there are power-seekers whose personal lives are ascetic (like Julius Caesar) and misers who collect money and valuables but ignore power (like Hetty Green) yet there are some who use their wealth to help them exert power, like certain newspaper magnates.

Psychoanalytic theory offers us an explanation of the development of these drives which is illuminating. Freud declares that the new-born infant is almost wholly preoccupied with the sensations which come from its mouth, and the satisfaction it derives from imbibing its mother's milk. Later, it becomes preoccupied with the other end of its alimentary canal. Its excreta are the first objects which it produces, and it finds

* The late Mary Douglas has done something of the sort in her book *Natural Symbols*. Though she starts from quite another viewpoint, she too perceives two axes in society, though her axes run at 45 degrees to mine. She calls them respectively Group and Grid.

them fascinating. It also learns to please its mother by producing them on demand or by holding them back when told to do so. These are known as the oral and anal phases of development. Finally, the infant moves on to a third phase, of interest in its phallus; it discovers it can achieve gratification without any help. At this time, it may also acquire anxieties if its parents forbid it, in horrified tones, to touch its sexual organ. There follows a quiescent period, until puberty, when sexual interests awaken and a new interest in the phallus as a specifically sexual organ arises. This is known as the genital phase. To those unfamiliar with psychoanalytic theory, these ideas often seem strange or disagreeable, the more so since discussion of them is tabooed in some families and groups. I shall only say that half a century of observation has borne out Freud's basic contentions.

Freud then adds the important proposition that each person has a certain amount of psychic energy (libido) to invest, and may fail to transfer it fully from one stage to the next, so that a certain amount of energy becomes locked up in each stage, causing 'oral fixations', 'anal fixations' or 'genital fixations'. Such fixations arise when the child's discovery of each phase is so treated by the parent as to become a source of anxiety. Thus house-training may be accomplished either by rewarding production on demand, or by punishing failure to retain. In the first case, the child learns the general lesson that productivity is good, in the second that retention is good—giving rise to retentiveness throughout life. Hence the miser. It is no coincidence that money is often described as 'filthy'. The anal type is also constricted in his ability to give love and in his personal relations. Where punishment is so severe as to breed resentment, the child may learn that it can revenge itself on its mother by unwanted production of faeces, and we get an anal-expulsive type. Again, it is no coincidence that we speak of 'smear techniques', and the crude, slanderous attacks on public figures and the debunking which are common in some sections of our society can be explained in this way.

I have dealt with the anal fixation in more detail, since the notion is still unfamiliar to some, though of course a great deal more could be said. I need only to add that when the fixation is genital the adult preoccupation is with power, or with the knowledge which gives power, either over people or over things. (Hence the scientist as well as the politician.) Intense preoccupation with political power can be a compensation for lack of sexual potency. (Of course, impotence can arise from other causes too, as can the urge to power.)

But Freud also noted that fixation can occur at the oral level: this seems to create a dependent character, so that we must group dependency with acquisitiveness and power-seeking in a trio. Now if we can have personalities displaying these three influences (over and above the factors earlier discussed), can we not have societies in which these trends are dominant? The answer is 'yes'. The Puritans were notably anal in their preoccupations, as I have described in some detail in *The Angel Makers*. Hence their success in business. (The curious association of protestantism and capitalism, which Professor R. H. Tawney described half a century ago in his famous *Religion and the Rise of Capitalism*, is hereby explained.) The Kwakiutl of the north-west coast of America, whom Ruth Benedict described, are greatly concerned to obtain power over one another. They hoard wealth, which they then destroy, the man who can destroy most acquiring the highest status and shaming his opponents. Thus while power-seeking they are certainly not anal-retentive. Finally, our own society shows strong dependency elements. In addition to a widespread tendency to demand support from the state (whether as subsidies to business or farmers, or as 'welfare' payments, health services, etc., for employees) we also show an immense preoccupation with food and drink, with its nourishing qualities, etc. The popularity of the smoking habit also betrays oral elements, and the relationship between sucking on a cigarette, cigar or pipe has often been compared to sucking on a nipple. The effect of sucking is calming, for it relieves unconscious oral anxieties; hence the tendency to light up in moments of stress.

The reason I advance these ideas is that they open up the much wider question of how far the methods we use to bring up children may inadvertently set patterns which bias the whole nature of society. If this is the case, attempts to modify society by merely political means will be ineffective; conversely we *can* modify society in desired directions once we understand how what we do affects adult character.

I must add that not all personality characteristics are formed in this 'environmental' kind of way. There are certainly inherited factors which affect the level of intelligence and probably the level of energy available. Some people are constitutionally energetic, some drift lazily or apathetically. And as Eysenck has shown, the tendency to neurosis seems to be inherited.

Nevertheless, this remains a topic of crucial importance in connection with the reconstruction of society, and I shall return to it in Chapter 10 when I come to discuss what we might be doing.

VII. *Conclusion*

Society emerges, in the survey I have been making, as a battleground of ideas—but still more as a battleground of personality patterns, for the ideas are the projections of varying personality structures. The really significant feature is the deep chasm which separates the types. The tough individualist simply cannot grasp what the tender nature-lover is on about. For the latter, to put a copper mine or a factory in the middle of a National Park or other wild scenery is not simply anti-social, it is a desecration: it is almost as if a factory should be set up within a church in which people are worshipping, and should clatter away during their prayers. The numen is dissipated. To the pragmatic individualist, however, all those rocks and trees are just a kind of God-given junk-yard, from which one may as well ferret out any bits and pieces which will come in handy. The parties simply don't talk the same language.*

The same deep gulf separates patrist and matrist. Let me give an example. Recently in Birmingham, England, a clinic was started for impotent men, whose impotence was psychological, based on a deeply-lying fear of women. It was arranged that women—all unpaid volunteers—should talk to these men, seek to allay their fears, and eventually, if it worked out that way, take them to bed. With the assurance that they would not be mocked if nothing happened, several of these men were able to recover their potency, and, once they realized that they were indeed men, the cure persisted. For some men, whose only experience of women was a dominating mother and a nagging wife, simply to talk to a warm and undemanding girl helped to change their entire attitude to women. However, a local dignitary, furious at what he described as organized immorality, contrived that the enterprise be closed down.

It might be thought that extreme views such as these are the exception—that most people congregate in a middle position. But investigation shows that people tend towards extreme views. In a study in which 22,208 people were questioned about the degree of conviction with which they held various social attitudes, it was found that most people agreed with the propositions 'I am in favour' or 'I am strongly in favour' (or, *not* in favour): only a small minority checked 'I am uncertain, but if forced would probably vote for the proposition' or 'I am undecided'. As the British psychologist R. H. Thouless pointed out many years ago, the fact that an issue is controversial does not make people uncertain what to believe, it makes them hold the belief with a high degree of conviction or reject it equally firmly. (We constantly see this in politics.)

The implications of all this for a revision of life-styles are crucial. It is absolutely unlikely that a majority of the population of a large modern society can come to agree on a life-style or even that they will consent to tolerate the life-styles preferred by those of different personality from themselves. On the contrary, they will seek to impose the pattern they prefer on their opponents. Thus Marxism cannot provide a solution

* Of course, there are chairmen of mining and other industrial companies who have beautifully situated country houses or take their holidays in beautiful scenery, while their firms ruin the scenery enjoyed by others. Doubtless this scenery means little to them; but if it does, they should be ashamed of themselves.

except for tough radicals. Fascism will only provide a solution for tough conservatives. Christianity will only provide a solution for tender-minded conservatives. Humane logical analysis (and that goes for this book, of course) will only appeal to tender-minded radicals.

In this tetralemma (and I could provide it with more horns if I used a more complex system of analysis) there is only one course which offers any hope: to use all the influence we can to crowd future generations towards the mid-position. There is a good deal of evidence that such attitudes are formed, or at least developed and reinforced, by early childhood experience, by education and by the values embedded in the culture of society. On the other hand, if there are hereditary determinants at work, the task may be hopeless. For my part, I tend to believe that such attitudes are largely or wholly acquired, and that we can shift them. I certainly believe this for patrism/matrism; I am less sure for tough/tender. This is a matter on which research is urgently needed.

What also emerges from the analysis I have been making is the very fundamental fact that in studying possible life-styles we are concerned as much with personality as with society. The gap between the two is bridged by the concept of *values*. Values are transmitted by society and determine or at least influence behaviour. For many people the language of values is more acceptable than the language of psychology which I have been employing. At the same time, few people can state with any precision what they mean by values, or explain how they work. So in the next chapter, let us rephrase the quest for the best of all possible worlds in valuational terms.

4

The Value of Values

I. *Introduction*

VALUES, everyone agrees, are changing. Some pundits tell us that
what we must do is to restore the old values. Thus Professor Martin
Bronfenbrenner, the Carnegie–Mellon economist who worked for the
US Treasury and the Federal Reserve Bank, regrets that 'we have diluted
the old value of self-reliance'. Others, however, declare that the technological age demands 'new values'—whatever they are—and that our
troubles arise from our failure to evolve them.

Despite general agreement that values are crucially important, it is
impossible to find a book which specifies how values are changing, why,
and what we ought to do about it. However, this deficiency can be
remedied. The last two chapters have made it clear how our values are
changing: patrist values have been largely replaced by matrist ones—
self-control has given place to spontaneity and expressiveness, to put it
as briefly as possible. And hard-ego values are now giving way to soft-
ego values, at least among the young: that is, individualism and competitiveness are yielding ground to group awareness and co-operation.
The reasons for this change have been adumbrated. What we ought to
do about it is to avoid going from one extreme to another. Each of
these values is valuable; our mistake is to overrate one of each pair and
to underrate its polar opposite. In a moment I shall explore this question of avoiding extremes more fully, but first let me touch on another
way in which values are changing.

Some authorities feel that values are not so much changing as vanishing. One of these is George W. Morgan of Brown University, who in
his perceptive book *The Human Predicament*, writes: 'Values are in dissolution. Many of us have no profound convictions concerning what is
good, just, beautiful or worthy—nor their opposites. Life-fulfilling
ideals are rare. Many people do not really believe that there are things
that merit respect, struggle and sacrifice. Few men are filled with a vital
sense of the genuine as opposed to the spurious.' It is the fact that we
now appreciate how enormously various societies differ among one
another in respect of what they value which has led, he thinks, to an
ethical relativism that empties the concept of all meaning. If we can
never believe that one thing is better than another, values become void,

and tolerance becomes indifference. We 'couldn't care less' and life becomes meaningless.

The cynicism which this generates can lead to the adoption of purely opportunistic, self-centred, short-term standards of behaviour. Robert Neidorf, teaching at a west coast university, reports with horror that he has heard three conversations often repeated: 'I have been told by members of the new generation that a man who lives up to an agreement that he would not make over again if he had a chance, is a hypocrite: thus integrity is now known as hypocrisy. I have been told that a man who labours at a project that provides no immediate sense of entertainment or gratification is a fool: thus foresight and love of wisdom are now known as foolishness. I have been told as a matter of absolute truth that there are no real truths and that any opinion about anything is as good as any other; it sometimes sounds as if the very sense of form and order that makes languages possible is being deliberately set aside.' This is a hedonistic, opportunistic, relativistic worldview and I understand Dr Neidorf's despair. If even half of this is true, the situation is clearly serious, and it is high time that the process by which values disintegrate should be explored, so that something can be done about it. For I believe this despair to be unjustified.

Before the discussion can proceed, however, I must start with some explanations and definitions—for there is no common background of ideas or even agreement on how the word 'value' should be employed.

Anthropologists use the word in a different sense from economists, who are preoccupied by economic behaviour. To the economist, anything an individual fancies is a 'value' for him and its value can be expressed in monetary terms as the price he is willing to pay for it. On this basis, of course, drugs of addiction have a high value, whereas in a social sense many people would maintain that they have a low or even negative value. The anthropologist is concerned with the motivation of behaviour in a much more general way: thus courage is, for him, a value—so is caution—even though neither can be purchased by individuals at a price. In particular he is concerned with certain basic assumptions he calls 'core values', which determine behaviour over wide fields of activity, and which are co-ordinated into a 'world view' or ethos. This is the sense in which I shall be using the word.

As I have implied, values are closely linked with behaviour. Many sociologists simply use the term 'values' as a kind of short-hand description of behaviour—if a person behaves in a self-controlled manner, he is alleged to value self-control. This is called a 'normative' use of the term, meaning that it is derived from norms of behaviour. But such a treatment of the matter is artificial, for the obvious reason that people often fail to live up to the values they hold. In other words, values describe a state of mind rather than a type of behaviour. I am not referring to the fact that people sometimes pay lip-service to values which they do not really hold. My point is that people can genuinely value a certain type of behaviour—frankness let us say—even though they fail to live up to it. Indeed, they may feel guilty about their failure. Conversely, people may behave in a certain way without consciously asserting it as desirable: they may even feel apologetic about it. ('I'm afraid I am an awful coward . . .')

Values, as here defined, are distinct from preferences, e.g. food preferences, in that they are quite general. A person who favours spontaneity is likely to favour it in fields as far apart as dancing or education, religion or married life. Similarly, they are distinct from means. To believe in the value of technology or the gold standard is not a value. (To believe in the value of flogging, however, is an expression of a general valuation of strict discipline.)

Notice also that the sociologist avoids making any judgment as between opposing values; he does not evaluate values. Spontaneity and self-control are just two modes of behaviour to him. He prides himself on having a 'value-free 'approach. But today people are dissatisfied by weak neutralism; they want to know whether one value is really more valuable than another. For if all values are equally valuable, what is one to do? How is one to run one's life? A navigator needs a guiding star. In this chapter, therefore, I propose to draw on the work of certain anthropologists and psychologists and to say how I think we can, without importing personal bias, extract a scheme of reliable values from the ethical mish-mash with which the sociologists have presented us.

Thus far I have talked of values as if everyone held clear-cut ideas on their values, but the truth is subtler. It has been pointed out by a team of Canadian anthropologists who made a study of the values held in a suburban community to which they gave the name 'Crestwood Heights' that what people do tends, in one sense, to be the opposite of what they say they believe. They also point out that men and women tend to take opposite views in such matters. For instance (they say, on the basis of their enquiries) women tend to be more optimistic and to think that things will get better, whereas men tend to take a more cynical and depressive view. Yet in practice, it is men who chiefly work for improvement and rail against the deficiencies they see, while women take a more realistic view and accept them. Or, to take another example, men tend to hold that reason is the best guide to action and to distrust emotion, yet in practice they often rely on 'hunches' and make snap judgments. Women believe you should trust your feelings, yet feel that one cannot be happy unless one learns something new all the time.

It is not surprising, in the light of what I have said about patrism and matrism, to find these authors saying that men tend to see order as a good thing in itself and regard freedom as a safety valve: if they indulge in an orgy it is only that they may work better afterwards. In contrast, women value order only as a means to freedom, and if they indulge in an orgy, then the orgy is the object of the exercise and not a means to an end. Again, men are doers, and hold that to be happy you must achieve something. Women are be-people and maintain that to achieve something you must be happy.

How far such distinctions would be found in other communities and in other countries would be interesting to explore. I mention these findings not so much because I think they are universally valid as to demonstrate that the schemas I have been describing are necessarily simplifications of reality, and because they are interesting in themselves.

Another set of differences, which has been too little explored, in any systematic anthropological sense, is that between the young and the old—not simply today and in the West, but in general. It is well known that young people tend to be more radical than old people. ('He who is not a socialist at twenty has no heart; he who is not a conservative at forty has no head.') I suspect that after a person's father has died, it becomes easier to follow his example—at least for those who rejected the father-image originally—and this may make for increasing patrism with age. Again, young people are more optimistic, in general, than old people, who tend to be cynical—but there are many exceptions. We may sum the position up by saying that the young tend to be more soft-ego and more matrist than older people.

Associated with every cardinal value are certain emotive words. Thus some of the emotive words for patrists are: old, traditional, respect, order, etc., and the cardinal value is conformity. The matrist's cardinal value is spontaneity and the corresponding emotive words include sincerity, impulse, equality, love. For the hard-ego type of personality, the cardinal virtue is efficiency, and emotive words are: new, effective, free and success, whereas for the soft-ego individual (whose virtue is selflessness) key words are communal, harmony, generous, natural.

This explains why, in a success society like our own, the most effective words to use in selling a product are 'new' and 'free', as every advertising man knows. The leaders of great corporations in their speeches repeat the themes of their advertising. Industry is creating 'a new world'. Mechanical devices will 'free' you from drudgery, make you 'free' to travel and so on. (But in the health food shops patronized by the soft-egoists, the key word is 'natural'.)

This preoccupation with key ideas also appears in the political field, and the diagnosis of our society as a hard-ego society is confirmed. Thus in a survey of the relative values of various political figures, made by Professor Berkley Eddins of the University of Buffalo (on the basis of their public pronouncements) it was found that the leading American political figures—Richard Nixon, Edward Kennedy, Edmund Muskie, Ronald Reagan, Hubert Humphrey, George McGovern and John Lindsay—all placed Freedom at the top of a list of five values covered by the study. Ralph Nader, however, placed Order at the top and Freedom at the bottom—as did Plato before him. (It is also interesting that Nixon, Kennedy and Reagan placed Wisdom bottom of the list: Plato rated it second only to Order.) These findings confirm very neatly the interpretation I have offered—that in its political aspect, the rethink which is now going on concerns hard-ego values versus soft-ego values.

Europe presents a somewhat less clear-cut picture, to be sure, since in many sections of society patrist rather than hard-ego values still obtain. 'New' is not automatically 'better' for the patrist, who is inclined to think that old ways are best. As a character in *Guy Mannering* said: 'Even an admitted nuisance of ancient standing should not be abated without some caution.'

II. *Value Alternatives*

The anthropologist Clyde Kluckhohn, Rhodes scholar and Harvard Ph.D., who died not long ago, made his name by an extensive study of the Navaho Indians—who have developed, incidentally, an extremely interesting combination of individualistic and altruistic values. His wife Florence describes herself as an educator, but could also claim to be an anthropologist. She has devoted her life to analysing the basic values people hold in different societies and to applying this analysis to practical problems such as mental illness, emotional maladjustment, cultural change, etc.

Her findings illuminate the analysis I have made; in fact, they go further in that they indicate quite clearly where we should aim, if we wish to reorder the values of our own society. She considers that there are five areas of basic importance, which she terms 'value orientations':

1 The relationship of man to other men
2 The relationship of man to nature
3 The relationship of man to himself
4 The relationship of man to time
5 The modality of activity.

In each of these areas we can detect the value choices I have been describing, but also a third alternative which is not so much a compromise between the two opposites as a third corner to the triangle, a new and more constructive position. Let us therefore consider each of the five in turn.

1 *Relation to Other Men* There are three ways, Florence Kluckhohn points out, in which a man can try to relate himself to other men. He can be an INDIVIDUALIST, competing with all other men and disregarding their views about how one should behave. At the other extreme, he can set up elaborate HEIRARCHIC structures, in which every individual is either senior to, equal to, or junior to every other individual (as in the army) and where behaviour is prescribed for each of these types of relationship. The third alternative is to form CO-OPERATIVE groups, organized internally, but externally in competition with other groups—as is the case in a society which has not yet reached the stage of monopoly capitalism. It is easy to see that the hierarchic pattern (Florence Kluckhohn calls it *lineal*) embodies what I have called the patrist attitude, while individualism reflects the hard-ego. The collaborative pattern, however, corresponds to mid-points on both scales: it compromises between hard and soft, between structure and lack of structure. And since mid-positions are best, this may be the reason for its success. Of course, we often speak of Western society, especially American society, as individualist. But, as Margaret Mead has pointed out, in her book *Co-operation and Competition in Primitive Societies,* our society is not wholly individualistic but displays co-operative effort too. And when co-operation breaks down, as in a strike or lock-out, great efforts are made to restore the will to co-operate. Both individualism and monolithic organization, being extremes, are less effective than co-operation: the first displays motivation but lacks the structure to give it effect, the second has the structure but tends to be weak on motivation.

Of course, it is not only industrial organization which is in question. The same principles apply to political organization, to churches and even to the family.

2 *Relation to Nature* Here again three attitudes are possible. Man can feel that he is weaker than nature and must live by its laws: he is SUB-ORDINATED to it. In contrast he may feel himself entitled to conquer and EXPLOIT it. Or he may seek to live IN HARMONY with it, achieving his ends by methods which do not damage it. Our new-born awareness of environmental problems has brought home to us the fact that Western man has long felt himself entitled to rape and exploit nature. It is a trend which perhaps began with the Romans. Our language is full of phrases like 'the conquest of the jungle', 'the rape of the earth', 'the exploitation of resources' and so forth. In contrast, many primitive peoples treat nature with respect. The killing of food animals is limited by taboos, and only what is needed is taken. Killing animals 'for sport'

to the point where the species is endangered (the fantastic *battues* of buffaloes in the USA in the nineteenth century are a key example) has no counterpart in such societies. In many such societies, even the felling of a tree is matter for thought: the feller apologizes to the tree and promises to plant another to replace it. Such attitudes are often attributed simply to economic good sense: the so-called savage realizes that he must not endanger the plants and animals on which he depends. However, we can also trace this to personality structure—to the soft ego which imbues plants and animals with a living soul, and which causes the man who destroys them to feel a genuine pang. Thus the exploitation of nature is a hard-ego manifestation (with elements of patrism, too, no doubt).

The third possibility is to live in harmony with nature. If we make a door, let us say, from a tree, the door will eventually decay and its components go to join the same natural cycles as if the tree had fallen in the forest. We have modified and lengthened the cycle for our own purposes, but we have not arrested it. If, however, we make the door of non-degradable plastic, we put a block in the natural cycle. We are no longer operating in harmony with nature. Similarly when we render a lake or river lifeless. The fact that today many people are advocating a change in our core values from exploitation of nature to living in harmony with it may enable us to consider this particular value without too much prejudice. In the case of some of the core values we are about to discuss detachment may be more difficult.

3 *Conception of Self* Man, it seems, tends to see himself as inherently EVIL, inherently GOOD or as a MIXTURE of the two—more reasonably, one may think. As I have shown, to think oneself irredeemably evil betrays a load of guilt, derived as a rule from severe parents and an intense Oedipal conflict. To feel oneself inherently good, in contrast, is a matrist attitude and appears historically as the Rousseauian belief in the Noble Savage. Both are extremes. Today, the belief that children are inherently good and need only to be left free to develop naturally is in fashion. The arguments I have advanced show that this belief in original virtue is just as false a view, in its way, as the belief in original sin. Man is a mixture.

In theology, each of these positions can be further qualified by whether the condition is immutable. Man may be seen as bad, but capable of redemption; as good, but capable of falling from grace. Christ, of course, promised redemption, but some sects were so imbued with the sense of evil that they declared redemption was restricted to a small number of people to whom it had been promised in advance, thus making redemption impossible for the majority; this formula enabled them to preserve the letter of Christ's teaching while changing the spirit. Moreover, the child who dies unbaptized, they held, must go to hell. We can contrast this with the guilt-free comment of the Christianized Samoans: 'Why spend so much time in remorse, when God is just waiting to forgive you?'

We can also detect these two contrasting positions today in attitudes to crime and punishment. On the one hand, the criminal, some say, should not be punished, for his criminality is not his fault but that of society. (Like the Noble Savage, he has been corrupted by civilization.) All that society should do is to try to reform him, to bring out his natural goodness. This is a matrist view. Furthermore, the matrist tends to judge actions by the intentions of the doer. 'He didn't mean any harm,' or 'He couldn't help it—it was the way he was brought up,' are seen by the matrist as satisfactory exculpations. Not so by the patrist, who feels that actions are good or bad in themselves, and that wrong actions should be punished, however good the intention. (Thus a man who murders a tyrant should be condemned.) Judges often emphasize this absolute view of the law, whereas juries often add riders, in such cases, about 'acting under great provocation'.

Thus, the patrist regards man as born to wickedness, for which he must be punished; he may be kept from misbehaviour by fear of punishment but cannot be reformed. It can easily be seen how the latter attitude associates with a belief in discipline, the former with a belief in spontaneity. If man is naturally good, we only have to strip him of the distortions of society and persuade him to be himself.

4 *Attitude to Time* Man can look towards the PAST, live for the PRESENT, or look towards the FUTURE. The Arabs provide an instance of a people who look towards the past, constantly citing historical precedents and parallels to what they do. This attention to the works of our fathers is obviously patrist in character. Americans, it is often said, look towards the future—although Margaret Mead has expressed the view that most Americans find it hard to look more than five or ten years in either direction, which suggests they live for the present. (Americans typically refer to a project ten years ahead as a 'long-term' one.) Looking to the future is associated more clearly with 'progressive' movements, including Communism. A rosy future is held to justify present suffering. The growth of 'futurology' betokens a shift of interest towards the future, and the belief that there is pie in the sky may be put down as matrist.

Future-orientation is associated, then, with optimism. The patrist, in contrast, thinks that things are not what they were, i.e. standards are declining. He is usually a pessimist. It is the matrist who feels that things are getting better.

The rational position consists, first, in realizing that the future is capable of being worse, the past capable of being better, than the present; and, secondly, in living for the present in the sense of extracting as much enjoyment or development as possible. The holiday-maker who is so busy focusing his camera that he does not really look closely at what he is photographing, typifies the kind of man who fails to extract the value of an experience because of preoccupation with a future event —to wit, looking at the photograph, in this case. Which is better: to see the Parthenon or to see a photograph of it?

5 *Modality of Activity* Recently the young have begun to draw a distinction between *do* and *be* people. To our fathers, action was essential. The stock phrase 'Don't just stand there, do something' would make little sense to a Red Indian, taught to freeze at moments of danger—a rewarding pattern in the forests but a dangerous one in many urban situations. In our society, activity is valued for its own sake: all sport is activity for activity's sake. (In the patrist view, Satan will find work for idle hands to do.) In a crisis an American feels an urge to take some action even when no useful action is possible—a situation satirized in the joke-phrase: 'Don't just do something, stand there!'

Suddenly, however, the ideal of a person who 'gets things done' is in disrepute: to sit passively, not even cogitating, but just enjoying the sunshine or one's inner reveries, has become a preferred way of life in some sectors of society. To the *be* people, action is unnecessary and pointless effort, which merely distracts one from living.

As it happens, DOING and BEING are the two extremes of Dr Kluckhohn's final category of value-orientations. Unfamiliar as this choice is to many of us in the West, to the anthropologist it is quite familiar. The Nuer of the Sudan, for instance, are do people. The Mexicans are be people, content to sit and relax.

As I have argued that mid-positions are best, it will come as no surprise when I say that both of these extremes are ill-advised. What then is the third alternative? Florence Kluckhohn calls it *becoming*. The Buddhist religion is cited as an example of a doctrine of becoming. Buddhists, while decrying a feverish physical activity, feel that change should come through natural growth and development. Dictatorial planning, therefore, is as undesirable as inertia. Political and social, as well as personal, change must develop from within.

By the same token, simple hedonism is as vain as frenzied action. It does not foster growth and development, but rather a progressive satiation which is the reverse of development. (Curiously we have no word for the opposite of development, except such specialized technical terms as 'regression' or 'dedifferentiation'.)

To sum up: in all five of these fundamental areas, there is a third position which is demonstrably superior to the others. Put in the form of prescriptions, man should co-operate with other men, live in harmony with nature, see himself neither as a child of sin nor as a Noble Savage, living in the present but ever developing, realistic in his outlook as between optimism and pessimism.

But these multipolar value choices, whose varied distribution fascinated the anthropologist, do not comprise the whole of values: there are others which are substantially the same throughout all societies, and can only be accepted or rejected. We might call them unipolar values.

III. *Naïve Pragmatism*

It is often said that Western society suffers from having 'wrong values'. We are too materialistic. We are preoccupied with success, meaning some kind of assertion of ourself as superior to others. We are given to believing that bigger is better, and hence that growth is good in itself. These charges derive from an underlying misvaluation, seldom mentioned. We rate competence and efficiency highly—too highly—to the exclusion of spontaneity and feeling: for a man who can concentrate on the performance of a complex task cannot allow himself to yield to impulse or to indulge his feelings. Indeed, we tend to be much more interested in means than in ends. Or, as it is sometimes put, our values tend to be *instrumental*.

I think it is more useful to specify what we *underrate* than what we overrate, because competence is fine in itself, and there is nothing wrong with material satisfactions in themselves: it is only when the pursuit of these goods results in stunting some other side of our nature that we should begin to worry. Most authorities agree that we tend to underrate the importance of the emotional and creative sides of our nature. The protest of those I have called the New Liners is largely about this, and the point may be treated as taken, intellectually, even if there are many people who feel no need to do anything about it. Less obvious is the fact that we underrate contemplation—the need to reflect on life and to try to 'understand' it. We need to incorporate what we learn about in our attitude system, instead of simply knowing about it in a detached way. (There is all the difference in the world between knowing that someone has been killed and experiencing the death of a person one knows intimately, and the same applies to less catastrophic experiences and, for that matter, to enjoyable and fulfilling ones.)

The human personality has, as Freud argued and as even his critics now generally concede, three levels: the super-ego, the ego and the id. Or, in more ordinary language, the feelings and impulses which come from the primitive part of the brain (= the id), the ability to think and co-ordinate behaviour, and to work to a long-term plan (= the ego), and the values, taboos and prohibitions which govern and limit behaviour (= the super-ego). Our age stresses ego-functions: that is, skill, competence, the ability to cope. We rate them higher than love and the capacity to feel, and we rate them higher than self-restraint, though this comes next in order of importance. In medieval times, self-restraint was placed at the head of the list, at least by the Church. In the pre-Christian Mediterranean world, the id was often placed first, the ego second and the super-ego last. Thus history can, for some purposes, be viewed in terms of the shifting balance between these three components.

As the sociologist Kenneth Keniston of Chicago University has pointed out, our age does not merely subordinate fantasy—if people do not exhibit a certain minimum of ego-strength, we actually lock them up. Yet many other societies can tolerate such people, and a few regard them as especially gifted. Probably the drop-out and the delinquent are more typical of human development than the hard-ego type that our society demands and admires. Further, Keniston suggests that our intolerance of schizophrenia, and the more inclusive definition we today give to mental disturbance, reflects this overdone preoccupation with ego-virtues.

The ego is important, to be sure, but there are moments when it should step into the wings and give the other sides of personality a chance to stand in the limelight. Unhappily, we tend to regard the ego as our better self, and to despise the id. This is what the New Liner means by 'uptight'. The price of this imbalance is high. The individual who is under the dictatorship of his ego suffers a stunting of his personality. The soft-ego person becomes alienated from a society which offers him no role. It is technology which demands, and which is created by, hard-ego people—a circular process in which the demands for ego-virtues escalate steadily, and have perhaps now reached the limits society can tolerate: there are no longer enough hard-ego individuals to fill the slots on offer. We have, therefore, as Keniston observes, only three options, to press on with technology, to turn back to the past, or to find a new society whose values transcend those of technology.

Many years ago, the respected sociologist Thorsten Veblen argued that there were two distinctively human modes of thought—which he termed instrumental and institutional—which shape all human actions. This distinction, which I believe to be faulty, was elaborated by the psychologist John Dewey and the economist Clarence Ayres, and has become influential.* According to these authorities, the instrumental attitude which is pragmatic and enquiring, corresponds to the ego,

---

* A good example of the instrumental assumption is the belief that a word can mean anything that people agree it should mean. The institutional view is that its meaning is defined by its deriviation and history.

while the institutional attitude, which asserts values, corresponds to the super-ego. Social change occurs as a result of the enquiring instrumental attitude, whereas the institutional attitude stands pat, as far as it is able. As good Americans and members of a success society, Dewey, Ayres and company approve unhesitatingly of the instrumental attitude and regard the institutional one with scorn.

What they fail to grasp is that instrumental values only concern *means*, they offer no help as to ends. Values like objectivity and self-control help us to develop science and technology, to build aircraft and split the atom. They work—but they do not tell us whether splitting the atom is desirable or what we should use the aircraft for. Only the values distilled by the cumulative thought and experience of those with time to absorb and contemplate reality offer guides to ends. The mistake these pragmatists make is to assume that institutional values are obsolete because they are old. For them the traditional is the fuddy-duddy and outdated. But absolute values do not go out of date: kindness is better than cruelty today, just as it was two thousand years ago. This is not to say that all the crystallized values of every society are desirable; or that that do not need reformulating in changed conditions. But neither should we throw away the accumulated wisdom lightly. To treat the past as unquestionably bad, the future as inevitably good, is as stupid as to take the reverse view.

Allen Wheelis shows he has taken the point when he comments on the battle between instrumental and institutional practices that the former tend to win over the latter, but that they destroy much without replacing it: for example, they weaken the family but have nothing to substitute. Moreover, as institutional values are undermined, the meaning of life appears to be lost, as it always falls within the institutional process. 'Institutions assert the existence of a social reality super-ordinate to the individual, declare that this alone has meaning, and that individual life only acquires significance by virtue of its place in this larger whole.' And as we shall see later, a man's sense of identity is founded on his, and his society's, values. Loss of identity is the price of attempting to proceed instrumentally.

George W. Morgan makes a similar point in more familiar language when he describes the modal personality of our time as 'the prosaic mentality'. In his book *The Human Predicament*, he writes: 'The prosaic mentality is characterized by a cluster of attitudes and interests that it raises to supremacy over others, which are ignored, denied or suppressed.' The prosaic man is interested in abstractions (which he calls facts), in methods, procedures and techniques, and in 'what I shall call clear-cut boundaries.' He stresses literalness and praises objectivity. These attitudes are central to science, though they do not make a person scientific, and have become central in our science-dominated world.

As Morgan demonstrates at length, such attitudes downgrade history and the arts and lead to consequences which dwarf and downgrade man himself. Just as man is reduced to physical insignificance by the sky-scraper, he is reduced to mental insignificance by the 'overmuchness' of the culture, by the flood of data too great to absorb. Morgan argues that there are several ways of apprehending things, of which science is only one. Historical knowledge and artistic knowledge are just as valid modes of apprehension as the scientific. But we take it increasingly for granted that 'the world' is limited to the scientific view of the world. Like a man crossing a busy street, we fail to see the sky because we are so busy looking out for the traffic. Because we concentrate on means, we fail to discover values.

But it is not quite enough just to say that we are preoccupied with efficiency and fascinated by means. Our trouble is that we neglect the many-sidedness of life and ignore the fact that human actions require to be assessed from many viewpoints simultaneously. I call this delusion 'naïve pragmatism'. Let me give an example.

When we prepare a meal, the primary object is, or is supposed to be, to allay hunger and provide nourishment. But in life as it is lived, meals simultaneously fulfil various other functions. They bring the family together—often, now that family prayers have gone out, this is the only ceremony which brings the family together with daily regularity. Meals also enable friends to meet, provide opportunities for the hostess to show her skill and taste, evoke good conversation, etc. They may also have a ritual component, recalling past occasions of importance, as in the case of the Passover.

Naïve pragmatism consists in overlooking this many-sidedness. If we assume that the only function of a meal is to provide nourishment, we shall allow members of the family to eat at different times, or to catch a snack on the way home. We shall be satisfied with tasteless but easily prepared dishes, served in a rough-and-ready fashion. We shall not be worried if people read or look at television as they eat, and so on. In so doing, we squeeze out of our life important components and there is no guarantee that we shall re-insert them elsewhere. Actually, the case of meals is by no means trivial: the loss of family structure consequent upon such changes as the erosion of the ceremonial and aesthetic elements in eating is certainly linked with social problems such as crime and suicide.

The naïve pragmatism which treats food simply as nourishment is evident in many other spheres. 'It is OK if it works' is the core of the pragmatist philosophy. The theory of the 'technological fix' is based on pragmatism. An interesting example of this approach is afforded by aversion therapy, in which people are treated for a neurotic compul-sion by conditioning techniques. Typically, a compulsive drinker is given an emetic drug until the sight of drink gives him feelings of nausea. Such treatment does nothing for the emotional condition which drove him to drink, and leaves him either to find some alternative ano-dyne, or in despair. That such a crude method could be proposed, let alone practised, is due to concentrating on the idea of stopping drinking and ignoring the other factors in the situation.

Other techniques which 'work' are derogatory to human dignity (e.g. tests of means as a condition of receiving benefits) to privacy, to friend-ship, to social life and so on. Anyone can think of examples. But human dignity is only one factor which the naïve pragmatists overlook, though the most important. A May-Day parade is not simply a means of getting from A to B. A fire is not simply a method of heating a room: it is the focus of a human group (as the word focus, which means a hearth, indicates). This is why, in human terms, central heating does not ade-quately replace an open fire, which adds life and movement to a room, as well as serving as a gathering-point. A car is not simply a form of transport: it is a status symbol, and a source of aesthetic pleasure. Sometimes it is the only elegant object a man possesses.

The pragmatists know this, intellectually, of course, but it means nothing to them. This is why they constitute a danger. We need to reaffirm the value of these values, if we want to create an acceptable world.

IV. *Absolute Values and Ethical Relativism*

Today many people feel that the growth of knowledge has destroyed all ethical standards. Because one society admires self-discipline, another spontaneity; or because one society declares marriage must be mono-gamous, another that it may be polygamous, people have come to feel that our Western standards have no absolute value, and they tend to retreat to opportunism and hedonism. All actions come to seem equally permissible. Furthermore, the effect of rapid social change is to under-mine the value of accepted values, forcing people to adopt a subjective position. Thus it is that today people no longer attempt to occupy a moral position but seek 'adjustment'. We do not say that the delinquent is wrong, only that he is maladjusted. (With the alternative view, equally misleading, that society is maladjusted to the delinquent, I shall deal later on.) But when nothing seems of value, life has no meaning. The existential despair so widely felt today springs precisely from this col-lapse of values. My argument thus far has partly destroyed this despair-ing position, by pointing out that many values are bipolar and that each of the pair has its good and bad aspects. One could also say the same of a value like courage. A reckless disregard of risk is hardly desirable, except perhaps in some extreme do-or-die situation. This is why we have two words for many such values: bravery when we approve, recklessness when we do not. Cowardice when we disapprove, prudence when we do not.

But there are other values which are not so obviously bipolar. Thus, honesty is good, dishonesty bad: truth is good, lying is bad. Still more, saving life is good, murder is bad. No one would seriously propose taking mid-positions in such matters. No one has ever admired weakness, vacillation and cowardice. True, a compulsive adherence to such values can become harmful because it then impinges on other values. To tell a person a painful truth unnecessarily cuts across the value of kindness or consideration. Even taking life is occasionally justified, notably when it prevents other lives being taken. Despite these special situations we have no real doubt about the absolute character of what we call moral imperatives. Anthropologists report that every society recognizes such imperatives, even though they may set different limits.

Primitive peoples are in any case a poor guide. They have little sense of a crime against society, as such, though they may fear divine retribution on the whole tribe and so interest themselves in an individual's crime. Again, they often restrict the operation of moral rules to their own group: to rob or murder a stranger may be quite permissible.

Most of the discrepancies between 'moral' codes in other societies and in our own which astonish or puzzle us fall in the sphere of sexual morals. But properly speaking, these are not moral matters at all; they are simply matters of custom and convenience. It would be futile to perform *Don Carlos* in Tibet where a father and his son commonly share the same wife. Principles like monogamy have no moral content, but arise from unconscious fears—in this case the Oedipus complex. They are taboos, literally. In the West we have recently seen the evaporation of the magical fear of masturbation, a practice which is certainly a poor alternative to normal sex, and which, like other forms of self-gratification, is harmful if over-indulged, but which is not in itself a sin, nor visited with dire penalties. To the Sherpas of Tibet, to hit a child or to kill a living creature is a crime worse than adultery. Who can be sure that they are wrong? (There is, however, one sexual taboo which is universal—that on incest, particularly mother–son incest. This, I suspect, has its roots in the need to wean the son psychologically from the mother, and thus is based on reasonable grounds.)

Despite all this, it remains true that the rules and customs of one society should not be imported into another on a casual basis. The conventions of any society fit together into a pattern, and if one is changed corresponding adjustments are needed elsewhere. Still less is it desirable for individuals to make their own rules. To greet a stranger by rubbing noses in a society in which people normally shake hands only causes confusion. To have two wives makes seating the dinner table very awkward in a formal monogamous society! Even the Arab practice of not eating until nightfall and washing only under running water during Ramadan disorganizes European landladies: Americans wash under running water anyway, of course. As these trivial examples suggest, every custom is embedded in a cultural context and to vary it causes inconvenience at least, genuine suffering at worst.

Ethics, however, are not the only sphere in which absolute principles can be invoked. There is one other: aesthetics. The notes of a major chord are mathematically related, as to their frequency of vibration, and an octave is an octave in India as it is in Europe. The proportions of the Taj Mahal appeal to the Europeans as to the Indians, because the rules of proportion are universal. Some colours harmonize, others clash. True, one may construct different scales of notes. The music of India does not sound like the music of Europe, nor does the Taj Mahal look quite like St Paul's Cathedral. Furthermore, the rule of contexts applies here too. In a long sequence of chords, a discord may have its legitimate place. Colours may sometimes clash to good effect. All rules can be broken on occasion. Judgment is all.

But we must not confuse categories. In Chapter 2, I pointed out how often moral (more accurately, ethical) and aesthetic judgments are confused. The patrist judges aesthetic issues on ethical grounds, the matrist does the reverse. The mid-position, one may now add, is that both must be taken into consideration. The work of art which is ethically degrading is not excused by its beauty or its truth to life. Neither is ethical behaviour satisfactory if it lacks grace.

To sum up: ethical relativism (provided we leave sexual convention out of it) is a bogy which does not exist.* Where unipolar values are in question, the principles are quite clear; where bipolar values are in question, a sense of proportion is all that is needed. It is perfectly true that in real life there are situations where it is hard to judge the right thing to do. Since we cannot foretell the outcome of our actions with certainty, there is always the chance that we shall misjudge. Our moral responsibility is limited to doing the best we can in an altruistic sense. In particular we should not fool ourselves that we are acting for moral reasons when we are really indulging a prejudice or a compulsive need.

---

* In textbooks on ethics a distinction is usually made between three types of ethical systems: the ethics of principle (Murder is wrong in all circumstances), the ethics of intentions (I did not mean any harm) and the ethics of results (It was a bit dubious, but no harm was done). I have not gone into this, because the only ethics we can work by is the ethics of intentions. If good intentions have bad results, we may feel guilty and we may be blamed—but this is after the event. Before the event, we can only mean well. I reject the ethics of absolute principle, because circumstances alter cases. In this limited sense, admittedly, I am an ethical relativist.

V. *The Need for Certainty*

To sum up, then: it is perfectly true to say, as people sometimes do, that our present crisis is a crisis of values. But the crisis arises less from the change in bipolar values—which is what strikes most people—than from the degrading of values and the subjectivism which has followed the abandonment of tradition.

In the absence of firm values, we are reduced to depending on our tastes or to following the preferences of the majority. (Since the majority are also doing the same thing, this leads to the endless 'hunting' or oscillation we call change of fashion.) The collapse of absolutes leads to cultural nihilism. A thing is good if you like it, and originality remains the one indisputable criterion. Thus a craze for novelty ensues.

Cultural nihilism leads in turn to a revolt against reason. When the products of reasoning are found to be unsatisfying—the word is perhaps inadequate, bearing in mind that the atomic bomb is one of these products—reason itself tends to be rejected. (As has been said: 'Man, having found that he cannot live by reason alone, seems determined that he will not live by reason at all.') Furthermore, as Wheelis points out, the products of reason tend to be converted into articles of faith, as happened to Marxism, for instance. Originally an intellectual product, it has become a dogma. When such dogmas are found lacking, and are rejected, reason itself tends to be rejected too.

At the bottom of all this lies man's desire to achieve certainty. Traditional teaching, including religion, offered certainties. Rejecting tradition, man has rejected certainty. But many people find it hard to live without certainties. As Wheelis says, 'It is possible for super-ego values to be lost in excess of the ego's ability to do without them. Many persons lose God before they are really able to live in an unprotected universe.' It takes a mature ego to handle decisions without reference to a super-ego, and that is precisely what we have not got—or rather what is harder to achieve than normally.

Only at a much reduced rate of change could we hope to absorb the shock.

The certainties offered by tradition are, it must be conceded, often wrong; the certainties offered by instrumentalism, though limited, are reliable. Thus we are faced with the choice between a security which is real but limited, and the security of religion or ideology which is illusory but unlimited. Some people find illusion easier to manage than insecurity. What people seek today is not *new* values, but *durable* ones.

It is sometimes asserted that what we must develop is a multi-valued society. If this means a society which offers openings for people of different types—for the ambitious as well as the lethargic, for the selfish as well as the unselfish, for the mystic as well as the man of action, then, as a short-term policy, it is reasonable enough. Society must try to accommodate the types of people it has got.

But if it is intended as an objective in the long-term for society as a whole then it is absurd. A society cannot be both selfish and unselfish, both co-operative and competitive, both creative and destructive at the same time without becoming disorganized. In a given situation, one must either compete or co-operate; one cannot do both. The prescription reflects a woolly belief that it is possible to have things both ways: to eat one's cake and have it. This is especially true of absolute values: one cannot value both kindness and unkindness, both truth and lies. That such a suggestion should be made indicates how little serious thought people give to the subject. The trouble is precisely that we *have* a multi-valued society.

In this chapter I have not attempted to explore the whole range of personal values which can become incorporated in social value systems. I might have spoken about acquisitiveness and power-seeking, about dependency and status-seeking, about aggressiveness and peacefulness. In some societies, such attitudes are the peculiarities of a minority, in others they may be so widespread as to influence the whole culture. But they are not necessary for the purpose of understanding the general trend of the times we live in and the reasons for our present discontents, which is my purpose here. Some references to them will appear at other places in the book.

The core of the problem, let me say again, is that we overstress ego-virtues (efficiency) at the expense of super-ego (morality) and id (impulse). This over-emphasis is maintained in many ways: in advertising, in political speeches, in the choices made by industrialists and business-men, by bureaucrats and technologists. To assert that a car or a nuclear power plant affords a convenience is not untrue—but it is only one aspect of the situation. The disadvantages are ignored. We need to affirm the importance of the id and the super-ego, of feeling and creativity, of contemplation and morality, with as much vigour and vividness, and as widely, as we affirm the advantages of material wealth and productive skill.

But it is useless simply to affirm this. The prosaic individual is not going to change his attitudes because he hears one's cries: he cannot, they are part of his make-up. (Neither can the 'drop-out' develop the prosaic mentality, when reproved by 'uptight' individuals for his un-committed attitude.) Thus the problem—and this is the core of my central point—is entirely one of how far we can gradually shift the modal personality of society, by education and still more by altered methods of child upbringing. But before we can open up the subject of what we could actually do, we must pass to the second section of the book and consider in more specific terms what is wrong with our society. In the next three chapters, I shall try to analyse its defects both from the viewpoints of the individual and in terms of the structure of society itself. What does a man expect of society? That is the first question.

II. Problems of the Present

The Psychological Slum

I. *The Psychological Slum*

IN February 1972 workers on the most highly automated production line in the car industry, in General Motors' plant in Lordstown, Ohio, finally went on strike, after a long run of sabotage of cars and equipment. They were not striking for more money, but for more interesting and lower-paced work. Many of them wanted to work on what they called 'the Swedish method', in which teams of men are responsible for entire vehicles, instead of simply carrying out one boring process repeatedly.

This earth-shaking proposal—that work should really be interesting, that money is not all—signals a new popular awareness of the fact that man has complex psychological needs and a determination to get out of the psychological slum in which most of us live. Since work occupies so much of our waking time, it is at work that most of our psychological needs must be satisfied. The notion that we can compensate during our leisure for the psychological insults we sustain at work, which has ruled for so long, is on the way out. It is an epoch-making moment.

The time is ripe to rethink the whole question of what human beings need: what are the conditions of a humane and civilized existence?

Towards the end of the Second World War an American paediatrician, Margaret Ribble, carried out a very significant experiment. Having noticed that the infants in a home for motherless children were pining and sickly, despite good physical care and feeding, she arranged that a group of them should be given special treatment: every day, for half an hour, a nurse was to take each baby and 'mother' it, rocking it in her arms and cuddling and stroking it. The results were dramatic: the babies brightened up and began to put on weight. Formerly, many had had breathing difficulties; these now disappeared. The mortality rate declined sharply.

As Dr Ribble subsequently showed, babies not only need tactile stimuli if they are to develop, they actually regress without them. In early life the nerves still lack their outer sheath of myelin, which, like the insulation on an electric wire, is necessary if the nerve is to function successfully. In the unfondled babies, the myelin formed before they were placed in the home actually began to break up and vanish.

Margaret Ribble also showed that the sensation of being rocked is necessary to the development of control of the breathing mechanism, which explained the respiratory difficulties. Other workers showed subsequently that human beings have a 'need to be held' and that this persists into adult life: no doubt this is connected with the fact that, in the womb, the infant is gently but securely held. It is this need which gives rise to cuddling and embracing in adulthood to express affection.

To my mind, the most interesting thing about this experiment is the way in which it dramatizes our extraordinary ignorance of human needs. Since we all know about hunger and thirst, about the need for sleep and the need for air, it is easy to assume that human needs are understood. But, if we take the obvious case of food, we see that it is only recently that we have come to understand the importance of vitamins, of protein and the nature of a sound diet in general. So, though we certainly have built-in mechanisms which drive us to eat and thus save us from starving to death, it is far from the case that we instinctively know what we require. Similarly, though mothers generally have a sound instinct to pick up their babies and 'mother' them, paediatricians like the late Dr Truby King did untold damage to a whole generation of children by urging that they be left in their cots and only picked up and fed 'on schedule', however much they cried. A little wisdom is a dangerous thing.

But if we are not really on the ball about such obvious everyday needs as feeding and mothering, how much worse is the situation when it comes to the more recondite needs. Nowadays people have at least a rough idea of their nutritive needs, and watch to see that their diet is adequate; but how many people could draw up a list of psychic needs, and use it to check whether their situation is satisfactory? They cannot be blamed for this, since so little research has been done on the subject and so little written about it. More than a quarter of a century ago the famous anthropologist Bronislaw Malinowski argued that a catalogue of human needs was the first step towards a valid theory of culture. But the hint was not taken. But when people feel a sense of boredom and frustration we can infer that psychic needs are not being met.

In this chapter therefore I plan to make some fundamental points about our psychic needs. Such needs fall into two groups: basic needs like affection, which apply to higher animals as well as man, and the complex needs which arise from the human ego, such as the need for self-respect, or the need to achieve an identity. It is because man has developed an elaborate forebrain, capable of abstract thought, that he is plagued by such problems. He has, so to say, created abstract needs. Though hard to define, they are of great importance to his peace of mind and much of the time of psychiatrists is spent in trying, rather unsuccessfully, to deal with them. These complex needs I shall discuss in a later chapter.

But before considering even basic needs, two general points must be made. First, in satisfying any need there is an optimum. Too much food is almost as bad as too little. Even vitamins become dangerous if too much is taken. Conversely, metals which we think of as poisonous, like lead and magnesium, are required by the body in trace amounts. This seems to be equally true at the psychic level: overpowering parental affection can be as damaging as too little. The point hardly seems worth making, until we reflect that there are areas in which we may be committing just this error. The philosophy of the growth economy is based on the assumption that there is no limit to the amount of goods which man should, in his own best interests, consume. But perhaps there is an optimum amount, beyond which we begin to feel nauseated? I shall come back to this.

Secondly, needs are not the same as wants. We may want ice-cream or sweets, but need protein or vitamins. We may want goods, but not need them. Still more uncomfortably, we may want more independence when we need more supervision, and sometimes vice versa. Again, the point is worth making only because it is so widely ignored. Our society assumes, in general, that things should be supplied when, and only when, there is a demand for them. To assert as I now do that demand is not the criterion of social action, but need is, challenges a whole range of hotly defended assumptions in modern society. Of course even our society draws the line at meeting demands when moral prejudice enters, as with drugs, pornography and sometimes alcohol and premarital sex. And it controls the sale of poisons (though many countries do not control the sale of guns). Apart from this, demand is king.

Let us now consider the most basic of all human, and indeed animal, needs, outside the physiological needs, namely the need for affection and the need to do something—the 'mastery drive' as some psychologists have called it.

II. *Emotional Investments*

As everyone knows, people have a strong need both to love and to be loved. It is perhaps more easily understandable that people should need to be loved: and if there is one thing psychiatrists have made crystal-clear, it is that the unloved child suffers permanent psychological damage. But the prisoner who feeds a mouse in his cell, the spinster with her dogs and cats, as well as the mother with her baby, demonstrate that men—and perhaps still more, women—need to love.

Hence it is obvious that a society which makes it difficult to form loving relationships, or which severs such relationships when they have been formed, is unsatisfactory and could be improved. Today when we read that in Victorian workhouses the men were separated from the women, so that husbands and their wives never met, we feel a shudder of revulsion at such inhumanity. But not only the decisions of bureaucrats, but the pattern of society as a whole can affect the possibilities. If we think about it, we see that the break-up of the extended family* has separated grandparents from their children and grandchildren (in comparison with pre-industrial society) to say nothing of separation from cousins, etc. Yet in modern life, we propose moving families from slums to new towns, and then are amazed to find that people are reluctant to leave the area where their friends and relations all live. Or again, we can think of the girl who goes to the big city, and lives alone in a bed-sitter: still worse, the elderly spinster or widow in such a situation: 'You don't realize it until you know it,' as one of these told British sociologist Peter Townsend, 'but loneliness is the worst thing you can suffer in life.' Social agencies have recently begun to uncover the extent of loneliness in modern society. Despite the existence of clubs and other organizations through which people can make friends and acquaintances, many people remain lonely, for lack of enterprise, lack of money or other reasons.†

Later, I shall raise the question of what, in the way of broad social changes, could be done about this, but first I want to develop the notion of emotional needs further.

People not only form emotional attachments to other people and to animals; they become attached to organizations (like their regiment, club, football team, old boys association and even sometimes the concern they work for). They also become attached to houses, towns, landscapes, regions and whole countries. 'Local loyalties' is a phrase which recurs when the central government wants to put through some scheme which people in the area object to. For instance, in England, where county boundaries of many centuries' standing are being changed for no convincing reason, strong feeling is manifested. When British soldiers were sweltering in the Middle East during the Second World War, they dreamed of a white Christmas—though if they had been at home, they would probably have been cursing the snow. Perhaps the most dramatic example of this emotional investment in place is seen when the authorities decide to flood a valley to make a reservoir and compel the inhabitants of the valley to leave. It is in the same spirit that people oppose destruction of the countryside by motorways, airports

---

* Anthropologists distinguish the 'nuclear family' consisting of parents and their children from the 'extended family' which includes grandparents, uncles and aunts, near cousins, grandchildren, etc.

† See Peter Townsend, in Josephson, E. and M. (1962), p. 331.

and other inharmonious intrusions. People also become attached to ways of behaving (cf. the Englishman's traditional devotion to changing for dinner, a generation ago) and perhaps even to ideas and principles—certainly to movements, such as the labour movement, birth-control, ecumenicalism, etc.

That such attachments occur is well known: the point I am trying to make is that they form an essential item in human satisfaction. The man who has few such attachments is emotionally deprived. If this is due to his own inability to form emotional links we say he is schizophrenic, and he is liable to end up under psychiatric care or in gaol.* Conversely, the emotionally healthy man forms numerous and diverse emotional attachments. And the relationship is two-way: he forms them because he is emotionally normal, and his ability to continue being normal is supported by his emotional investments, which give him an emotional return and a purpose (or purposes) in life.

All right; now let us turn from the individual to society. We can see at once that some societies may facilitate such emotional investment, others may handicap it. We can even say that a healthy society could be defined as one in which there is a rich network of such relationships, and a sick society as one in which the network is thin and impoverished. A society in which people move their place of abode incessantly, or one in which there is no extended family, is likely to be emotionally hungry. But this is just what our society does. It imposes on people an emotional poverty, amounting in the worst cases to destitution.

If I seem to labour the point, it is because people seem curiously insensitive to it. We recognize that emotional investments exist, and there we stop. We fail to see that they are a central feature in personal happiness and that it is the business of society to take them very seriously. The English, particularly, distrust emotion and tend to dismiss it as 'mere sentiment'. But what is so 'mere' about sentiment? Thinking is much more 'mere' than feeling, which developed earlier in the evolutionary story. Thus, when it is planned to flood a valley (to revert to the earlier instance) the general feeling is: too bad about the inhabitants, but the desire of people to take showers and wash their cars (which lies behind the need for additional water supplies) comes first. But does it? Water to drink, water to wash in, is essential, to be sure. But the marginal uses of water are far less productive of human satisfaction than the attachment of people to their homes and gardens and familiar surroundings, to say nothing of the destruction of the community as

* The term schizophrenic, or 'split mind' denotes a divorcing of feeling from thought and action, and not, as is often supposed, a 'split personality' in the sense of an alternation between two character patterns. A typical case is found in the murderer who not only feels no emotion as he slays his family but who is equally impassive when he hears his own death sentence pronounced.

such. A great evil is done to some hundreds of people in exchange for an imperceptible improvement to a much larger number. But this formulation understates the situation. For the water-consumer can find other solutions to his needs, but the man who has spent a lifetime in a certain place cannot, in any way at all, replace even a fraction of what he has lost.* He does not have another lifetime to invest.

A further point. People cherish what they love: they seek to improve as well as to protect. If organizations do not provide an opportunity to serve and contribute to their members, they lose support. So, when we come to consider the implications of all this, we shall need to ask how far society offers opportunities for service not just to society itself but to all those specific objects and patterns and ideas to which people devote their love.

Just as the need to love expands into the larger idea of emotional investment generally, so the need to be loved is simply the nucleus of a larger emotional reality. People need to feel that their family, their community, their club or regiment and ultimately society itself, value them and need them. The concepts we chiefly use in discussing this aspect of the question are that of *prestige* on the one hand, and *social* services on the other. It is a mark of the ill-organized nature of our thought that these two ideas should seem to be so little connected.

Finally, it might be added that people seem to need to have a sound emotional relationship with themselves. A person who is disgusted with himself is in bad shape, and so is a person who is infatuated with himself; Freud coined the term 'narcissism' to describe such relationships, pointing out that, though narcissism can take a pathological form, there is a basic preoccupation with the self which is natural and indeed essential. The impact of society on self-love is a dual one. If it forces a man into actions which revolt him, it deals him a psychic blow from which he will not readily recover, if ever. And if, during infancy, the relationship with the self is damaged, he will show the signs of it throughout his life. But these matters call for a consideration of the

---

* Though I do not want to stress the topic of water supplies too heavily—it was only introduced to provide a concrete instance—it may be worth justifying the assertion that other solutions can be found by pointing to two or three relevant facts. First, water could be made more costly, whereupon economies in its use would be effected, and the need for a new reservoir might be avoided. The loss would then fall on the purchasers of the water, who would have to reduce expenditure elsewhere by eliminating their least rewarding purchase—so that their loss is, in the strict sense, marginal. Second, much water is consumed by industry, where economies could also be effected, or alternative methods of cooling, quenching, etc., found. The cost of so doing would appear as a trifling rise in the price of the article manufactured, with a similar effect. Since serious water shortages are due to develop in Britain, the USA and some other countries in the near future, these considerations may soon become public issues.

difficult subject of the ego, which I deal with in a later chapter. For the moment, let us stick to the basic human needs.

One gloss is called for. One often sees love described as *one* of the emotions, the others being fear, anger, jealousy, etc., but brief consideration shows that fear, anger, etc., are only *reactions* to a situation: love is the only emotion which comprises a *need*, and so should not really be grouped with the reactions.

But there is a human need even more basic than love, and one which is increasingly frustrated: the need to cope.

III. *Coping*

The most deeply built-in of all mechanisms is the tendency to do something about the environment, to cope. The lowly amoeba withdraws from uncomfortable conditions, such as acid or heat, and seeks its optimum environment: birds build nests. Man, likewise, is a creature deeply committed to action. Moreover, he not only feels impelled to cope but he positively enjoys it. This is why people climb mountains, engage in sports and games and so forth. It is not for the end result, but for the pleasure in the activity itself. (Of course, some games have been 'professionalized' and even amateur games may be for an award, but this does not alter the fact that many people play a game like golf just for 'the exercise' or, more accurately, for the pleasure of exercising a skill.) As a matter of fact, this may be true of animals: rats which have learned to get food pellets by pressing a lever will often continue to get them this way even when pellets are freely available. Indeed, animal play, like human play, is an instance of functions being exercised for their own sake. The truth of this at the simple physical level is shown by the way in which children will test their newly acquired ability to balance by walking along the top of a wall or other narrow place—and anyone who has been in charge of small children knows how they insist on such opportunities.

Such behaviour knocks a wide hole in the theories of behaviourist psychologists, who claim that all creatures, man included, only act to obtain a reward. When the rats in their 'Skinner boxes' press the levers, are they doing it for food or for the fun of the thing? Of course, if we agree to use the word reward so as to include 'the fun of the thing', then the proposition is true. And in the case of man, at least, there may be additional rewards in public admiration and approval. The boy who dives into the river does so primarily for the fun, perhaps also because he feels a sense of achievement at a well-executed dive; moreover one's own approval is also a kind of reward.

What I have called coping corresponds closely to what some psychologists have called the 'mastery drive', and I have used this term myself in earlier writings. Today, I think it is too narrow. We are considering a range of activities which start with simple physical manipulation—the child's pleasure in moulding dough which leads on to the skill of the model-builder, the watch-maker, etc. The scale runs on from bodily control (as in diving) to sports and games, where planning and strategy begin to supplement physical skill. Industrial managers, barristers conducting a case, etc., get their satisfaction from coping at this cognitive level, and this is perhaps also the source of the pleasure of the scientist. I think we can also distinguish behavioural coping, as in oratory or even the achievements of a Casanova or a politician. But there is no need to press the analysis to its scientific limits: my purpose is to establish the profound importance of coping behaviour to human satisfaction, as a preliminary to asking how far modern society in fact satisfies this need.

One can sum the matter up by saying that men respond to a challenge and like doing so, so that they demand challenges to respond to. The challenge, however, must not be ludicrously easy nor impossibly difficult. There is no pleasure (for example) in playing tennis against an opponent so much better than you that you cannot return the ball at all, and none in playing with a 'rabbit'. Tennis players team up so as to get 'a good game', i.e. a closely fought one. But, as we shall see in more detail presently, our society, when it presents people with challenges, tends to present them with impossibly difficult ones or ones which are too easy. Thus the workman carrying out a repetitive process on a production line, or the girl wrapping matchboxes or decorating fondants, is bored by the simplicity of the task. The manufacturer, understandably, does not want some of the jobs done well and others badly, so tries to simplify his processes until they can be done by the least skilled, least intelligent employees, thus guaranteeing boredom and frustration to the more skilled and more intelligent. At the other extreme, economic processes may throw a man out of work, presenting him with an insuperable difficulty in maintaining himself. In a more primitive society, he could cope by clearing a plot of land and planting it, for instance: in modern society such solutions are not, as a rule, available.

As these two examples show, the incompetence of our society in providing opportunities to satisfy the coping-need may occur at a simple daily level, or may involve one's entire life, with various possibilities in between. Hence the popularity of hobbies, sports and pastimes, which enable the individual to restore, to some extent, what is missing from his life. The desk worker, who lacks opportunities for physical mastery, may play football or go sailing at the weekend. The manual worker, if nothing else, may ruminate over his football-pool coupons. Incidentally, the wide range of possible hobbies and pastimes reminds us that people's preferences are rather specific. One seeks the exact combination of physical and mental effort, the exact level of difficulty and the specific types of skill which answer to one's make-up. Ideally, then, work should also be matched closely to one's inherent requirements. In a crude way, it often is. There is no point in a manager giving an employee a task for which he is mentally or physically quite unfitted, and no one but a fool chooses a job or profession at which he has no hope of making good. But in detail the picture is much less satisfactory. It is very easy for an employer to keep a man who is good at his job in the same position, when in fact it may be much too limited to make full use of his capacities. Employers tend to move the man who is bad at his job because this sticks out, while sighing with relief when a job is done well and thinking no more about it.

IV. *The Work Situation*

When men attempt to manipulate their environment for useful ends we call it work. So it is primarily in the work situation that we must expect to find the need satisfaction of which I have been speaking. Let us therefore consider how far work today meets human needs, even though to do so takes us into areas of need which have not yet been discussed.

First, does work provide a challenge to our skills and abilities? For professional men and women, in general, the answer is yes.* The barrister pleading a case, the surgeon, the author, the politician, the scientist . . . all these can bring their full powers to bear on their problems and solve them or fail to solve them as the case may be. At the other extreme is the production-line worker. Lynda King Taylor reports how employees often leave a job, saying at the exit interview: 'I really didn't have a *job* to do.' In between, there are jobs with a certain degree of achievement embedded in them: a bus-driver has to make a series of decisions and can drive with more or less skill, even if he is not fully stretched. Second, and closely connected with this: does the job provide variety? Obviously the repetitive jobs do not.

Another need which work can satisfy is the need for prestige: a man likes to feel that the community values his contribution and that his skill is recognized. Here again, the professional man's skill is generally recognized and rewarded, while the production-line worker is not asked for skill. In intermediate positions, the pressure may be for maximum output rather than for a high standard of work. Young men entering industry often find this discouraging. As a young plumber said to me: 'They don't want a decent job. They just want output. It makes you fed up.'

From one's skill derives one's self-respect, but self-respect also

* But Lord Reith, the man who built the BBC, complained that he had never been 'fully stretched' in his life.

depends on feeling that the work one is doing is worth while. A man who grows food, a man who cures the sick, even an entertainer or a scholar, and quite certainly a good cook, can legitimately feel that he, or she, is making a genuine contribution to society. This is much harder for the man who, let us say, compounds a worthless patent medicine or markets mink belly-button brushes. Though we all have a tendency to justify our actions to ourselves, so that even the purveyors of trivial devices and marginal services may claim to make people a little happier, yet there can hardly be the consciousness of personal worth which comes to a man in a job without which society could not carry on. Hence, as output expands and incomes rise, there is a tendency for contributions to become more and more marginal.

Moreover, people desire to see a complete end-product. It is one thing to be able to say, 'I made that chair,' quite another to say, 'I drove nails into a hundred chairs, which other men cut, smoothed and polished.' Thus the subdivision of labour and the complexity of technical processes generally tends to undermine personal involvement in the product. (This must be qualified by saying that a well-defined team can take pleasure in a joint achievement.)

Finally, not to lengthen the list, work should contribute to one's life purposes. For most people, today, it does so only inasmuch as it is paid for, and one needs the money to live. But, as an author, I am not only concerned with the money my books earn: I am also rewarded by the feeling that I am provoking discussion and advancing ideas which may affect people. In working out these ideas before I start to write, I am also developing my own mind and bringing myself into a better relationship with the complexities of the world I live in. (I am also fortunate in producing an identifiable end-product, in acquiring a specific status, whether it be low or high and in being seen as an individual and not an automaton.) The person, in contrast, who does a meaningless job cannot have his heart in his work to the same extent. To decorate a room for one's own use yields a deeper satisfaction than to do it for a stranger. One has moved, when the job is finished, a little nearer one's heart's desire.

One more brief point: we all like to work at our own pace, sometimes speeding up, sometimes slowing down, sometimes stopping for a breather or a change of occupation. The industrial worker, generally speaking, cannot do this but must follow the pace of the machine and take his breaks, if any, only at prearranged times. Even if the pace of the machine or moving belt is set near his average output, it will sometimes seem too slow for him, while at others he will feel under pressure. Having worked under pressure of this kind during the war, I know how harassing this can be.

Enough has been said to demonstrate that many jobs are extremely frustrating and that the tendency, as industry grows more mechanized and streamlined, is for the frustration to grow. It is true that technology creates new challenges, too—airline pilots, computer programmers, even television repairmen can be instanced here—but on balance the situation seems to be deteriorating. It is certainly very different from the position in a primitive community. When the Samoans wish to build a boat, the whole community turns to: there is music and gossip. The skill of the adze-men is manifest. Since fish is the main source of protein the boat certainly serves the community's life-purposes. The pace of work varies, and is broken by pauses. The end-product is identifiable. Commitment is underlined by a religious or magical ceremony of blessing the boat.

All this has been said many times before: the degrading and frustrating nature of much industrial work was criticized by many nineteenth-century commentators, notably Karl Marx, although the analysis they made of the reasons was much less thorough than I have made here. Yet the problem still persists.

Marx believed, strange to relate, that all these ills would be cured if only the workers owned the instruments of production, and so escaped the necessity of taking orders from the owners, to whom they were bound in a sort of slavery. Now there may be arguments for the co-operative ownership of the tools of production, and in a moment I shall discuss them, but, whether there are or not, it is clear that state-owned production lines also suffer from almost all the drawbacks we have just been considering.

It is often claimed that the high wages of men on production lines in the automobile industry are made possible by the efficiency of the process, so that they are recompensed for the boredom and frustration by the money. As the personnel manager of one of the largest British motor manufacturers once told me: 'After a while, the men get fed up with the boring nature of the job, and leave. But within a few weeks they're back again, because they can't get the same wages elsewhere. They've committed themselves to a standard of living, hire purchases and so on, and they can't manage without the money.' He seemed to think this a good thing. When I suggested that a situation in which men were held in a frustrating situation was likely to lead to a high level of strikes and stoppages, such as the motor industry is noted for, he dismissed the idea, saying that the strikes were simply due to 'bloody-minded shop stewards'.

A strike, of course, provides almost all the psychological satisfactions that repetitive work lacks. It presents a challenge; it has a definite end product. It makes for variety. There are opportunities for social contact, and so on. Indeed, in *Are Workers Human?* I suggested, not altogether facetiously, that every well-managed firm would arrange to have a strike about once a year for the benefit of its employees. People would work so much better after it, with reduced absences, that the increased output would probably make up for that lost during the strike.

Recently the thought that frustration at work might be connected with the incidence of strikes and absenteeism has been put forward by a few far-out management consultants, and there is talk of trying to modify jobs to make them more interesting. This is called, in the jargon of the trade, 'Job Enrichment'. In addition, it has been shown that routine jobs lead to a loss of efficiency, a numbing of the intellectual powers and symptoms of depersonalization such as social withdrawal. They also lead to high labour turnover and increasing absence from work, which is a source of costly inefficiency.

When a tedious task is made more interesting the increase of effectiveness can be dramatic. S. Wyatt and J. A. Fraser of the Medical Research Council's Industrial Fatigue Board showed this in an experiment with pairs of women operatives in the tobacco trade. One woman had to weigh and cut off 30-gram quantities from a roll of twist; the other had to wrap them. When the two women changed jobs half-way through the shift, the daily output from five pairs of workers went up an average of 11·2 per cent on that achieved with no changeover. But when the changeover was made twice, it went up 13·8 per cent; everyone was happy. It didn't cost a penny.

You might imagine that the good news would soon have penetrated to industry generally and that managers would have been busily increasing the element of variety in work. When I mentioned it to the chairman of Britain's biggest firm of tyre manufacturers, he scoffed, saying that money was the only thing that employees were interested in. Actually, studies of employee attitudes in the USA reveal that money is by no means the only, and not even the chief, of the things the worker wants. Again in the careful study made by Hall and Locke at the Rowntree chocolate factory, pay was found to be only one of half a dozen factors affecting satisfaction; and when S. N. F. Chant asked 250 shop employees what made a job worth while, they placed 'good pay' below security, opportunity of promotion, freedom to use ideas and freedom to learn.

These are not new ideas: half a century ago Max Weber observed 'no man easily yields to another full control over the effort, and especially over the amount of physical effort, we must daily exert'. When fifty-three workers on a conveyor belt in a cannery were questioned, every single one expressed a preference for a different kind of work.

Actually, job enrichment is not a new idea. A quarter of a century ago, during the Second World War, the Cadillac people were faced with employing unskilled labour to manufacture aircraft engines. Completely unskilled women made a precision aluminium component for these engines, each one turning out a finished product. Every girl worked from a chart which showed her just what to do next and why. (In later experiments on these lines tape-recordings were used to take the employees through the sequence of operations.) Peter Drucker, reporting the Cadillac experiment, writes: 'The worker did nothing but unskilled motions which were easy to learn; in fact it took no longer to train these women than it would to have trained them for orthodox assembly-line work. But every girl did a whole operation, which brought into play one muscle after the other, thus giving the whole body a chance to rest and a chance to develop a working rhythm. Also each girl could work at her own speed and vary the speed, in itself one of the best means of combating fatigue. And each girl produced an entire product with all the satisfaction that goes with it. As a result, there was not only a highly satisfied and happy labouring force; there was also an extremely efficient one which produced more than could have been produced on an orthodox assembly line.'

The difference between the position of professional classes and manual workers is brought out by a survey of six different professions plus skilled and unskilled workers. For the professions, the proportion saying they would choose the same job if they had to start again ranged from 82 per cent for journalists up to 91 per cent for mathematicians. But only 16 per cent of the unskilled workers said they would do so, and from 40 to 50 per cent of the skilled workers.

Blauner, the author of the study, comments that these figures may understate the position, since to run down one's job is to criticize oneself.

Apart from the industrial implications, the prolonged frustration of basic needs has long-term effects on the personality. 'As a craftsman he had been responsible for what he did and required to exercise foresight, judgment and care as to choice of means. Under the factory system, these faculties were never called into play. As a personality he was ignored; he was paid by the hour and not for the job . . .' writes the psychiatrist, Lewis Way, adding: 'Man was taken from a social and family environment and herded with an army of employees recruited from various sources. He lost the background of a stable and integrated environment which is necessary for complete social adjustment.'

The efforts of sociologists and management experts to humanize work have been criticized as 'cow sociology'—an attempt to lull the workers into placidity. For those who think that revolution is the only answer, of course, the more exasperated the workers become the better. But after the revolution, the problem will remain: factories will still be required, and work methods will not be vastly different from those existing under private ownership. And for those who have less faith in revolution as a prescription, surely anything which humanizes the life of an important section of the population is highly desirable?

No, that's not strong enough. The reconstruction of work so that it satisfies human needs is essential: since the work situation is where we spend the largest single chunk of our waking life, if it is frustrating the object is lost. Even if humanized work involved some loss of output it would be worth it. And as yet we have hardly begun to study the problem of finding ways of rehumanizing work.

This is an idea which goes deep into our whole philosophy. As Dr E. F. Schumacher, the economist, has said, if the ideal with regard to work is to get rid of it, every method that reduces the work-load is a good thing. 'Hence the ideal from the point of view of the employer is to have output without employees, and the ideal of the employee is to have income without employment.' Thus arises the problem of leisure, in which we try to restore to life all the fun that is missing from work, or are bored if we do not know how to do so. But should life be dichotomized into boring work and unboring leisure?

I have written of work solely in relation to personal needs; this does not mean that I think it has no other functions in relation to man. The Buddhists hold that work has three functions:

1 To help a man to develop his faculties
2 To overcome self-centredness by making him join with others in a common task
3 To bring forth the goods and services needed for a becoming existence.

Western society has concentrated on the third of these functions to the neglect of the other two. These wise words should be blazoned over the desk of every manager and management consultant.

V. *Other Needs*

It is often said, or lightly assumed, that one of man's most clear-cut needs is for security—economic security is usually meant, now that physical security is reasonably well protected; but emotional security is important too, and is often neglected.

However, the situation is not actually so simple. Too much security can be cloying. No one likes to be treated like a child. A man in bed in a hospital is pretty secure, but when he ceases to be ill, he soon becomes bored. The fact is, most people do not want to have security provided so much as to be in a position to create their own security. Man has a need to run his own life, to make his own decisions, which we may call the need for self-determination. Thus, just as we can have too much food or too much love, we can have too much security.

What people really dislike very strongly is to be in a situation over which they have no control. We hear a lot about economic security because the vast, impersonal forces in modern society present people with problems far beyond their control. A man who loses his job because of a general industrial slump, and who consequently cannot get another, does not know what to do. No constructive action is open to him. And since people know that this is the situation, they may feel insecure even when they are in a job. Still more, the direction society is taking is unattractive to many, but they feel there is nothing they can do: 'one feels so helpless'. Bertrand de Jouvenel, famous as a lecturer on economics and a diplomatic correspondent, a member of the French Commission of National Accounts and President of 'Futuribles', an organization for studying possible futures, has observed that: 'Life in Western society is a new fatalism, a feeling that our future is determined for us by the autonomous course of a superhuman agency, whose god-like nature is acknowledged by the reverent use of the capital: Technology.' In most primitive societies, in contrast, though they may be physically insecure in the face of tempest or of drought, for instance, action to avert the danger is usually possible. And in the absence of natural disaster, their economic security is usually firmly based.

As psychologists have shown, we feel anxiety most when there is nothing we can do. When we can struggle to overcome a danger we are too busy to worry much.

This important truth is little understood by those in power, those who think they are meeting the problem by providing 'social-security systems' of a paternalist or charitable kind, instead of creating the conditions in which self-help and independence are possible.

All human needs have a dynamic character. We maintain our bodies by taking in material and getting rid of waste products; we are not kept in a state of equilibrium, but keep ourselves in it, just as a tightrope walker keeps his balance by constant adjustments. Our psychic needs are equally dynamic.

In short, we do not simply need to be given security, we need to achieve it for ourselves. We do not need to have the problems of living mastered for us, we need to master them ourselves. We do not simply need to be loved, we need to love.

It may also be said that man needs variety and dislikes monotony. Properly speaking this is not a distinct need so much as a qualification of the needs we have been discussing in terms of the time scale. We need food but we do not wish to eat the same dish every day. We need to face challenges but not the same challenge repeatedly.

Here again, variety is not an absolute requirement. What we actually seek is a happy medium between monotony and over-stimulation. Both are deadening, as people who try to cram in too many new sights and places into one vacation often discover. In most periods of the past, one imagines, the danger was monotony: an excess of input is something peculiar to the modern age. The constant presentation of new images, facts and ideas via 'the media', notably through television, dulls the capacity to observe detail and inhibits the reflection and consideration which is necessary for new materials to be incorporated into one's mental stock.

The desire for stimulus varies widely among individuals. As Professor Eysenck has shown, extroverts demand much more stimulus than intro-verts. They eat more, drink more, smoke more and have intercourse more often. They enjoy parties and social intercourse, and take more risks because of the 'excitement' involved. They also make more expan-sive gestures. So great is the difference that a level of excitation which is boring for an extrovert may be painful and exhausting for an introvert. (Personally, as one who finds loud noises painful, I am often astounded at the calm, even approval, with which extroverts suffer them. Similarly, Muzak and other kinds of background music are irritating to me, but are welcomed by many others. Clearly, I am an introvert.) I suspect there is a tendency to lower the threshold as one grows older: the young tend to welcome noise.

When a person does not receive the amount of stimulus he requires, he first becomes bored, but eventually develops 'stimulus hunger' and goes out and seeks to justify it. This may lead to what has been called an 'arousal jag'—the equivalent of a blow-out after a period of short commons. It has been suggested that stimulus hunger is an element in the causation of delinquency: to risk capture by the police provides a 'thrill' and gives the feeling of 'really living'. As Eysenck says: 'Many of the activities of the juvenile delinquent seem to stem from boredom, from a desire for stimulation, and from an apparent willingness to take more risks.' Driving a car recklessly fast—even better, a motor-cycle—provides thrills, too.

The inference is that our society provides too little excitement for extroverts, especially for young extroverts. Little thought has yet been given to the question of how to reintroduce it.

Drugs, including alcohol, influence the arousal level temporarily. The introvert is helped by alcohol, which makes him more sociable, where the extrovert simply becomes too noisy. The use of marijuana and other drugs, I suspect, is connected with this need for a shift of threshold. When it is lowered, even a calm environment is sufficiently stimulating. (Actually, the process seems to involve a transfer of attention from external to internal stimuli. The introvert, like the marijuana-depressed extrovert, has enough going on inside him not to have to worry about what is outside.)

Though human beings desire a measure of variety, they also demand a high degree of consistency from the environment, and it is important that these two factors be clearly distinguished. We learn that certain actions are rewarding: if they suddenly cease to be so, or, still worse, if they switch back and forth between effective and ineffective, we are flummoxed and feel completely at a loss. Anyone who has tried to establish contact with a mentally disturbed person will remember the sense of bewilderment and even fear which overcomes one as one finds that accustomed approaches evoke an unexpected response. Our technological society, while providing us with more variety, has a chequered record as regards consistency. In some respects we can rely on the environment more, in others less. The woman who cooked on a wood or coal fire knew it would always heat her pots; the woman who cooks on electricity may have her plans thrown out by a failure of the supply. A car goes wrong more often than a horse. But it is not at the technological level that the shoe really pinches; it is in the pattern of life itself. A century ago, a man who bought a cottage in the country took it for granted that it would still be a country cottage when he died. Today, he may find himself in the middle of a housing development or next to a motorway a few years after he has moved in. Government action, inflation and other forces may make nonsense of decisions on which people have founded their whole lives. Against this the greater reliability of some minor features is inadequate recompense.

The only professional psychologist who has tried to categorize human needs in the kind of way attempted here and in my earlier book *Conditions of Happiness* is Professor Abraham H. Maslow of Brandeis University, whose *Motivation and Personality* was published in 1954. The groups he arrives at are substantially the same as mine, except that he distinguishes as 'safety needs' the tendency of an organism to drop other activities when its physical safety is threatened, and to cope with the threat. What he is really pointing to is the fact—and it is an interesting one—that, way below the conscious level, our brain has a pretty good idea of the priorities and switches its programmes accordingly. However, it needs certain signals to be able to do this, and can fairly easily be misled. For example, it does not respond to radioactivity, which it has no means of detecting, or to odourless gases such as carbon monoxide.

Maslow goes further than me, however, when he claims that there is a need for self-actualization. 'This tendency might be phrased as the desire to become more and more what one idiosyncratically is,' he writes, 'to become everything that one is capable of becoming.' Certainly, it is desirable that a person should realize his potentialities, and if a person realizes that he is capable of more than he is doing he will feel frustrated.

Yet is one to say that a man born long before the aircraft was invented, yet equipped with just the kind of capacities which might have made him a good pilot, is frustrated? In that case, there must be many who are frustrated because mankind has not yet evolved the function for which they are fitted.

Maslow makes the point that we need the opportunity to use our cognitive capacities just as much as we need to use our emotional capacities. Jobs that do not present a challenge, therefore, cause a loss of zest and (he says) a depression of bodily functions.

Admittedly taking figures from the air, Maslow suggests that it is 'as if most people were 85 per cent satisfied in their physiological needs, 70 per cent in their safety needs, 50 per cent in their love needs, 40 per cent in their esteem needs, and only 10 per cent in their self-actualization needs'. He goes into considerable detail in showing how the person who has achieved self-actualization differs from the one who has not. 'A man who is thwarted in any of his basic needs may fairly be envisaged as a sick man or at least less than fully human,' he declares, the second phrase hedging the first a good deal. 'The good or healthy society would then be defined as one that permitted man's highest purposes to emerge by satisfying all his basic needs.' With that conclusion I am in full agreement, though I suspect complete satisfaction of all needs for everybody to be an ideal far beyond attainment and should prefer to say that a good society is the one which achieves the maximum satisfaction possible in the given circumstances.

VI. *A Need-oriented Society*

Summing up, there are for practical purposes three groups of needs, physical, emotional and functional. There may be others. It is not clear to me whether there is a specific aesthetic need, or whether this simply represents a special combination of cognitive and emotional responses. Again, is it possible that there are rewarding modes of experience which we never miss if we do not know about them? One can see that a person who has had the Beatific Vision will hunger to have it again; but are those who have never even heard of mystical experience frustrated by its absence from their lives? More work on the subject is needed. Our society has a long way to go before it satisfies them to a reasonable degree. Obviously complete satisfaction of all needs all the time is an unattainable ideal, but we could certainly do a good deal better than we do at present. Even if we cannot live in a palace, we need not live in a slum.

It is this awareness of the deeply unsatisfying nature of most industrial jobs which is driving many young people (and some older ones) to turn their backs on the 'rat race' and seek some simpler existence in which demands are kept to a minimum. They have discovered that you can live quite happily with very little money. Paul Goodman has argued that the frustration of the more-or-less delinquent youths with whom he tries to deal is due largely to the fact that society offers them no hope of a challenging and worth-while role. As he says in *Growing Up Absurd*, to hold down a job and then be related to life through consumership is not enough.

Though it is not my intention to pursue the subject exhaustively, perhaps one gloss should be made to avoid misconception. It is a human trait to convert the means to ends into ends themselves. Thus socialists may propose nationalization of industry as a means towards a juster or more efficient society. They soon pass to regarding nationalization as an end in itself, even if it can be shown (in some particular case) to be unsuitable. In the same way people may come to regard something as essential to their self-esteem, and suffer real pain if it is unavailable. Clothes may not be needed in a centrally heated room, but one might feel painfully embarrassed to be naked, or even incompletely dressed. Society thus has to cater for many pseudo-needs. Again, one kind of satisfaction may be adopted as a substitute for another; and if this is lost sight of the person concerned will fight to retain the substitute. Similarly, a person may fight to retain symbols of prestige, rather than prestige itself.

In the extreme case we have the obsessions. The guilt-ridden person who continually washes his hands might be said to 'need' to wash his hands. The person whose sexual desires have become associated with a fetish may be said to 'need' the fetish object. The reason for drawing attention to this is that it makes the point that we are not simply concerned with satisfying wants. In the extreme case just quoted, social policy must be directed towards reducing guilt and fixations of the sexual instinct, not just to turning out more wash-basins and high-heeled shoes. Yet this is how the system works at present. It satisfies market demands, whether they are rational or not.

Equally, it ignores, too often, what it would be wise to demand. Just as a child may want sweets when it needs vitamins, people often fail to see where their real interests lie. Obvious though the point might seem, people constantly make this mistake. They drive to the top of a mountain because it is 'less effort', when climbing it on foot might have been productive of more genuine satisfaction. They demand central heating when perhaps stimulation of their body's own function by exercise might be better for them. They watch football on television when perhaps they should be out taking exercise themselves. There is thus great need to educate people in making the right choices. We have already learned we have to do this with physical needs, such as diet; we have still to learn that we also require to educate people how to meet their psychological needs.

The next few years will see, I believe, a growing recognition of the fundamental importance of our psychological needs, and of the fact that they require to be satisfied directly and not by substitution and distraction. In particular, the present situation in which we expect a man to be ingenious and discriminating when he comes to buy a hi-fi or drive a car, yet to be undiscriminating and moronic as soon as he enters the factory gates, cannot persist much longer.

What has happened in our society is that we have attempted to meet our psychological needs by the supply of goods. In the primitive world, goods are intended to meet *physical* needs: they comprise food, clothing, houses, weapons. Now we have a new kind of goods, designed to meet non-material needs. (Sometimes, we try to achieve both ends at once, as when we buy a larger car or house than we need, for status reasons.)

In a natural society man gets exercise by swimming or dancing, or in the course of his work; today he needs a car and a bag of golf-clubs or a sail-boat. In a natural society, he gets status from his skills; today he needs to purchase status-symbols. Once, his fantasies were supplied by a human story-teller; now they need the elaborate machinery of television. Where he made his music by singing or playing, he now depends on radio and phonograph. But is the satisfaction they yield as great?

We have harnessed our psychological needs to the service of the goods-producing society, and the more it frustrates us, the more we are driven to produce still more of these goods. It is not surprising, then, if workers demand more money. To buy a car, for instance, may be the passport to the psychological fulfilment they cannot find in their work. Thus the fact that employees ask for money does not mean, as some employers claim, that employees are not interested in job enrichment, and this is true even if the employee himself does not perceive the nature of his own motives.

We have created a world of substitute satisfactions. We have also created a world of distractions. The hypnotic appeal of television is that it conceals the emptiness of one's life. Driving about in cars at the weekend conceals the fact that one has nothing better to do. Drugs and 'excitement', such as is provided by spectator sports, fill the same role. All keep the wheels of industry turning, as direct satisfactions would not.

To conclude, we need to establish a 'need-oriented society' in place of our present goods-oriented society. So far, we have barely scratched the surface.

6

Social Suicide

I. *What Community Is*

'PARIS is a loose merger of many, very many, small provincial communities, each of which is self-sufficient and pleasantly or offensively clannish. "Do you live here?" they will ask in the little local shops, and your answer makes a difference, not only in the prices but in the service. A policeman won't arrest you if you live on his beat; the accredited street-walker won't pick your pocket; they will see you safely home. Even though you are a foreigner, you may still be a *petit Parisien*, an insider, more French than a Parisian from some other quarter; he is the stranger.'

This passage from Lincoln Steffens' autobiography graphically expresses the notion of community. Mary Mitford, the novelist, put it even more crisply in the 1820s, when she wrote of her village as 'a little world of our own . . . where we know everyone and are known to everyone, interested in everyone and authorized to hope that everyone feels an interest in us'. This sense of community is vanishing in the modern world, as everyone knows. Many of our problems are due to the fact. It is constantly asserted that we must 'restore a sense of community'. The communes now being set up so widely in the USA, in Germany and elsewhere, *are* communities in the Mitfordian sense, and their members are driven to join them precisely because modern society is so lacking in a sense of community.

Yet, despite these reaffirmations of the need for community, society in general continues on its way, blithely undermining community right and left. Ignorance and self-interest are among the reasons for this, but perhaps more important is failure to recognize the enormous social and personal costs of so doing. In this chapter, therefore, I want to define quite clearly what makes for community, what its advantages and disadvantages are and what are the costs of absence of community, or, as is sometimes said, of living in a mass society.

The definitions of community offered by sociologists are not very helpful and often psychologically faulty. Perhaps the best is: 'The mark of a community is that one's life may be lived wholly within it.' However, this is not an essential feature, so it is better, I suggest, to think of it as a network of interpersonal relationships and emotional investments. It is a system of mutual obligations, of mutual assessments and of emotional links. Let us take a look at these three components.

Mutual obligations act so as to restrain selfish or asocial behaviour. The owner of a field cannot be unpleasant to the farmer who rents it, or he will not receive the free load of manure which he usually gets; the farmer on his side cannot neglect to keep up the fences and hedges or he will not find his lease renewed. In many primitive tribes mutual obligations are created in a quite deliberate way, especially when two groups (such as two families) come into contact for the first time. Often presents are given, creating an obligation to repay at some later date with even more splendid presents—a fact not always appreciated by visiting Europeans who accept all the hospitality without any sense of commitment. In modern society, in contrast, mutual obligations are generally defined by contract; provided its terms are observed, no general obligation results, no sense of social pressure is felt.

However, it is not only mutual obligations which link people in a community. Intermixed with them are positive emotional commitments: love of some, admiration of others, distrust of some, perhaps dislike or even hatred of others. To these we may add gratitude for help received, jealousy and envy on the negative side and yet others, such as respect or envy.

In 1946 I put forward the idea that there is a natural social unit for which I suggested the name 'assessment group'—being the largest group in which every individual can form some personal estimate of the significance of a majority of the other individuals in the group, in relation to himself. Depending on how large a majority we regard as the criterion, and other factors such as geography and ease of contact, I suggested that 1,200 was about the maximum size for such a group; above this level the proportion of the group which any one person can assess falls away until at about the 2,000 mark it ceases to be a face-to-face group. (It is perhaps significant that when industrial concerns expand they run into organizational problems at about this stage.)

As many writers have pointed out, human beings have a great need to be recognized as individuals, not treated as ciphers. In a village community, we are assessed in the light of fairly extensive knowledge of our entire personality. We know that the doctor is short-tempered, but we know he is a good and conscientious physician. We know that our neighbour drinks too heavily, but we also know that he recently lost his wife. When a customer is slow in settling his bill at the village shop, the proprietor knows whether he is out of a job or could well afford to pay. In the anonymity of mass society, however, one unpaid bill is just like another, and the computer does not take into consideration that the defaulter lost an arm rescuing a comrade in the mine.

I have mentioned the importance of emotional investment in other people within a community. Even more frequently overlooked is the importance of emotional investment in places—in familiar scenery, in one's home town or village and one's home itself. If people live in a place for many years, they become emotionally attached to it: the trees, hills, buildings, etc., all spell 'home'. Associated with the scene are specific past events which have personal significance: a picnic here, a first job there, the place where Mrs Smith had a heart attack, etc. No matter if the milieu is ugly or beautiful, it is bound up with one's life.* Rare is the man who has no sentimental attachment to his home. Often people, at the end of their lives, return to their home environment. (In the past few weeks, as I write, three people have said to me that they finally felt that they had to settle in the part of England where they had spent their childhood, and the poet W. H. Auden has returned to England for the same reason.)

To dismiss such feelings as 'mere sentiment' is to miss the point. If such attachments give pleasure or a sense of security and belonging, they are highly important and we should encourage them, and make them easier to maintain, not laugh at them. Sentiment is never 'mere'.

Feeling for place under-props community. A person who has spent his whole life in one place becomes identified with it, fusing his feelings for the scene and the people in it into a single pattern.

It needs little stressing that the forces of modern society are undermining both the permanence of personal relationships and of involvement in place. Now let us consider why community is so widely held to be a desirable thing.

II. *Pros and Cons of Community*

Communities offer much greater physical and psychological security than does a mass society. They also exert social controls which, though they can in some circumstances become oppressive, usually have the effect of making life safer and more agreeable.

The driving force of a community is the general human desire to stand well with others plus the knowledge that one may need help one day: it is better to have friends than enemies. In a community, if your house burns down, neighbours will help put the fire out, or shelter you if it is destroyed. They may also help on less dramatic occasions, finding a job for a man who is out of work or lending a hand to a mother who is sick, and so on. In a mass society, in contrast, it is possible for a person to be murdered in public while onlookers take no steps to help,

---

* The reluctance of slum-dwellers to leave their slum is due as much to this as to loss of contact with friends: the scene to which they move is often unappetizing in human terms, even when it is aesthetically superior or more convenient.

as was demonstrated in New York on a now-famous occasion. In a community (such as the one I live in) it is inconceivable that no one would go to the help of a member in distress—for the price would be that one day the tables might be turned.

Where the number of people herded together becomes too large for an individual to recognize most of the people he sees, and where he lives his social life with a different selection of people from those he meets in his business or economic life, and where his neighbours are strangers, community vanishes.

But the assessment group also provides psychological security. There is some evidence that whenever we meet strangers, unconscious anxieties are aroused until we can determine whether they constitute a threat or not—whether it be a physical threat or a threat to our psychological position. (This is why, when people meet for the first time, they ask 'Where are you from?' and are delighted if they both come from the same town, i.e. are really members of the same community, with common interests and assumptions.)

Secondly, the community bestows status, or more accurately prestige, in accordance with a person's total contribution and personal worth. Everyone wishes to have a sense of his own worth and most people prefer to have that valuation endorsed by the community they live in. As has been said, people need both achievement and success—to have done something and for it to be acknowledged that one has done something. This question of status and prestige is so important and so poorly understood that, instead of discussing it here, I shall devote the next section to it.

Thirdly, the community exerts social controls, primarily on the basis of the nexus of mutual aid to which I have referred, but also because people are receiving from the community non-economic benefits, such as status or hospitality. The shopkeeper cannot overcharge or put sand in the sugar if he wishes to keep his status position as sidesman at church, or if he wishes to be invited to social gatherings by neighbours. His business life is not divorced from his personal life. If he ignores such pressures he may be ostracized—but most people feel a strong need to stand well in their community and are restrained from anti-social behaviour by this fact long before ostracism becomes a threat.

It is the fact that the various sides of life—economic, personal, political, social—are integrated, so that one affects the other, which is the real hall-mark of community. In the mass society, in which one's economic relations are with one lot of people, one's personal relations with another, exploitation and anti-social behaviour cease to attract social penalties.

It is certainly true that in some communities these social pressures become onerous. Even if we have no personal experience to go on, we have all read of the narrow-minded, censorious, prying communities so common in the nineteenth century, especially in Scotland and rural America. And the fact is, if people's personalities are vindictive, they will make a vindictive society. The fault does not lie in the system of mutuality we call community, which on the whole tempers even vindictiveness, but in the corruption of personality, and the problem has to be dealt with at that level. (See Chapter 10.)

Sometimes one hears urban life praised 'because one is so free' or because no one pries into one's affairs. This is understandable but the penalty is that one is insecure, and may be lonely. It may be reasonable to flee from a mean and narrow-minded environment, but it is still better to move into a broad-minded and generous one.

The small community also may suffer from offering too narrow a range of choices. If it is merely a question of finding a particular job, the difficulty can be met by moving elsewhere. But if it is a question, say, of having a wider range of friends, only a larger community can supply the need.

These objections apply primarily to the completely closed community such as today is found only in conditions of geographical isolation, or where religious convictions sharply define membership, as among the Amish. The open community, which admits all who wish to join—may even woo those who have something special to contribute—which maintains links with others and whose members have the means to travel elsewhere from time to time, to refresh body and mind, need not suffer from these drawbacks.

III. *Functional Status*

T. N. Whitehead, in his *Leadership in a Free Society*, tells the story of how a new hand joined a works where prestige had long depended on skill with the cold chisel, although this tool had actually been displaced by power machinery. The new hand aroused considerable dislike as an individual, but the men reserved their verdict on him until a break in the work, when they gathered to watch the new hand demonstrate his skill with the traditional tool. He did this very successfully and ever after retained respect as a man who 'certainly knows his cold chisel'. Prestige, which depends mainly on one's occupation, and one's skill at the job, is an important element in human satisfaction. The word status, thanks to works like *The Status Seekers*, has come to mean prestige. Correctly, *status* refers to a position in the social structure, a slot into which a person fits. Some status positions are marked by high prestige, others by low prestige; others may be equal in prestige but different. *Prestige* defines the regard in which others hold a man, the respect they have for him. In an organic society, an individual's prestige depends

primarily on the contribution he makes to the community, and is therefore linked to his job. Thus a doctor tends to have high prestige regardless of his personal characteristics. However, a person who contributes
effort to the community in his spare time naturally wins respect, and
respect is also displayed to people who are felt to be exceptional individuals—for instance, especially saintly or very learned—even if they
do not contribute in an obvious way.

In an organic society, therefore, prestige is *functional*, i.e. derived
from one's function. But in a mass society we cannot judge how useful
a person's function is nor how well he performs it. We therefore tend to
judge by indirect clues, sometimes called status badges. We guess how
successful someone is from his clothes or his car, or his standard of
living. However, wealth is naturally an unreliable indicator of social
value, and in any case the badges of status can be faked to a considerable
extent. Thus many people acquire prestige who do not deserve it, and
others fail to win the prestige they merit. This arises from three causes.
First, the complexity of modern society, which makes it hard for us to
judge whether an accountant or a scientist (say) is really contributing to
society; second, the fact that wealth is not simply used as an indicator of
achievement, but is actually the goal. In a society which makes the
struggle for wealth (rather than for knowledge, for power, for holiness,
etc.) the principal goal of society, naturally success at the activity of
accumulating wealth really confers prestige, just as success at playing
football confers prestige on a footballer.

In addition, the division of labour and automation of industrial
processes has made it impossible, in many trades, for the worker to
display exceptional skill, strength or ingenuity. One cannot win respect
by repeating the same simple movement all day long. The village community which loses its best ploughman or woodsman feels a sense of
loss. The loss of a production-line worker can be filled immediately.
Thus the worker is deprived both of the sense of achievement and of
success: he can only attempt to buy prestige by maximizing his earnings
and using the money to buy status badges.

This brief account of status in modern society needs supplementing
by two points. First, I have not referred to hereditary status. This is
seen in its purest form in kingship. It is natural that the leader of an
organic society should have prestige. Kings were, and in some countries
still are, leaders. They may or may not be good ones. There is little
to be said for filling high status positions by the hereditary method; it is
not the prestige of the status position which is unnatural, merely the
way in which it is filled.

Societies often bestow marks of high prestige on those who have
made an outstanding contribution: honorific titles are one such reward,
and they serve both as an expression of respect, and as a signal to others

who may not know of the achievement that respect is due, as with the French Legion of Honour. In Russia, too, there are Stakhanovites and Heroes of the Soviet Union.

As society grows more anonymous, these marks of status become increasingly important and it is essential that they be distributed appropriately. In countries, Britain for example, where the distribution is in the hands of political parties, honours are given too often to party supporters or to those who have pushed the process of industrialization even further or to 'popular' figures (e.g. the Beatles). Often it seems that the object of the patronage committee (as it is, with unconscious humour, called) is to 'send up' the entire system. Those on the left are inclined to see the giving of honours as a ridiculous and obsolete practice, when in fact it is an essential social mechanism.

Second, one should add that deference is commonly paid to those who have power, if only for the reason that they might use that power to aid or to damage you. This is why, in the army, where you may easily encounter someone not known to you by his features, badges indicating the position in the hierarchy of power are worn as well as badges of personal worth. Thus the slots in the power hierarchy are also status positions, and the status of the feudal lord or of the eighteenth-century landlord, not to mention the parson and the bishop, depended more on his power-position than on his contribution to the common good or personal worth. Hence for status to be functional, it is necessary that no members of the community should have power over others, except when licensed to act for the community, as in the case of government officials, etc. If a man can deprive me of my house or job, I am forced to defer to him. Unhappily, even where power is diffused, people may put their heads together and form a clique in order to enhance their power.

A discussion such as this would have been readily intelligible in the nineteenth century, when everyone accepted the existence of different statuses, even though they failed to see that they should be based on function rather than power or wealth. Today it may be rejected owing to the fact that many people cynically feel that *all* prestige positions are phony, and deny that respect need be shown to worth or experience, still less to power. It is because they feel that they themselves are not respected that they refuse respect to others. The cure is to reconstitute society so that men do receive the respect that is their due; in short, to restore functional prestige. For man's deepest need is to feel, and have acknowledged, a sense of personal significance. 'Respectability' has become a derogatory word, because of its bourgeois perversions. But true respectability is something we all need.

IV. *Erosion of Community*

Why is community vanishing in the modern world? To answer this question let us first consider what are the factors which favour the development and maintenance of a community. Basically, it is the existence of things held in common by members of the community, and not shared by others with whom they come in contact. These include common interests, institutions, rituals, values, skills, techniques and common visible markers, such as a style of clothing, or a particular dialect or accent or skin-colour. Common interests, especially work interests, loom large: mining communities are a well-known example of a community based on work, and tied to a particular territory. The armed services have a certain sense of community, and we also speak of 'the legal community' and the 'business community'. Involvement in a particular industry, such as coal-mining, by creating common interests, fosters community. Religious beliefs may also hold people together, as with the Hutterites. But at the basis of community lies territory, for if people do not meet regularly, on a social as well as a business or work basis, then the integration which is the special feature of community cannot occur. Territory also contributes to the sense of unique identity which fosters community-feeling. But the territory must be definable in some way; an island, a village or an area with a natural boundary.* Unique styles of clothing, hairdressing or even methods of preparing food not only distinguish the member from members of other communities but also provide common interests and support the sense of identity. Common rituals, undertakings and institutions also have a unifying effect.

One might go further and say that, if common values are a mark of community, common personalities must also be a feature. And it is true that in one tribe bravery is valued, in another miserliness, in another avoiding making trouble, in another respect for elders. Such common elements in personality arise from common methods of child-training.

What then is responsible for the erosion of community? Urbanization is often blamed for the undermining of community but it is not the most important force at work. As sociologists have shown, there can be within cities strongly knit communities—in ghettoes and foreign-immigrant sections, particularly, and in suburban dormitory areas. (There are still villages within cities like London and Paris.) In fact, whenever language and dress clearly mark membership, or when the geographical area is well defined, and when there are institutions which bring the members of such groups into contact, religious affiliation

---

* Until they were drained in the eighteenth century, the East Anglian marshes were inhabited by people dwelling on boats, who formed a community quite separate from the land-dwellers.

being the commonest source of such institutions.* Of course, it remains true that the greater part of large cities lack these conditions and do not constitute communities.

However, much the most important distinctive force at work, I suggest, is mobility—both change of abode, which we may call residential mobility, and daily movement to and from a fixed abode. It is obvious that the emotional investments which I have described, both those involving people and place, cannot develop far where individuals or families move in and out of the group every few years. Conversely, where residence lasts a lifetime, the emotional network will become more elaborate: marriages and friendships will develop between children, further cementing the relationship between parents, and so on. This is even true when the children themselves go to live elsewhere.

To say that low residential mobility is a requirement does not mean, of course, that individuals should not be free to move about, within reason, on a short-term basis. A man may still be attached to his community even if he is a commercial traveller or a schools inspector and moves about during the week. Nor does it destroy a sense of community to take one's holidays elsewhere. Even if some member of a family removes to the big city to work, he may still be regarded as a member of the community, if he maintains his personal relations by frequent visits and in general displaying interest, and especially if it is believed that one day he will return to live there.

The mobility conferred by the car does make it possible, however, for a person who nominally lives in a community to place all his interests outside it. Obviously if a large number of members behave in this way, the community disintegrates; this is what happens in some suburbs or when a village is absorbed by the spread of a town.

Another serious aspect of day-to-day mobility is the way in which it enables large numbers of strangers to flood into a community for a short period. This has long happened with beauty spots, and more recently with young people at 'rock festivals' and similar occasions. In addition to the severe physical problems of feeding, sanitation, etc., and the incidental noise, damage and loss of privacy for members of the community, the actual cohesion of the community is undermined if the process continues, as happens in beauty-spots, especially when they suddenly receive widespread publicity. No longer can one recognize and assess most of the people one sees in a daily walk; no longer can one be sure that there is no hidden threat. This aspect has so far been underestimated. A special case is afforded, however, by the community

---

* One reason the British people have the reputation for good citizenship may be the fact that they live on an island, so that the community is clearly demarcated. It is interesting that Wales and Scotland have been absorbed fairly peaceably into the larger community, whereas Ireland, another island, has not.

which receives weekend or summer visitors in large numbers. These may develop a real attachment to the place, and contribute something to it, but in emergency they can always pull out and the possibility of a change of plans is always present, so that they cannot really be accepted as members of the community, and by their presence they dilute its character.

Modern communications also undermine community by focusing attention on national and on world affairs rather than on local issues, and by conveying information about other patterns of behaviour, other benefits. Obviously, some interest in world affairs is desirable, especially now that we have made a world in which we can easily be affected by things that happen far away. But the balance has swung too far, and this is mainly the result of economic gigantism. Local papers merge and vanish, national papers become fewer, because it proves profitable and because the law admits the formation of such developments. Communications also convey information about other patterns of behaviour, and implant new ambitions. This too is fine in moderation and if pros and cons are presented fairly. But they seldom are.

The third force eroding community is the generalization of culture—coca-colonization as it is often called in recognition of the American influence on other cultures. But it is not just a question of goods, or even fashions. Technology itself tends to destroy local variation. When a community had a special manner of building, or a special skill, like the sword-makers of Toledo or Damascus, or even a special wine or farm product, like the strawberries of the Vale of Evesham or the wine of Orvieto, let us say, its definition was increased thereby. It gossiped about different things from the neighbouring communities, perhaps wore distinctive clothing or trimmed the beard a special way. Today, we have a generalized culture. Less and less do clothes, accent, skills, food preferences and so on indicate membership of one community rather than another. We seem headed for a universal culture, in which whisky can be bought in Japan as readily as saké in Los Angeles or Coca-Cola in Scotland. Some think this a good thing, and it obviously has some advantages. But they come at a high price.

Finally, community is eroded by 'immigration'—meaning the entry of a considerable number of new members with different values, conventions and interests. The occasional entrant tries to become assimilated, and if he does not, it is no great matter. A large group of new entrants, especially if they all come from the same source-community, tend to stick together, forming a community within a community, and so threaten the host-community. Today this chiefly happens with the arrival of people distinguished by a different skin-colour, as well as markedly different beliefs and customs. Thus the objection of the members of the host-community becomes tinged by racialism. Racial prejudice, it hardly needs saying, is indefensible; it is therefore unfortunate that the perfectly real issue of maintaining community and cultural continuity, which is a reasonable desire, becomes confused by the racial issue. Just as a village community might resent being swamped by an influx from a new housing estate, it is perfectly reasonable for a community to object to being swamped by people from another country. 'Are they going to fit in?' is the question one hears when newcomers arrive, whether it is in an old people's home, a regimental mess, a village or a dramatic society.

For all these reasons, community is being destroyed in the modern world, and a new type of social pattern replaces it. The nineteenth-century sociologist Ferdinand Tönnies said that community (*Gemeinschaft*) was being replaced by *Gesellschaft*, which is rather inadequately translated as association. But disintegration has gone further than he foresaw and today we are seeing the emergence of mass society.

V. *Mass Society*

'Mass society' is the term coined to indicate a society in which community is weak or absent. In a community we recognize the other members as individuals: even if we do not know them personally, we know something about most of them. In a mass society, most of the people we meet in the course of a day are strangers about whom we know nothing. And there are too many of them. If we hear that a member of our community has suffered a misfortune, we offer to help. But we cannot help all the people in a great city who need help, or even find them. So the spontaneous impulse dries up and, at best, we support some charitable undertaking.

The cost of this depersonalization is high. Transactions lose their social content and become purely economic, and so tougher. A man can bring himself to sell a dangerous toy to children he never sees; he would not give it, however, to the children of his personal friends. The shop assistant can be uncivil to a customer she is unlikely to see again (or vice versa), but the village shop must keep its customers; equally, they depend upon the shop.

The mass society undermines the psyche of its members in other ways too, as we shall see. 'In cities a man gains his freedom, but loses his sense of direction,' as the sociologist R. E. Park once aptly put it.

In the mass society, as we have seen, status ceases to be functional and a 'phony' status system is substituted, giving rise to a continuous battle for status.

Insecurity becomes marked, since one can rely on no one for help. So serious is this factor that the state is obliged to step in and provide aid for those in trouble—not only incomes for the unemployed but food for the elderly, supervision of child upbringing, aid for victims of fire or flood and much else. Indeed, and the point is often overlooked, the state only came into being as a result of the decay of community. At least one eminent historian traces all our modern troubles to the emergence of the state as a final source of all good things (not merely of power). To ask for the restoration of community is to ask for the 'withering away of the state'—as the original Marxist theoreticians realized.

But the aspect on which I should like to throw the emphasis is a different one. In the mass society, a man forms economic links with one group of people, social links with another, political links with another. He gets his medical care from yet other people, his education from yet others and so on. In his life he has transactions with tens of thousands of people, many of them unknown to him except as names at the bottom of a letter, and sometimes not even that. This we might call multiplex society, in contrast with the community where the same people are related in several different roles simultaneously. It is complexity and specialization which give rise to anonymity and impersonality in the modern society. And it is this which causes the lack of involvement, the absence of commitment, which is so noticeable today.

What, then, could we do if we seriously wished to restore a sense of community, or at least to arrest its decay, in our society as it exists? Evidently, we should have to persuade people to settle in one place as far as possible, and discourage employers from moving people about, for one thing. This would often be difficult: a diplomat, a sailor must inevitably move around. A large firm, like IBM, may wish to move its employees, so that they gain experience of different methods and types of work. We have to weigh the advantages of such restlessness against the disadvantages, and keep such movement to the minimum. Clearly, this sort of thing cannot be done by compulsion. It is a question of creating a climate of opinion and feeling which discourages unnecessary mobility and makes the costs known.

Similarly, we would have to create a climate of opinion in which people would seek to keep a proportion of their interests within their local community, and devote a certain amount of their time to local activities—as still happens in many local communities, happily. It is in the cities that the problem becomes acute, because the communities lack natural definition. Rather subtle measures would have to be taken to preserve the individuality of a suburb: at present we consciously merge it into the main mass. One reason we do so is the overwhelming human passion for consistency. If the standard of street cleaning is higher in Section A of the city than in Section B, we start to complain; if the street signs are differently lettered, we start writing to the papers to say how confusing this is. In the long run, the answer must depend on reducing population densities, and this means reducing the total population in a country like Britain where there is an average of 1,000 people to the square mile, when the mountainous parts are excluded.

Finally, we should have to resist the ruthless appropriation of cultural items from other groups, whenever those items are a source of pride to them. A military regiment would be incensed if members of the public appeared wearing its uniform, and in most countries laws exist to prohibit this, since it is obvious that such a development would undermine the cohesion of the unit and render the uniform useless. In Scotland, however, the various tartans fulfil, or used to fulfil, an identical function, assuring clan members of their identity and distinguishing them from members of other clans. Yet the fashion trade has taken the tartans (incorrectly known in the USA as plaids) and has made them universally available. The same thing is happening to the differentia of other cultures, and not only in the sphere of clothing.

Is it possible to turn back the trend towards a world culture, or even to arrest it? Probably not, except within certain communities which, like the Hutterites, are strongly determined to preserve their individuality and can enlist the children born within the community to carry on this purpose. If it is impossible, then we must recognize that we are headed for a mass society on a world basis, with all that that implies. Is it possible to reduce residential mobility, as I have called it? This is not quite out of the question, but at present the problem is not appreciated by individuals or by authority. Governments move people out of cities to new housing estates, displace groups of people to make roads and reservoirs and so forth, with no more compunction than is needed to avoid a serious loss of political support.

Let me stress that I am not arguing for total immobility or total diversity of culture. The in-turned community suffers limitations, just as does the out-turned one. As always, it is a question of the happy mean. In the past, the danger was too little contact with the world; today, it is too much. Another turnover point has been passed.

What I wish to establish is that small, stable groups such as all men lived in until the days of Rome and most men lived in until a century or so ago offer psychological and social rewards which are steadily becoming rarer. The setting-up of communes is thus a spontaneous attempt to restore the organic quality to society. The unsolved question is: can it be restored for the entire population of a country, or can it only be achieved by minorities who opt out from the normal pattern of society?

But before coming to this vital question, there are other aspects of contemporary society which call for consideration, since they add to the stress which is felt by its members.

VI. *The Anomic Society*

Some twenty years ago, two American scientists performed an experiment which not only threw some light on individual behaviour, as it was meant to, but also, as one can now perceive, cast a piercing light on social processes as well. They placed a cat on a stand opposite two panels or windows and applied a light electric shock to the surface on which it was standing, to induce it to jump through one or the other aperture. The question was, which would it choose, in consideration of the fact that it received a food-reward if it chose one window, but bumped its nose if it chose the other? Naturally, if the reward was always given at the left-hand window, the cat soon cottoned on and jumped consistently towards the left.

But here the fiendish part comes in. After a while they made the system random: the reward was as likely to be at one window or the other. Now an exceptionally intelligent and self-controlled human being in similar circumstances might realize that the only rational course was to jump at random, and get the reward 50 per cent of the time. No other policy could do better, though to jump always at one window would do as well. What most of the cats did, however, was to sit there shivering and refuse to jump at all. The situation had become unpredictable and they did not know how to cope, so they gave up trying but continued to display tension and anxiety. The fact is, that the brain, whether of cat or man, is a device for extracting pattern from the environment and making adaptive decisions: it is not a device for producing random decisions. In fact, it cannot do this, and when people are asked to write down numbers (for instance) purely at random they prove unable to produce truly random sequences, unconsciously favouring certain digits and sequences of digits.

Reflecting on this experiment, I suddenly realized its relevance to a society in which reward is not accurately related to effort—a society like our own, in fact. Of course, reward is not entirely random throughout our society, but neither is it well correlated with effort. A man who works hard and honestly for many years may remain poor and unrecognized; a man who finds minerals on his property, who corners the supply of a scarce commodity or engages in socially useless financial manipulations, may become rich overnight. I need not lengthen the list of examples, for the situation is well known. In addition, a man may become rich by some chance event, such as a win in the 'premium bonds' or a state lottery, or may be impoverished by some action of government, such as changing the hire-purchase regulations, the prohibiting of the import of items in which he was accustomed to trade, and so on. Compulsory purchase of his house may deprive him both of expected market value and of the unpriceable advantages of the fact that he has adapted it to his own needs and tastes in a unique way, and now must start again. Actually, government action—including the action of other governments, and also subsuming under this the action of local authorities, etc.—has become the main factor making life unpredictable, especially in highly planned countries like the UK. Inflation too is a factor which makes plans, which seemed good when they were made, unworkable. Devaluations, changes in the tax laws, even budgetary changes—say, the amount of money provided for motorways or for university research—also make nonsense of individual planning and effort.

In such circumstances, it is not remarkable that many people feel tension and insecurity, and some give up the struggle whether by emigrating, committing suicide or simply by minimizing their commitments.

Some of the cats in the experiment I have described, however, did not become quiescent. They became furious with rage and attacked the whole experimental set-up, scratching at the doors and trying to destroy them, and snarling at the experimenter himself. Do we see in our own society people who simply want to destroy the whole system and to shoot the gang who maintain it and operate it? We do? Perhaps inability to see what course to pursue to fulfil ourselves is one of the reasons for this. Of course, this is not the whole story. As I showed in the last chapter, life has other frustrations, and there are other reasons for withdrawing from the struggle or becoming a destructive revolutionary, as we shall soon see. But the shivering tabbies of Masserman's torture chamber vividly present an aspect of modern society which is often ignored.

For some seventy years now the state of affairs I have described has been known by the term of *anomy* or *anomia*, a Greek formation coined in the sixteenth century for lawlessness and borrowed by the French sociologist Emile Durkheim, who first systematically explored the idea of social frustration. Durkheim came upon the notion while writing about the division of labour in society, and it led him to one of the first great sociological surveys, a massive study of suicide.

In Durkheim's view, the anomic condition of society was a principal factor in the suicide rate. At the time this was a startling concept. To suggest that suicide, apparently the most individual of acts, should have a social basis, seemed to many wilful paradox. But Durkheim made a brilliantly ingenious use of existing statistics—his work is still a model to sociologists. Carefully sifting the figures from all over Europe, he showed that—despite popular stereotypes, such as that Latins commit suicide more readily than Nordics—there are in fact certain regularities which persist in every country and from year to year. Because the figures often did not give him the details of marital status, children, etc., that he needed, he got his student, Marcel Mauss, laboriously to tabulate by hand the data concerning 26,000 suicides in documents held by the French Ministry of Justice.

Durkheim concluded, in essence, that people commit suicide when life has become meaningless. This may occur for some personal reason, such as the death of a loved spouse; or because of the failure of a business, each of which wrecks one's plan of life. But it may occur because life as a whole just begins to seem pointless: because there is no goal which seems both desirable and attainable, or because efforts to reach the chosen goal are proving fruitless. Durkheim said: 'All man's pleasure in acting, moving and exerting himself implies the sense that his efforts are not in vain and that by walking he has advanced. However, one does not advance when one walks towards no goal, or—what is the same thing—when one's goal is infinity . . .' 'To pursue a goal which is by definition unattainable is to condemn oneself to perpetual unhappiness,' he said.

Durkheim came to the conclusion that social goals become unattainable when the economic system is working erratically, and that this was due to lack of regulation, whether by the state or by the decisions of producers. In a large market, with much subdivision of labour, he said, an entrepreneur could not take in the scope of the market at a glance, and so made incorrect decisions. This is why he chose the term *anomia* (unhappily translated by some American sociologists as 'normlessness') for the phenomenon.

The concept was developed further by the Canadian sociologist Robert M. McIver, who declared that, when effort proved vain because of social conditions, people rejected the rules of society and heeded only their own interest or whim: such people he called anomic individuals, meaning people with no sense of social responsibility or commitment. Thus the term quietly came to be applied to a state of mind of individuals rather than to a state of society, causing a good deal of ambiguity. The American sociologist, Robert K. Merton, developing this aspect, pointed out that American society requires you not merely to seek to be rich, but to be richer than other people. However much money you have, you could always have more. As Merton observed, however rich society as a whole becomes, in such a system one must always struggle for more: there is no end to the process.* (When Americans of many different income levels are quizzed as to what they would call a satisfactory income, they all named about 25 per cent more than they were actually getting.)

---

* Merton was especially taken with this aspect of anomia: the objectives approved by society and the approved means of reaching them. (Thus if wealth is the objective, burglary is not an approved means, but gambling is.) He felt that anomia was primarily caused by setting ends which were unattainable for the majority, given the approved means which he called norms.

This theory receives some confirmation from the way in which suicide is distributed among the various occupational classes in the USA:

	Average annual rate per 100,000
Professional and managerial	35·4
Sales and clerical	11·6
Skilled workers (craftsmen)	14·3
Semi-skilled workers (operatives)	20·5
Unskilled labour	38·7

Apparently, it is those who are at the bottom of the scale, who presumably see no hope of advancement, and those at the top, who have to struggle perpetually to maintain their position, who are the most likely to kill themselves. These figures can be supplemented by a two-year study made in the city of Tulsa, Oklahoma (population 250,000) which showed first that the class which, of all persons, was the most likely to commit suicide, was the retired—those who had no occupation and so no purpose, and for whom life was therefore without meaning. Over a twenty-year period, retired persons showed a rate of 89 suicides per 100,000 of the population, nearly five times the average rate. At the other extreme, certain professions—authors, editors, reporters, college professors and the clergy—showed no suicides at all. These, I note, are all professions in which the individual is free to make his own decisions and to deploy his time as seems best to him in relation to his goal. Other professions with low rates per 100,000 also have this characteristic of personal self-determination: carpenters (5), accountants (7), truck drivers (12), engineers (15) and so on. (In contrast, nurses and doctors, who also have some power of self-determination had very high rates. Possibly, one speculates, because the battle against sickness is unending, so that eventually one feels one can never win.)

Stress in general is not a cause of suicide, however. In concentration camps, rates of suicide were low; nor do people commit suicide in conditions of danger. Suicide is a way out 'from the collapsing enterprise of life' itself. Essentially, then, anomia refers to the condition of society when large numbers of its members 'opt out' in the sense of feeling no commitment to its rules and conventions, which have become too frustrating; and so feel free to pursue their life-aims by means which society rejects (crime); to express their frustration by hitting back (violence); or by withdrawal from it (communes); or by apathy (drop-outs); or by suicide. The use of drugs like pot provides another kind of withdrawal.

The concept of anomia can also be applied to specific groups within society, such as the family. The family in which all actions are tolerated is anomic for the child—for if one cannot win love and praise by being good, how can one win it? 'Permissiveness' makes effort meaningless. (The solution is to find some form of behaviour so intolerable that parents are driven to forbid it, then one can demonstrate goodness by refraining.) Condemnation of anti-social or objectionable behaviour is a *sine qua non* of happiness for the child as well as the parents, R. D. Laing's views notwithstanding. Inconsistency in bringing up children, of course, produces an even more frustrating situation.

Anomia also strikes at the middle class in a period when its standards are being forced down in favour of the working class. Nor is it solely a question of economics. The middle class sees its values threatened: its belief in standards of clothing and cleanliness, a particular way of life, even its desire to preserve the buildings and landscapes of the past. It sees little hope of reversing this trend. Small wonder if its members feel hopeless or desperate. The desperation of the very under-privileged is well understood. The desperation of the ever-less privileged is no less real.

On the other side of the penny is the desperation of youth, who do not see how to succeed in a culture which in so many ways embodies values which differ from their own. And for those whose aim is a radical social revolution, success may also seem unattainable—hence the resort to violence. Where social mores are unacceptable, one must resort to rebellion.

However, suicide is not my theme: it is significant as an index of anomia, and the fact that suicide rates are rising in most Western countries indicates that anomia is a crucial problem. It is equally important that—like the cats—some people respond to anomic situations by violence, either because they reject the rule of society as being too frustrating and decide to become their own masters and make their own rules, or else in a fury of vengeful rage.

When people find society too intolerably disorganized they turn in desperation to anyone who will restore order and define unambiguous social goals. Such was the position in Germany in 1930, when 10 per cent of the population were out of work and savings were vanishing in a spectacular inflation. Hitler, proclaiming a clear goal, defining for each person his position in the social hierarchy and giving him a clear task to do, was welcomed: any reservations as to his methods or eventual aims were obscured by the relief from anxiety which his system brought. Thus anomia, if severe, leads to fascism. It is the growing disorder of US society today which makes a new dictatorship a distinct possibility.

The sociologist, Leo Srole, demonstrated that the link between anomia and authoritarianism exists by questioning people in Chicago (*a*) about their attitudes to authority and (*b*) their feelings about society. There was a 0·5 correlation between those who felt 'You wonder if anything is worth while any more' and an authoritarian attitude. The criminologist L. Radzinowicz, in his *Authority and Crime* shows how crimes against the person, against property and against public order flourish in conditions of social disorganization. It is striking that in England, where observance of conventions is stronger than in the USA, the murder rate is about one-twentieth of America's.

Another thing which restores a sense of unified purpose and imposes discipline on an anomic society is war. In war, all minor aims and rivalries can be forgotten: people are united in the common aim of victory. 'The peacefulness of war' is a phrase which succinctly expresses the reduction of anxiety which (at least for a time) war procures.

One of the consequences of anomia certainly seems to be depression, the incidence of which is rising in modern society. H. B. M. Murphy of McGill University and his colleagues, who made enquiries in many parts of the world about the frequency of basic depressive disorders, found that this was related *not* to class, to place of residence, to nature of religious belief or any of the usually proposed factors, but solely to the degree of cohesion of the community. (They also noted that guilt feelings were associated with this depression only in areas where the Judaeo-Christian tradition obtained, which is interesting but starts a hare which I will not pursue here.)

VII. *Origins of Anomia*

The most obvious factor causing anomia is a rapid rate of social change. If a man buys a house in the country for his retirement and then a suburb springs up round it, his entire life-plan for his old age is frustrated. If a man invests his savings in, say, government bonds and government action causes these bonds to drop in value, the same thing happens. Similarly, new technical devices can make decisions obsolete, as when the noise of aircraft makes a house undesirable, or when a new technology renders a hard-won skill obsolete.

Crowding and high immigration rates, which I have already discussed in connection with community, may also contribute to anomic conditions.* The immigrant, by definition, comes with different social norms and may or may not be able to find opportunities to fulfil his life-aims. Crowding, by increasing interaction, breaks up accepted patterns of interaction or renders them inappropriate.

These aspects of anomia have been much debated by sociologists, but it seems to me that there is another side to the question, equally important but generally neglected. What about the life-aims themselves?

* The case of immigration into Israel is obviously a very different one, since it brought together people of a *similar* culture, and, as one might have predicted, the signs of anomia in Israel are very low.

These may contribute to anomia in two ways. First, they may be unrealistic. Donald Crowhurst, the yachtsman who wished to be the man who had sailed round the world single-handed but whose skill and courage were inadequate, is a good example on the personal scale. Having circled about in the South Atlantic in an attempt to steal victory without really carrying out the task, when he found that his deceit was not going to succeed, he committed suicide. Having failed to live up to his persona as a dashing and capable sailor, he could not carry on. Of course, there have always been individuals who overestimated themselves. Today, I suspect there are unusually large numbers of people who believe that achievement is easy, and who consequently find themselves frustrated. Some drugs, notably LSD, seem to enhance this tendency. If such people do not withdraw in despair, or become vagrants or spongers, they blame society for their failure and become violent. In a later chapter, I shall try to explain why I think this over-optimism comes about. (Just as we once heard a great deal about people with 'inferiority complexes', today we can observe many people who have 'superiority complexes'.)

However, without pursuing the psychological aspect here, it is a commonplace that television, advertising and the media, have presented people with visions of a way of life that, while attainable by some, is certainly not attainable by the majority, at least in the current state of world development. In this sense, at least, it is possible for people to form unrealistic ambitions.

Secondly, and this also is no academic point, society may be split into two or more groups with incompatible aims. Today, for instance, we see in most Western countries a middle-class group which is losing ground and a working-class group which is gaining ground, in a socio-economic sense. Obviously these two groups have opposing aims. That is what the class war is about. I simply wish to point out that the consequences are anomic for the losing class, and if they constitute a sizeable proportion of the whole society, then they are anomic for society.

But the socio-economic split is not the only one. Much less well-recognized but, I suspect, even more important, is the value-split between those whom I have called the hard and soft egoists, between those who are concerned by issues like starvation in underdeveloped countries, torture in dictatorships, war in Vietnam and India, reform of prisons and mental institutions at home and the whole range of social issues, irrespective of socio-economic class. Here again, some reformers tend to feel that their aims are unattainable, and to resort to violence or despair. But note the interesting thing: this split cuts right across the socio-economic one. Support for social measures is certainly not confined to the working class, and (*vide* the 'hard-hat' phenomenon in the

USA) it is often the manual workers who favour authoritarian and re-actionary measures.

It follows that a satisfactory existence for individuals is only feasible in a society which is reasonably united as to basic values, and where the aims of life are not unrealistic. As Robert Merton stressed, society influences us to phrase our aims in certain forms, and if we phrase them in terms which are unrealistic—such as to be richer than any one else—this converts realistic aims into unrealistic ones.

A high rate of social change also causes other problems. People form a conception of themselves, usually termed a *persona*, to which they try to conform. Thus, if it is part of their ambition to be brave, and to be seen as being brave, they will go to great lengths to appear brave, however acute their internal trepidation. Thus the impoverished gentleman may continue to change for dinner, even though he can only afford a boiled egg; the *nouveau riche* who continues to tuck his napkin into his collar, to prove that he is still a common man, as he attacks his grouse and burgundy, is the complementary example of the same mechanism. In conditions of social change, like those today, people often find it hard to maintain their personas; and if people have to abandon their persona, they usually crack up entirely. Thus a high socio-economic mobility—often praised as desirable, especially in the USA and by those who expect to rise—may have disastrous effects.

In addition, as I have already related in the previous chapter, social change disrupts the social machine in ways which make the attainment of goals more difficult.

Technology is the ultimate author of these iils and especially too much technology too fast. We need a breathing-space to find ways of handling the technological novelties we have, before we are presented with any more. Violence, insecurity, suicide, loneliness, these, and more, are the price we pay for living in a mass society, and for the 'wider horizons' and the 'freedom' which it provides. When we come to understand the conception, we may begin to wonder whether the price is too high.

To sum up then, to restore community and cure anomia, we should have to reduce the rate of social and technological change, reduce the mobility of the individual and perhaps even discourage communications; we should have to limit the inflow of new members to communities and we should have to preserve the 'uniques' in each cultural sub-unit, accepting cultural diversity rather than standardization and a common culture as a social aim.

These are aims which go against the whole trend of our times, and to many will seem retrogressive. But since my case is that our culture is proceeding in the wrong direction, it follows inevitably that it must abandon its present course. In Chapter 8, therefore, I shall examine just what the implications of such a programme would be. But the sense of boredom, the feeling that life is meaningless, is not wholly explained by anomic conditions, and in the next chapter I turn to the question of personal identity and uniqueness, which lies at the very root of the crisis of our time.

Who Am I and Where?

I. *Introduction*

UNDER the obviously symbolic name of Inburn, the sociologist Kenneth Keniston describes a student whose personality he investigated. Externally normal enough, if rather reserved, inside he was deeply dissatisfied with society, the world and himself. Typical of his comments were: 'I have very little in common with any of the people I meet,' and 'The idea of trying to adjust to society as it now exists fills me with horror.' His sense of identity was weak: 'Sometimes I feel I am the plaything of forces beyond my control.'

Keniston compares 'Inburn' with Ishmael and with the character in Melville's *Moby Dick* who sometimes became so enraged with everyone and everything that he would go to sea until the mood had subsided. Inburn was as contemptuous of himself as of the rest of the world. He told Keniston how he and his even more cynical friend Hal 'were full of magnificent disdain and fed it with all the knowledge we could get— and what wouldn't fit we disregarded'. They read Kafka, D. H. Lawrence, Hume, Rousseau, Voltaire, Shaw, Jung, Freud, Marx. 'We read voraciously, but not the right things and not enough.'

He wrote stories for Keniston, as part of the enquiry, in each of which he appears as an outsider, looking in. Keniston comments that the 'central and unifying themes in Inburn's fantasy life centre on the rage to re-enter the "insensible" sanctuary he had had with his mother'. Characteristically, when asked how he would reform the world, he replied: 'I'd like to have us all go back to the womb.'

The 'outsider' is evidently an anomic individual and Inburn is typical of a certain type of maverick and destructive social critic whose discontent arises less from the defects of society than from deep neurotic problems of his own. Keniston was primarily concerned to analyse Inburn in psychoanalytic terms, as part of a wider study of how people live their lives. Inburn had what I shall later show to be a very typical pattern, a warm and possessive mother and a cold or absent father. To make things worse, he was an only child. This combination invariably leads to a boy having difficulty in taking up the male role, so that he rejects authority and all father-figures, and has great difficulty in relating to women, whom he fears as overpowering. (Inburn had only platonic relations with girls, and masturbated excessively.) At the unconscious level, there are incest fears. It is a classic variation of the Oedipus situation.

So little social feeling did Inburn have that he could declare: 'It is better to murder, which is just an act, than to make no acts at all.' Here is the *acte gratuite* in clearly expressed form: the motiveless crime. Freud would say that the acts Inburn felt he could not make were sexual ones, and the desire to murder expressed the frustration due to this impotence. Long before Freud, Blake put the same thought quite explicitly: 'Sooner murder an infant in its cradle than nurse unacted desires.'

Later, I shall go into such underlying psychological factors in some detail, but here I want to examine the objective social factors making for a sense of alienation. Whatever the cause, alienation is an extremely serious phenomenon, and it is growing. Society cannot afford to harbour many such alienated figures (though the presence of a few may be a useful critical stimulus). Equally important is the fact that they themselves are miserably unhappy. What, then, are the social origins of alienation? How can we reverse this trend?

II. *Where Am I?*

To be alienated from society means to feel one has no part in it, no involvement in its purposes or methods; perhaps that one feels rejected by it. One cannot influence it, one feels, and one tries to live without being influenced by it. It is to be out of love with society. Robert Nisbet puts it well when he writes of 'a state of mind which can find a social order remote, incomprehensible or fraudulent; beyond real hope or desire; inviting apathy, boredom or even hostility'. And he comments: 'It has become clearer that alienation is one of the determining realities of the contemporary age . . . implicating ever-larger sections of the population.'

A person does not only feel alienated from society as a whole; he may feel alienated from other people, from work, from certain institutions, from political reality, from nature and place, from the past and even from himself. Total involvement in everything is, no doubt, impossible, perhaps even a form of madness. It is reasonable to feel alienated from things which are evil—from a fascist state, for instance. But if the sense of alienation spreads to include nature and the past, and finally the self, it becomes a serious sickness; and if many people in society are thus alienated, society itself is diseased.

The idea of alienation first arose in connection with industrial work. The poet Schiller, observing the early stages of the industrial revolution, indicted what he called 'the separation of gratification from labour'. Hegel and Marx took up the idea and termed it alienation. For

Marx, alienation was synonymous with exploitation: the worker felt alienated (*a*) because he did not himself decide what he should do and (*b*) did not own the product of his work. This was a reasonable, if incomplete, diagnosis—though Marx's belief that ownership of industry by the proletariat would completely resolve this problem was wildly over-optimistic. Ownership implies control. The individual craftsman can decide whether to sell the shoes he has made, give them to a friend or keep them for himself. The worker on a production line in Soviet Russia, though in a remote sense a part-owner of the cars he is helping to produce, cannot decide on how they are to be disposed of.

Alienation from work comes not only from the boring, non-challenging nature of the task but from wider factors such as the ultimate value to society of what is being produced. One cannot be deeply involved in compounding a worthless patent medicine or trivial gimmick, for instance. As society grows wealthier more and more people are involved in making things or providing services of less and less significance—as I have already argued.

Erich Fromm has pointed out that modern man is alienated not only from the process of production but also from the *objects* produced. Once people loved and valued their personal property—clothes, dishes, beds, books—for they were hard to replace. To acquire them was difficult, involved taste and effort. To tear or break them was a minor tragedy. To part with them was painful: to give something away was to give part of oneself. Today we live in a throwaway society. A broken jug can be replaced. A gift can be found, if money is available, without reducing our own store. Fashion is stimulated to encourage us to discard even what is not broken or worn out. We lose something when we cease to relate to objects.

This consumer attitude then spreads to other fields. The spectator consumes the game he watches, consumes scenery,* consumes a party without becoming involved in it. He can watch a building on fire without any pang or any wish to help in extinguishing it. Finally, he can watch a murder being committed and do nothing.

Furthermore, modern man does not know how most of the things he uses are made, or how they work; he only knows how to manipulate or consume them. They remain objects to him. Fromm considers that our ever-increasing need for more things, more goods, arises from this.

The fact of alienation from economics is an old story. It is compounded by alienation from politics and from institutions. We feel alienated from politics when we have no sympathy with the aims of

* See *The Doomsday Book*, p. 280, for a summary of an article 'Consumers of the River' by Wendell Berry, a poet, describing how empty and destructive it is to experience a river just as 'scenery'.

government, as distinct from means; and when we feel we have no power to influence the choice of aims. Today when all governments seem intent on economic growth, at whatever cost in the disruption of personality and the environment, many people feel alienated in this way. Furthermore, as Sir Geoffrey Vickers has pointed out, people become alienated from the institutions on which they depend because they feel that the officials in charge are governed by what he calls 'institutional standards of success'. All institutions desire to grow, and their managers feel they have succeeded if growth occurs, failed if the institution contracts or vanishes. But the real question is whether the institution is meeting human needs, not whether it is expanding. This is true of industrial giants, but even truer of local government units, which are often dominated by business considerations and minimizing the level of local rates and taxes, rather than the good of the local community in all its aspects.

When people feel alienated from politics—that is, when political leaders appear unable to run the country so as to meet their basic needs —they are apt to transfer their allegiance to a leader in whom they place an excessive trust and whom they identify with, a process sometimes known as Caesarism. The German trust in Hitler, which arose from the despair engendered by the mass unemployment of the late twenties, when some ten million people were out of work, is the best-known recent example. Franz Neumann has examined this process which, as he points out, depends on the presence of anxiety, this anxiety being revealed by conspiracy theories, according to which some evil group is plotting destruction. (Thus the French revolution was ascribed to the Freemasons.) The Caesaristic solution institutionalizes this anxiety, i.e. accepts it, puts it in the open, provides an explanation and proposes a cure. In the case of Germany it was the Jews, of course, who were made the scapegoats: but the anxiety *was* present, and no account of the rise of the Nazis which overlooks this is adequate.

In short, when anxiety co-exists with political alienation, the risk of dictatorship is high, because existing political parties, in most Western countries, do not admit effective alternative policies or parties. Should anything occur to arouse strong anxieties, in any such country, a dictatorship will spring into being, and a scapegoat will be selected.

In the absence of such anxiety, we shall see increasing political apathy on the one hand, increasing political violence on the other. The zealots will cause explosions and assassinate individuals; the majority will ignore the news and seek to escape from the impasse by winning the state lottery or private football pools.

While most of us are dimly aware of these types of alienation, we are more apt to overlook the importance of alienation from nature, from the great natural cycles and from the mysteries of birth and death. The pollution of the environment and the destruction of rare species and entire ecosystems springs from this kind of alienation, which in turn springs largely from living in towns, but partly from an attitude of mind. Coupled with alienation from nature is alienation from place—the failure to form emotional links with particular scenes and places—to which I have already referred.

And to this catalogue we may perhaps add alienation from what existentialists call 'the mystery of being'—or, as some would say, alienation from God. It manifests itself as a loss of the sense of wonder and awe. Professor Henry Winthrop of the University of South Florida has put it very well: 'This type of alienation occurs whenever men have lost the ability to wonder how anything ever came to be—a concern, of course, of the modern cosmologist. It also occurs when they cease to marvel at the many forms of human love, whether these reflect *Eros* or *Agape*. [That is, sexual or spiritual love.] We see it once again when men have lost the ability to witness with respect man's capacity for self-transcendence, his expressions of social altruism and his concern for social justice. In general this form of alienation also includes the ability to experience or understand the religious impulse in others—those invisible bonds of sentiment and fellow-feeling which prompt men to be concerned with and underwrite one another's welfare.'

Finally we come to the strange notion of a person alienated from himself. As Fromm puts it, such a person is 'estranged from himself. He does not experience himself as the centre of his world, as the creator of his own acts—his acts and their consequences have become his masters.'

A person's relationship with himself is a puzzling thing, as we can gather from expressions like 'I was not myself yesterday,' or 'It was good for my ego.' Both these phrases imply that we have a conception of ourselves which we may not continuously live up to; when we say that some comment was good for our ego, we mean that it enabled us to believe that we approximate more closely to our ideal conception of ourself.

If, in contrast, we think of this other self as performing actions which we despise and we lose our respect for ourselves, we have an identity problem. Our identity differs, in actual fact, from the identity at which we aim. So, at this point, the alienation crisis is linked with the identity crisis. A man cannot feel self-respect, as Fromm points out, if he 'does not experience himself as the active bearer of his own power and richness', but feels himself 'an impoverished "thing", dependent on powers outside himself, onto whom he has projected his living substance'. (And he italicizes these words.) As elsewhere, this also is true in the political context: the man who makes himself dependent on a Führer is himself enfeebled and self-disgusted.

In conditions of total alienation people react either by violence or by despair. The negativism, boredom and 'couldn't-care-less' attitude so common today is the direct consequence of alienation. This alienation stems from loss of community. And according to Fromm it is now 'almost total'.

I have mentioned the phenomenon of alienation from oneself, but it calls for further discussion, for it is part of a key psychological process known as the formation of identity. 'Who am I?' is a question everyone has, at some time or other, asked themselves. In three short words it raises issues of great subtlety and importance for today, which psychologists have recently begun to analyse under the label of 'identity problems'. Thanks mainly to the work of Erik Erikson, this elusive idea has been pinned down and defined in a way which makes its implications clear. Erikson has been concerned mainly with the development of identity in the growing child and with the clinical problems arising. Another psychiatrist, Allen Wheelis, has taken the lead in relating these ideas to society, and I shall draw on his brilliant book *The Quest for Identity* in what follows, though of course he is not responsible for my conclusions.

III. *Personal Worth*

Most people (perhaps all) need to have a sense of *personal worth*, and feel a deep-lying disquiet if this sense of worth is threatened or is absent. They also wish to feel that they are in some sense an *individual*, with unique attributes, and not simply a cipher, a robot or carbon-copy of other people: this is what psychologists mean when they write about 'the search for identity'. These two ideas are closely connected, since without a sense of identity one cannot have a sense of worth. I shall take them together.

Our sense of worth is naturally derived from the same kind of standards as those by which we recognize the worth of other people, so that it is our social value, our contribution to the social group, which normally provides the basis of it. But our estimate of ourselves is influenced by what society thinks of us. The man who makes an outstanding contribution—whether it is breaking a speed record, curing the sick, producing a work of art or growing the food on which everyone depends—can certainly feel that he is worth something, and particularly if his contribution is unique. Thus the artist is certain of his identity: he is the man who painted *La Gioconda* or whatever it was, and no one else past, present or future, can say the same. Ditto for writers, composers; ditto for scientists. In a lesser way, anyone who excels can claim to be in some degree unique. 'He is the best football player in the county . . . the man who discovered the electric lamp . . . the builder of the fastest boat on the lake . . .' Such descriptions bestow an identity on people.

In modern society, unfortunately, many people find it hard to achieve such an identity. The man who performs a repetitive operation on a production line cannot point to the delivery line and say, 'I made that refrigerator.' He is certainly not unique, as far as the factory is concerned; if he fell ill, or died, another man would step into his place, and his absence would hardly be noticed. The production line is a constantly quoted example; but much the same is true of many jobs from the bus-driver or shop assistant to the civil servant or computer programmer. This is due to several trends which I have already discussed, notably the fact that industry has rejected the skills and individuality of the worker.

Professional men, such as lawyers and architects, do make a personal contribution; writers and artists, etc., of course, are even more uniquely individual, as are performers and public personalities. I suspect that these fortunate people completely fail to grasp the desperation of those who are entirely replaceable. (It is even worse if one can be adequately replaced by a machine, which is why the computer is often seen as a threat by a class which was previously well-placed in this respect.)

Loss of community is also a factor: the village shop assistant remains an individual, known to most of his customers and knowing them. More insidiously, the state treats men as ciphers, and with the growth of computer methods will do so even more. Letters from people who object to being 'simply a number' are constantly printed in the papers and reflect this feeling. To the administrator, this is 'sentiment' and administratively impractical. The victim can reply: 'Sentiment is what matters to me, and I am not concerned with your administrative problems. You must find another solution to them.'

To no small extent, our conception of ourself is expressed by the objects with which we surround ourself. These are not only evidences of achievement, they are status symbols in the proper sense: indications of our tastes and interests and our 'walk of life'. This is why it is so hard to get rid of the affluent society: stripped of his peculiar possessions a man becomes indistinguishable from other men; he loses his identity.*

But technology undermines this element in personal uniqueness too. Mass production means that most people have much the same sort of possessions. Attempts to restore uniqueness by 'personalizing'—by adding initials or extras, or by recombining basic units—are now a commonplace. The growing demand for antiques, for hand-made jewellery, etc., expresses the wish to escape this impersonality. Modern life also treats people as objects, assigning them a number and treating

* I owe this thought to Professor V. A. Mitscherlich's *Society without the Father* (1969).

them mechanically, on the basis of a few recorded facts, whereas a human being usually treats you on the basis of his total knowledge and impression of you.

As soon as we realize that the inhabitants of technological society are suffering from a loss of the sense of personal value and identity, we see that this explains many types of behaviour. For example, today people are excessively preoccupied with status, and bitterly resent anything which seems to derogate their standing. Trade unions fight to maintain 'wage differentials' which put their members above those of other unions on the status ladder. Demarcation disputes in industry arise from this too. If a man is identified as a welder, he is seen as having a special skill which is in limited supply; then if riveters start welding not only is his economic position threatened but also his sense of identity. The economic position could easily be protected: the sense of identity cannot, which is why such disputes are so intractable. People resign their jobs because they were asked to do something beneath their dignity, and so on. Moreover, people often resent the respect accorded to those who have achieved high standing, and attempt to debunk them, or pull them down from their pedestals. 'Who does he think he is?' is a cry which refers quite palpably to identity. Such actions reflect inner weakness: the man who knows his own worth can afford to ignore the disrespect of others. In the same spirit, people often insist on 'their rights', though do not use them. People dislike taking orders, which they feel demeaning, though it is natural enough in many circumstances to receive orders. A healthy independence gradually becomes an unfounded attitude of arrogance.

The status battle also leads to competitiveness, which must be distinguished from emulation. In past ages, one sought to do as well as outstanding people; now it is necessary to surpass them. But to surpass the achievements of the past is increasingly difficult, and (except in technological matters) often impossible. Few can manage it. Hence changes in fashion. Artistic life becomes a matter of vogues and cliques: the desire to please or to intensify vision becomes the desire to shock.

As Lewis Way points out in his penetrating book *Man's Quest for Significance*, as morale declines, this frenzied competitiveness turns to aggressive individualism, discontent and anarchy.

While a person's identity is definable in terms of what others think of him, it is even more a question of what he thinks of himself. We gradually evolve aims in life, and standards of behaviour, and we see these as a coherent whole. 'No, that just isn't me,' a person may say, when some course of action is suggested. They perceive that they have a style to which they must remain true. Equally, we recognize this as being true of others, and may say: 'That just isn't like her, to do that.'

It is not only that one chooses a role but also that society recognizes in some sense the role one has chosen. When we choose a role, we expect society to treat us in an appropriate way, just as it expects certain behaviour of us. ('Call yourself a yachtsman, and you don't know how to coil a rope!')

Women are particularly hard hit by this loss of identity, since the state has taken over so many of their functions. Their maternal lore has been replaced by the district nurse; their role as cook by the dietician, the school meals service, and the pre-cooked food. Their role as educator of their children, even in the earliest years, is usurped by the kindergarten or so-called 'infant' school. Once they provided clothing and even medical know-how: these contributions too are much reduced. It is this loss of sense of worth which has given rise to the Women's Lib movements—naturally first in America, where this defeminization of woman has gone furthest. True, women suffer economic handicaps —but economic equality can do little to restore the sense of inner worth which has been lost. In addition, the assimilation of the sexes, I suspect, weakens women's sense of being uniquely different from men and vice versa, and so intensifies the problem for both sexes.

It can also be seen that the search for an unique identity explains the numbers of young men who seek to become photographers, dress designers, television producers, graphic artists or, for that matter, star footballers or boxers. All these are unique individuals, in the sense that if Mr X produces a certain programme, that programme is unique to him, even if it is bad. Better to earn little as a person than earn a high salary as a robot. It also explains the people who commit a murder, or hijack an aircraft, and explain afterwards that they did it in order to 'be somebody'.

A characteristic of our society which no longer strikes us as strange is the excessive general preoccupation with 'public personalities'—television performers, society leaders, political figures. The explanation, once again, is that in a mass society, only a small number of people can emerge as individuals, since the number of people a single individual can recognize is limited. Since most people are deprived of such recognition, they can only assuage their sense of depersonalization by identifying themselves with such figures. It is not required that they be heroes, or models (as in the past), only that they be strongly individualized.

As we grow older, our identity becomes more clearly marked. Our achievements or failures mark out what kind of man we are; our attitudes, derived from our experience, become ingrained. Subject to this slow crystallization, identity is normally stable. Occasionally we say of someone: 'She's become a different person since her husband died.' When this happens it is usually because some crushing external force has been removed, releasing us to realize the personality which was always there, or because some overwhelming burden has crushed our identity. Illness, both mental and physical, can have the same effect; 'I am not myself today,' we say, a phrase which shows vividly that we have a precise conception of ourselves.

During the Second World War the Nazi administration issued a decree dramatically known as the *Nacht und Nebel*, or Night and Fog, decree. Certain persons, under this law, could be deprived of their identity. Every record concerning them would be destroyed, even in the concentration camp in which they were incarcerated, as well as birth and marriage records, insurance policies, anything they had written, etc. They would have only a number, no name. And they would be told that this had been done. 'As far as the world is concerned, you have never existed.' In addition, they were moved from one camp to another at frequent intervals, so that they could never build up acquaintance-ships or become known as individuals even to guards and other in-mates. The effect on these individuals was catastrophic. It destroyed them.

IV. *How Society Undermines Identity*

'Identity is a coherent sense of self,' says Allen Wheelis. 'It depends upon the awareness that one's endeavours and one's life "make sense", that they are meaningful in the context in which the life is lived.' It is our aims which impart the desired coherence to our activities. A man who is trying to carve a farm out of a wilderness will have to carry out an enormous variety of disparate actions, but they all contribute to his main end. Even his recreation can be seen to play a part in his life-plan, since it restores his energy and enthusiasm for the main struggle.

But if his efforts are rendered fruitless by the decisions of a highway authority to drive a road through his plot of land, his efforts cease to make sense; his aim is frustrated. As the instance suggests, the modern world often reduces the efforts of individuals to nonsense, due as much to the rapidity of social change as to the larger scope of public plans. It is primarily because we live in an age of change that identity is so much weakened today. But if this seems a new idea, the impression is a false one. More than half a century ago, the German sociologist, George Simmel, declared, 'the deepest problems of modern life derive from the claim of the individual to preserve the autonomy and in-dividuality of his existence in the face of overwhelming social forces.'

Erik Erikson stresses that identity should show stability over a period of time. He calls it 'a persistent sameness within oneself and a persistent sharing of some kind of essential character with others'. Thus in periods of change we must either modify our identity or end up with an inappropriate one: society begins to expect of us a pattern of values and behaviour which is not our own. The person who rigidly preserves his identity risks becoming obsolete, his aims and attitudes old-fashioned, his values out-of-date. He becomes 'square'. Thus change can destroy our sense of personal worth.*

However, in a changing world, personality itself may become fluid. Wheelis puts it: 'The social character now coming to prevail seems sculptured to fit a culture of change. In order to survive, it would appear that the individual must become progressively more able to modify himself . . . The key words of our time are flexibility, adjustment and warmth—as, for our grandfathers, they were work, thrift, will.' However, the flexible personality may not be the one best fitted for survival, for survival is likely to depend on the ability to pursue distant aims with unwavering determination.

The individual who avoids committing himself to any aim or attitude, and who holds himself ready to trim his sails to every wind of change, suffers a sense of having lost himself. 'Not knowing what he stands for, he does not know what he is.' This state of mind gives rise to persistent anxiety and anxiety, by a circular process, feeds the need to stand well with others: the social conformity or 'other-directedness' to which David Riesman drew attention in his celebrated *The Lonely Crowd* (1961), but whose cause he was unable to explain.

With the abandonment of overt ambitions and the retreat into the self, the desire for achievement becomes replaced by the desire for human warmth, and 'adjustment' becomes the aim of life, rather than 'achievement'.

A further cause of loss of identity lies in the simplification of culture.

As Margaret Mead has observed, though the culture of the United States seems fragmented to a European—and is—yet there is a sense in which it is highly simplified and homogenous. The Californian not only drives the same sort of car as the New Yorker or the Wyoming cowboy but he responds to fundamentally the same imperatives. This is true increasingly of the rest of the world. The culture is becoming homogenized. Two centuries ago in Britain, a Norfolk reedsman, a South Downs shepherd, a hunting squire, a Scottish clansman, led lives which were substantially different. They wore different clothes, ate different

* And while one can recover from a single major set-back, few people can bounce back twice. This was noticed in the great slump of the thirties. A coal-miner made the switch to working in a stocking factory. He found great difficulty in adapting to this 'cissy' job, as he thought it: he felt less of a man, now he was no longer facing the dangers and demands of coal-mining. When, through no fault of his own, he was laid off from this job, he went to pieces altogether. It has also been noticed that people who commit suicide are typically people who have been a double failure—in two roles, for instance, at work and in their marriage. They have nothing 'to live for'.

food, even their language differed past the point of comprehension. Today, the world is coca-colonized: the word was coined to express just this fact. Today you can travel round the world and still find the same drinks, the same gadgets and the same clothes.

But in a homogenized, coca-colonized world it is harder to be an individual. One becomes a cypher. The distinctive features which identified you as a shepherd rather than a fisherman or a don are stripped away. It is this loss of individuality which motivates minorities to fight for the preservation of their local culture, as the Irish fight for the use of Gaelic, the Welsh for self-rule, and indeed in nationalism everywhere. This too explains black nationalism and the desire to learn black history from black teachers.

Another force making for loss of identity is the ubiquity of communications. Thanks to the media, and above all to television, the same facts pour into every home in the land. The minds of all are concerned with the same set of problems, are cognizant of the same public figures. Thus the furniture of the mind comes to resemble the furniture of everyone else's mind. This may simplify communication, reducing it to an exchange of stereotypes, but it destroys individuality and eats away the sense of personal uniqueness, and hence of worth. For if one is replaceable, if one has nothing unique to offer, one is not an individual.

Finally, there is the fact that our sense of identity depends not only on how we think of ourself but on how other people think of us. They attribute an identity to us, and as a rule we try to live up to their expectations of us. The man who knows he is regarded as the life and soul of the party feels obliged to maintain this reputation; the man renowned for bravery is all the more unwilling to seem a coward on some later occasion.* In mass society, we are cut off from such expectations: people expect only what we assert of ourselves—which imposes on us the burden of choice. In all these ways, mass society is the source of the identity crisis: the only way to restore indenitty is to revert to a non primitive kind of society.

Perhaps one should also blame universal education for opening up to people ambitions which, in the nature of things, most of them can never achieve. The ploughman's son was content to become a ploughman too, or, at most, to take one of the other jobs of which he had direct experience. Today, education familiarizes the ploughman's son with

* Sometimes society, or a group of people, attributes to us an identity we do not recognize, and we may feel impelled to adapt ourselves to it. The coward who is mistaken for a hero, and desperately tries to live up to this conception, is a stock theme of comic books and films. More serious is the case where society, in effect, tells someone he is worthless and unwanted, imposing this identity on him until he comes to accept it himself.

everything from computer programming to fashion-modelling, and this may plant in him ambitions far beyond his capacities, if he happens to lack brains or beauty. I do not say that it is bad to open up such possibilities, only that it has—like most things—a bad as well as a good side. If it helps some to achieve identity, it frustrates others and we have no figures to show whether the first group is larger than the second.

V. *Autonomy and Bureaucracy*

Deep in the human psyche lies the need to feel that one's actions are determined by oneself. Today many people have the feeling that what they do is determined by other people, by the state, or even more generally by the system under which they live. In a literal sense, the state (in all its manifestations, both local and national) imposes regulations and compulsions: the volume of legislation and statutory orders grows incessantly. In a more figurative sense, one travels to work every morning because it is the 'done thing', the line of least resistance, and not from an urgent desire to get on with a particular job. Contrast this with the settler going out to fell a tree to make a stockade with: he is deeply committed to getting the job done. In short, people feel they have lost autonomy, and an automaton is not a person. Hence the general fear of computers: if they are going to do the thinking, while other machines do the work, what have we to contribute? The sense of depersonalization is often encountered by the alienist, and in certain types of insanity people claim that 'thoughts are being thought for me'. Many people, who are still nominally sane, are being pressed by our society in this direction. (Inburn felt himself the victim of impersonal forces.)

The main reasons why the state interferes increasingly in the life of the individual are twofold: a combination of technology and population density. Technology increases people's power to annoy or harm other people. A man with a car can kill half a dozen other people, as he never could have with a pony-trap or even a coach. A girl with a transistor radio can annoy the neighbours without even the effort of raising her voice. (I knew a deaf woman who, because she could not hear her alarm clock go off, used to leave her radio switched on all night with the volume control at FULL. At six o'clock every morning her neighbours were all woken up by stentorian announcements of the day's programmes and kept awake without respite.) But our power to annoy or harm is greatly increased if we are crowded together. A man in a remote cottage can leave the radio on and annoy no one, just as a man can drive inattentively on empty country roads without killing anyone. The crowding together of human beings is due partly to the increase in population, partly to the tendency of people to crowd together in cities and suburbs. But both of these are the products of technology, so, in the last analysis, it is technology which is to blame.*

The ramifications of state control will certainly stretch much further, before long. As Sir Geoffrey Vickers has put it, we are nearing the end of the period of 'free fall' in which technology has been applied indiscriminately, without regulation, and about to enter an era of absolute control.

It is a paradox that man, in becoming freer in some senses, has become less free in others. Boosters often tell us that man is freer than ever before: free to travel anywhere, free to eat and drink exotic foods and beverages, free from sexual taboos and so on. But in another sense he is less free. As we have come to understand physical laws, we find our freedom limited to working within them. As Wheelis puts it, you cannot build an aeroplane without allegiance to determinism. And as social and psychological mechanisms become clearer, we see that our actions are not free: we are the creatures of environment or of heredity.

Thus, for this reason too, man finds himself less of a person, more of a cypher. Perhaps the reason we talk so much today about the importance of the human person, about dignity and the potentialities of man, is precisely because they are being continually diminished.

But neither does the recognition of an indeterministic element in nature help us: where the outcome is chancy, there is little we can do to control events. In our helplessness and lack of autonomy, we lose our self-respect and we find ourselves again reduced to cyphers.

Man's sense of loss of autonomy has a further important consequence. The human *will* seems to have little importance when human affairs are settled by forces over which the individual has no control. This weakening of will has been observed by many psychiatrists in their patients, as Wheelis observes. The psychologist William James believed that a sense of personal integrity depended on being able to will effectively. If we hear a great deal today about human rights and the dignity of the individual, it is precisely because that dignity has been reduced and those rights eroded.

Parallel with the devaluation of will has gone a devaluation of courage, for courage is the sign of will. The man who rejects the system or strikes out against it is derided as an eccentric or dismissed as an anarchist or rebel. Some people take on dangerous tasks or sports, such as mountain climbing, in order to prove their courage and determination to themselves, but most people regard this as peculiar and confess without a blush: 'Of course, I am an awful coward.'

---

* Two other factors in the current loss of autonomy may be that bureaucracy tends to become more powerful and requires techniques enabling it to handle more detail—this is the real threat of the computer; this, and a tendency to regard such control as desirable or inevitable.

To recapitulate, technological society destroys the sense of unique individuality in many of its members by (1) the mechanization and sub-division of labour; (2) the size of administrative units and centralization of decisions; (3) the growth of regulation which is based on population density and man's increased powers; and (4) the rapid rate of social change when measured against the yardstick of a human life-span. All these are trends which are continuing with accelerating rapidity, and which only a titanic and revolutionary effort could stop or reverse. Unless this effort is made, the drama of identity will reach crisis point.

VI. *The Identity Crisis*

The identity problem is felt with especial force by the adolescent, stand-ing at the threshold of adulthood. Now he or she must commit him or herself: now an identity must be chosen. As people sometimes say, 'I need to find myself,' or 'I must find out who I am.' Erikson,* who has studied the process of finding an identity in detail, tells the story of an orphaned American-born girl who told a detailed story of her childhood in Scotland, in a town which she named and described, even simulating a Scottish accent as she did so. Erikson, realizing after a while that the whole thing was an elaborate fabrication, sympathetically asked her why she had developed this elaborate deception. 'Why, bless you, sir,' she replied, still in character, 'I needed a past.'

Erikson has studied how the growing child assimilates and repudiates various identifications, combining them in new patterns. In the course of this it is much influenced by the way in which society identifies it. If it is told that it is idle, for instance, it may say, in effect, 'OK, if I'm tabbed as idle, idle I shall be.' Or it may reject the label, and work harder. Ambitious and superior parents, who make excessive demands on a child, often have this effect of causing it to form a 'negative identity' —that is, to adopt perversely all the roles which have been presented as dangerous or undesirable, and so to become a black sheep. This is especially likely if such behaviour has been seen to win attention, or love, in others. A child shares its parents' identity: it is simply 'Mrs Jones' little boy'. In the eventual struggle to become Mr Jones in his own right, strong rejection of parents is liable to take place.

But the identity crisis of contemporary youth seems due more to the failure of society to offer it acceptable roles than to the struggle to escape parental domination at the identity level. Youth is naturally idealistic and has been trained to believe the world should and can be improved. Opportunities for improving it, for attacking the real prob-lems of society as distinct from churning out more goods for the benefit of the more privileged, are few.

* See in particular *Identity: Youth and Crisis.*

Hence the readiness of young people to protest, to attach themselves to causes; hence too, their rejection of the standards of a society which in so many respect ignores these ambitions. Hence the readiness to follow gurus, or teachers who preach a less material, less anonymous existence.

The moment at which the individual chooses a career or decides on a life's ambition commits him almost irrevocably. Thus adolescents are faced with a decision of far-reaching importance which they may or may not be ready to take. They need, as we sometimes say, time 'to find themselves'. In the past, when a boy followed his father's trade unless he felt a very explicit impulse to break away, the need for decision was less acute. Today, especially in a matrist age, few people feel bound to follow in their father's footsteps, and the question of 'what to be' can be harrowing. For women too this has become more of a crisis, now that home-keeping is no longer accepted as a sufficient full-time occupation, and now that many girls are given educations which make a career a reasonable possibility.

The choice is even harder, however, if one is still confused in one's values and uncertain about one's aims. This, too, is the situation of many young people today and lies at the heart of the student protest. They receive an education which provides them with the skills to attempt more than their parents, but which does not give them a value-structure or a philosophy which enables them to decide on how to use those skills.

Wiser than we, primitive societies assist the transition from childhood to manhood by ceremonies (known to anthropologists as *rites de passage*) which clearly demarcate the two states. In principle, these ceremonies are designed to show that the young man has in fact developed the skills and courage needed to sustain a man's role. Thus among the Dyaks the boy must go into the forest and return with the head of an enemy. In other tribes, he must carry heavy logs or succeed in killing game. Tortures are often applied to demonstrate courage; these are sometimes absurdly severe, in others they have dwindled to the merest ceremony. A boy cannot marry until he has passed such tests, and sometimes the test is itself the marriage ceremony, or is administered by the women. (Most such rites also show elements symbolizing rebirth, or involve circumcision and similar ceremonies, which do not concern us here.) The same element of testing is present in 'marriage by service', in which the suitor works for the father of his intended for several years before being approved as a husband. (As in the Bible story of Esau.)

In our society, we still speak of 'coming of age', but most of the privileges of that state are granted sooner, while we further confuse the issue by having different ages at which one may become a warrior, qualify academically, or begin to vote. We believe ourselves to have got rid of a meaningless rite; actually it is sheer folly not to mark clearly the achievement of manhood, and to make its privileges dependent on providing some evidence of fitness.

VII. *A Sense of Purpose*

'He who has a *why* to live can bear with almost any *how*,' said Nietzsche.

Perhaps the most fundamental of man's demands is that life should have a purpose or a meaning.* Jung once remarked that he was besieged by men in their forties and fifties who had made money and launched a family and now wanted to know the meaning of life, and when Victor Frankl questioned his patients at the Vienna Polyclinic he found that 55 per cent felt life was *not* meaningful.

The intensity of modern man's search for meaning has two causes. When we are starving, to find food becomes our dominant purpose. The instinct to survive is fundamental, as that Greek philosopher demonstrated who, when a friend declared that life was not worth living, plunged his friend's head beneath the water. The friend struggled to survive. When we have ensured our own existence, our next object is likely to be the production of children and their launching into the world. It is precisely because these simple objectives have been met that we now look for some ulterior purpose.

It is generally possible at this point to engage in some larger social purpose, in helping one's fellows or improving the state of the world. But today there is a widespread suspicion about the worthwhileness of such effort, a suspicion which is intensified by the threat of the nuclear holocaust. (Of course, when war breaks out, people find a new purpose in life, which is why war is often welcomed.) Bernard Shaw relates how he quite deliberately constructed an identity for himself, and then found a purpose in Fabian socialism. He said he was fortunate in possessing a combination of critical faculty with literary resource. But there was one thing lacking at this stage. He 'needed only a clear comprehension of life in the light of an intelligible theory: in short, a religion, to set it in triumphant operation'.

Another possible purpose is to seek to develop one's own potentialities. However desirable, this is somewhat selfish: it is a superior form of hedonism.

---

* The truth of this was shown in the appalling conditions of concentration camps, where, as Victor Frankl describes, people invented purposes for themselves. One determined to rejoin his children, another to revenge himself. Thus armed, they could survive. After his release, Frankl founded a school of psychotherapy on the proposition that the basic driving principle of human beings is the will-to-meaning —and not the will-to-pleasure of Freud or the will-to-power of Adler.

There are those, not few in number, who do not ask the purpose of life, because their daimon tells them what they have to do. Michelangelo did not waste time in questioning but knew from the start that he had a talent to apply.

When long-term motives fail then many people settle for a simple hedonism. As the writer of Ecclesiastes says: 'Go thy way, eat thy bread with joy, and drink thy wine with a merry heart; for God hath already accepted thy works . . . Live joyfully with the wife whom thou lovest all the days of the life of thy vanity; for that is thy portion in life . . . Whatsoever thy hand findeth to do, do it with thy might; for there is no work, nor device, nor knowledge, nor wisdom in the grave, whither thou goest.'

The Chinese have taken a similar view, and Lin Yutang has expressed it in simple words: 'The question which faces every man born into this world is not what should be his purpose, which he should set about to achieve, but just what to do with life, a life which is given him for a period of, on the average, fifty or sixty years. The answer that he should order his life so that he can find the greatest happiness in it is more a practical question, similar to that of how a man should spend his week-end, than a metaphysical proposition as to what is the mystic purpose of his life in the scheme of the universe.' Unqualified hedonism rapidly becomes boring, however, and self-improvement alone seems unduly self-centred. Helping others remains, despite the cynics, the most worthwhile purpose. There are, in any culture, many worthwhile ends. The problem is commitment. Paradoxically, we find a purpose by committing ourselves and achieve identity too. As Allen Wheelis says: 'To commit allegiance and will and energy to valued ends means to define the self in terms of these ends and to find in them the enduring meaning and purpose of life.' A judicious combination of all three ways may be the best of all—hedonism, self-development and service to others.

Some people, to be sure, can find a purpose by adopting a religion. The function of religion is to give meaning to life: if every action in the world plays a role in determining our future in another world, or another reincarnation, then no action is without meaning. Thus, even if such theories are untrue, they serve a useful purpose and the realist would say that people should be left with their religious beliefs, even if they are illusory, rather than cast them into doubt and despair. Today, when religion (and not only the Christian religion) is everywhere being undermined, people are left with an unsatisfied thirst for meaning. 'What is it all for?'

If the universe were clearly seen to comprise the unfolding of a vast pattern ('God's purpose') this would provide something solid to cling to, but the scientists tell us that the seeming pattern is the result of chance, and that what seem to be absolutes are relative.

In these circumstances, theories, however wild, which imply the existence of a pattern in the universe are welcome: hence the popularity of astrology and the 'fringe' religions.

The alternative to a religion is an ideology, which is a kind of secular religion. The appeal of Marxism lies in the fact, on which Marx insisted, that society is *inevitably* developing towards Communism and the classless society. Marx and his followers bitterly criticized those who merely said that man *could* make a better world, if he made up his mind to do so. This difference, which might seem small, converts Marxism from a political doctrine to a religion.

Victor Frankl maintains that we can discover the meaning of life in three ways: by experiencing a value, such as love; by suffering; or by doing a deed.

However, he also seeks to support his patients by arguing that there may be a meaning which we cannot grasp, just as an ape used in a medical experiment cannot understand why it is suffering pain or developing a disease. Explaining the unknown by the still more unknown should not be necessary if his former proposition is true.

But to understand the 'meaning' of life implies rather more than to find a purpose in life. Here we can turn for help to the philosopher Michael Polanyi, who has made the important discovery that the meaning of anything cannot be arrived at by the scrutiny of particulars. We can never learn the shape and appearance of a wood by simply studying the trees. Entities are arranged in hierarchies, and we can never infer the properties or purpose of higher members from the scrutiny of lower members. Science, however, is precisely the scrutiny of particulars, and their subdivision into ever more basic entities. Thus science cannot tell us the meaning of life. Moreover, says Polanyi, 'an unbridled lucidity can destroy our understanding of complex matters . . . the damage done by the specification of particulars may be irremediable.' Nor can philosophy—though it can help us to avoid error. For awareness of meaning comes from contemplation of the whole, and pondering what one sees. Modern life keeps us too busy and too distracted to ponder, and alienates us from nature and from the experiences most worth pondering over.

If, then, our problem can be summed up by the words 'alienation' and 'loss of identity', what ought we to be doing about it? Obviously, there is no easy solution. I have mentioned many things which, if we had the sense, we should do: reduce the rate of social change; live in communities; improve our political system; live in the country; reject the consumer mentality; simplify bureaucracy; avoid 'busyness'; reflect. In short, we should have to return to a simpler and in some respects more primitive kind of society.

Above all, we should have to limit the rate of application of new technology—and this is the real case against technology: that it produces alienation. This is why the optimism of the technocrats is so hopelessly, hopelessly wrong. In the last chapter, I shall return to the question of our obsession with technology, for it is at the heart of our difficulties. For those who are repelled by the idea of an ever more unnatural and gadget-ridden society, there are basically two problems to consider, each unsolved. The first is how one could run a reprimitivized society: the second is whether one could achieve the change of attitude throughout society. Is it administratively possible? Is it psychologically possible? To these questions we can now turn.

III. Prospects for the Future

8

The Paraprimitive Society

I. *Introduction*

IN what kind of society would a sensible person choose to live? Many people have sought to answer this question and have described the legal and social arrangements of Utopias. But the correct answer is of quite a different kind. A sensible person would choose to live in a society whose other members were also sensible. He would not want to be assaulted as he walked home; he would not want his home burgled or his daughter raped. Nor would he want to buy unsafe, ill-designed goods, or to be exploited by corrupt politicians. All along the line he would prefer to associate with people who were unselfish, unprejudiced, conscientious, friendly and intelligent. And even if the laws and customs were unsatisfactory, a sensible citizenry would speedily modify them—whereas a cruel, corrupt or selfish public would soon pervert sound laws and customs.

Obvious as the point may seem when stated, it is apparently not obvious in fact, for in every account of Utopia known to me it is taken for granted that the bulk of the inhabitants will be sensible (if I may use this word to sum up a bunch of desirable traits) and the writer devotes his time to describing the laws and customs, and perhaps some of the technical arrangements. But it is precisely the creation of a sensible populace which constitutes the problem.

Moreover, it is a proposition which conceals a joker. For it implies that we have to design a society in which people different from ourselves would be happy, and in which *we* might well be unhappy. We should find no outlets for our obsessive needs—no exaggerated luxuries, no pornography and no brothels, no boxing or all-in wrestling, no gambling or football pools. Whether we should like such a society or not is no guide—though it does make it harder to bring such a society about. The main error we make is to work at bringing about a society in which *we* could be happy. But fundamentally the task is impossible. Ideal societies cannot be made with imperfect people.

Unhappily, the converse is also true. The sensible person cannot ever be as happy and fulfilled as it lies within him to be in an imperfect society. Society sets limiting conditions to our personal quests for happiness. In Chapter 10 I shall survey the possibility of producing more 'sensible' people.

In this chapter I want to ask: in what kind of society would sensible, non-anxious, non-obsessive, non-neurotic, non-prejudiced, balanced people wish to live? When I say 'balanced' I mean, in particular, balanced in respect of bi-polar values, such as patrism and matrism, hard and soft ego. In preceding chapters, I have discussed many of the desiderata in detail: now I shall try to summarize and bring all the threads together.

The conclusion towards which the discussion in the preceding chapters inescapably tends is that, if we were aware of our own best interests, we should try to restore to some extent to our own technological society the structured character of a pre-industrial society. Can we not combine the advantages of the former with those of the latter? Or, if we cannot have the best of both worlds, should we not find some compromise position?

Obviously, it is not a question of turning our backs on technology. No one but a saint or an ascetic would willingly do without running water and electric lights, or without anaesthetics and antibiotics, to name only a few of the most obvious benefits of technology. It is simply a question of whether we have to embrace technology on an all-or-nothing basis. The cries of 'Ludditism' which greet any suggestion for restricting the impact of technology miss the point. Indeed, some of the latest technology is more desirable than the earlier: who would refuse to replace a dangerous pesticide with a safe one?

Moreover, some recent technological developments are rather favourable to the paraprimitive society. Foremost of these is the prospect of small, independent sources of power. In the last analysis, the modern world is made possible by the fact that man does not have to rely on his own muscles, or even on those of horses, but commands vast stocks of energy, equivalent to hundreds of horses for each person. Many of our pollution problems arise from our lavish consumption of fuels. What gives a community independence, without sacrificing living standards, is access to cheap power which is under its own control. Many a remote island or mountain valley becomes habitable, in principle, as soon as power is available. Since the sun is the prime source of energy, solar power sources constitute the best bet, and are non-polluting too—though the unreliability of sunshine in many parts of the world makes methods of storage equally important. If the methods by which plants store light-energy so successfully can be imitated, both problems will have been solved.

For a society which tries to combine the advantages of primitive group structure and satisfactions with those of technology we need a descriptive term, and more than twenty years ago I put forward the expression 'a paraprimitive society' meaning one which is parallel to or similar to a primitive society. It is not ideal, for many pre-technological societies were far from primitive, in the sense in which the word is often used; and anthropologists dislike the use of the word even for the simplest pre-literate societies, pointing out that their cultures are often complex and show signs of a long evolution. But the alternative, a *metatechnological society*, does not convey its meaning satisfactorily and I shall stick to using the original term suggested until a better one is found. Actually, I suspect it is the eighteenth century, in advanced countries, which can teach us most, if we need an idealized epoch in the past to serve as a rough model for the future. Though far from primitive and in many respects more sophisticated than today, it retained in considerable measure the social structures, work patterns and values which we have been discussing. It was also, to be sure, marked by privilege, corruption, dirt and poverty: let us not glamourize it. Yet many people contrived to be happy and productive, free of stress and existential despair.

However much room exists for discussion of details, it is relatively easy to consider what we would retain from technology, because its products are there in front of us; and it is relatively easy to see what we do *not* want to retain from primitive society—the blood-curdling practices, the diseases, the elaborate taboos and rituals, and so on. What is harder to pin down is what we *do* want to retain from it. The essential features which we want to restore are, I suggest: (1) the personal nature of relationships, including economic and administrative ones; (2) what I have termed 'mixed motives', meaning that the decisions should always embody non-economic as well as economic considerations; (3) activities, especially work, which are meaningful in terms of each person's life.

Where then might we be in fifty years, given the will, and provided we are spared war, famine, plague and invasion from other planets?

II. *What it would be like*

In classic depictions of Utopia, there is a distinctive scene to describe—whether it is some idyllic community, full of sun-burned, laughing people in long white gowns, or whether it is the busy crowds, clad in fantastic plastic garments on the moving walkways of a roofed-in city, in the vein of H. G. Wells.

I suspect that the possible Utopia of forty or fifty years on will not look so very different from now, except that hopefully we shall have cleaned up the air, water and junk-yards, pulled down most of the slums and jerry-built factories, and set some limits to the use of the internal combustion engine. I trust it will also be less noisy.

On a closer view, we might see that the smaller towns and villages are thriving, that some remote areas where the population was declining, are now busy again—especially some of the islands. Correspondingly, in the large cities, bulldozers will be clearing the drearier areas and returning them to fields and parkland, thus breaking up these hypertrophied centres into more manageable units. If we go inside the factories too, we might find a different set-up: fewer long production lines and vast rooms full of people doing tiny, repetitive jobs. Instead, groups of people making complete products at their own pace. We might notice that they start and finish work at different times of day, as suits the group's convenience, and other unusual details.

But the really dramatic changes would be invisible, for they would concern personal relations, legal and administrative arrangements, economic and tax structures, the nature of education and the atmosphere of home life.

For instance, the tax system may have been modified to discourage people from congregating in large towns and cities, or to discourage them from producing goods of marginal happiness-value. (We already use taxes in this way when we tax alcohol or, as in Britain, remit purchase taxes on articles of necessity. We could go much further: for instance, we could tax gadgetry like electrically operated car windows, and remit taxes to firms which showed a low or declining rate of labour turnover.)

Education will, I am sure, have been greatly changed and in a moment I shall come back to this. So will methods of child-upbringing. But perhaps the most startling of the invisible changes underlying the conventional surface of Utopia will be some kind of policy for regulating the rate of adoption of innovation. As I have already argued, too high a rate of change can be as costly and frustrating as too static an existence. There is a happy mean in everything. Our current policy of adopting every innovation which can be marketed at a profit in our creaking economic system cannot persist for much longer. In medicine we have learned that it is better and cheaper to prevent disease than to pick up the bits: the same applies to social disruption. Will there, then, be an Innovations Board considering every major invention? In our society, such a board would be subject to intensive pressure from those who felt they could make a dollar from it: it would probably shilly-shally and delay, and be the object of public criticism. Some smarter method, based on computer analysis of the invention's likely effects, taken in conjunction with the rate of introduction of other inventions, is more likely. It will have to be a high-power operation, led by men of the highest possible capacity, acquainted with people as well as things.

But the most significant changes may not be the dramatic administrative ones so much as changes in the way ordinary people choose to lead their daily lives. They may have a clearer idea of their own real needs, and see that happiness and convenience are often different, or even radically opposed.

Many proposals for a new society envisage the population grouped in small communities of five hundred people or so spread uniformly over the land, with little in the way of towns and cities.* I believe this concept is impractical as a general policy, ill-considered and unneeded. True, it is easier to maintain communities if they are somewhat apart from one another: there is less need for arbitration where their interests clash, less physical and cultural invasion to cope with, and so on. But as I have already argued, community can be developed within large towns and even cities given the right conditions, and there are reasons why we should retain this well-tried structure. A group of villages needs the support of a town to supply the larger and more costly items which cannot be held in stock in a village; and areas need regional capitals at which even more rarely bought items can be held. Regional capitals can also support theatres, concert halls and other services which depend on large buildings and accessibility. However, there is probably no real need to go above a hundred thousand people, except possibly in a national capital. Long before a million is reached, the concealed costs of such a concentration begin to outweigh the advantages of further size.

This kind of structure corresponds closely to the way the population was distributed a century or so ago, with the difference that today transport and communications are far easier, so that living in such conditions would be much easier, access to medical and other services simpler, and so on. It still corresponds to the more rural areas in developed countries. It implies, however, a decentralization of the population in large cities. This is necessary to restore the contact with nature and with the non-urbanized community which is lacking in the cities.

Thus I can foresee changes within cities designed to give the units within it a stronger sense of cohesion. I can even see people turning their backs on giant cities—say, those of a million people or more—because they prefer to exchange its advantages for cleaner air, less noise, more contact with nature and a less impersonal existence. It would be valuable to know what proportion of people living in large cities do so because they really wish to, and how many do so because the work is there, or because they have already made a life there.

In countries like Britain, Belgium, Holland, etc., decentralization would be wholly impractical unless the population was greatly reduced. There is simply not the space to put them, short of creating a sort of

* For example, the 'Blueprint for Survival' issued by the British periodical *The Ecologist* in January 1972.

suburban sprawl over the whole country. (In England, each community would have a square plot about 1,200 yards on a side, or rather less if mountains and marshes were excluded. This is without allowing for roads, airfields, hospitals, factories, docks, power stations and so on, and assumes the sacrifices of all parks, gardens, woods and common lands.)

III. *Localization*

If decentralization is not the precondition for the development of community, what is? Members of the nascent community must place the greater part of their economic and emotional transactions within the group. In practical terms, this means that you must do at least some of your shopping at the local store, garage and post-office, and minimize buying by post and expeditions to the shopping centre or the big smoke. You must also place many of your social and personal contacts within the group, take part in some of its festivals and ceremonies, and support its group aims and interests, preferably by effort rather than money. For lack of a better word, we might call this the 'localization' of interests.

Moreover, the community must have real power to decide on local issues—which means it must have an effective local (parish, commune, county, Ort, etc.) governing body, and must support it by voting, attending meetings, candidacy, etc. For such localization to develop depends not simply on the willingness of the members but on the extent to which the central and regional authorities are prepared to delegate power. At present, as we all know, the tendency is to centralize power more and more. Strong arguments can be advanced to support this policy: more efficient administration, greater uniformity of standards and the like. The disadvantages are seldom stated or even recognized. In plain words, we may have to accept less efficient administration, less uniformity of standards and so on, as the price of community; though obviously we should work to minimize such drawbacks.

Localization can also foster corruption, because it is easier for people who know each other to connive than if they are unacquainted. (However, corruption also occurs in large-scale organizations and we could do with more research into the social dynamics of the subject.)

But it is not only a question of localization of interests: there is a further very awkward factor which is seldom given the consideration it deserves: we shall have greatly to reduce both the amount of physical mobility and the pace of social and technical change. Communities cannot continue to cohere either if their members constantly leave them, or spend large parts of every day outside them; nor can they if they are constantly invaded by members of other communities, either coming in as short-term residents, or merely flocking in for the day.

Finally, we need to reconstruct the productive and distributive system, tying productive units into the local community, rather than integrating them into business empires or public corporations.

Technically this may not be as difficult as it sounds, since the average size of factory in Britain, even today, is about 100 people. Certainly, there are some activities which cannot be localized: systems requiring nation-wide organization and standardization obviously require a considerable degree of centralized structure. (Even so, there are private telephone companies in the USA and in England; Newcastle has had its own, very efficient, municipal service for decades.) Centralized organizations vary a good deal in the extent to which they move individuals about, and in general respond to local preferences. Local people can take pride in the appearance of their local railway station, but seldom get an opportunity to be proud of their telephone exchange or transformer sub-station.

There are some activities—say, air traffic control—which clearly cannot be localized. There are others which could, if one really wanted. Cars do not have to be made all on one site, but can be assembled from components made by a variety of firms in many different places. Even watch-cases do not have to be made by watch-makers, and in France there are factories making nothing but watch-cases employing 100 or 150 people. Some of the large-scale industrial activity we see is brought about by financial advantages which result from the nature of our economic system, rather than from any real efficiency bestowed by size. For instance, if a large sum of capital can be borrowed at cheaper interest rates than a smaller sum, the man who builds a big factory will do better than the man who builds a small one. A big firm can 'lean' on its suppliers, forcing them to absorb costs which a smaller firm would have to carry. (Thus automobile manufacturers insist on the suppliers of components storing them until required, with penalties if they deliver earlier or later than a given date.) From a social point of view, this is actually less efficient, since any failure to supply parts (as might be caused by a strike or fire at the suppliers) can bring the whole assembly process to a halt. Conversely, where a big supplier supplies many small firms, he can 'lean' on them. Large organizations tend to be relatively inefficient, as so much effort has to be spent in co-ordination.

In some cases, size seems to result from a naïve belief that larger is necessarily better, or at least sounds better, or from following the general trend to larger sizes blindly. The fact is we have really not tried to push the technology of 'smallerization'. We 'blow up' designs, but we seldom deflate them.

IV. *The Standard of Living*

The question which someone invariably asks, whenever any proposal to improve the quality of life is made, is: but won't it lower the standard of living? To which the quick reply is: don't you mean the *material* standard of living? Because pure food, unpolluted air, agreeable work, even psychological security, are just as much part of the standard of living as is the possession of goods. In America particularly, the (material) standard of living has a holy, untouchable quality, before which all other considerations bow. This is ironical, since the standard is so high that Americans could take a cut in material standards and feel it less than in most European countries.

But I believe we could free the resources needed for social advances without any real cut in material standards, simply by trimming the fat, or perhaps a better metaphor would be draining off the excess water from a case of dropsy. Consumer societies produce many things which add little or nothing to satisfaction, or which are only wanted because of the imperfections and frustrations of such a society. The point is so important that I will point out eight examples of what I mean.

1 *Obsolescence* Built-in obsolescence simply makes it necessary to manufacture replacements more often than necessary. The fact that a car like a Rolls-Royce is still functional after thirty or forty years gives us some indication of how unnecessarily short the life of the average car is. General Motors laid the basis of its commercial success by inventing the annual style change, exploiting the status-need *not* to be seen driving last year's model. As everyone knows, numerous other devices to hasten obsolescence have been devised—such as ceasing to manufacture replacement parts. This goes for many things besides cars.

The whole business of fashion-changes is another kind of artificial obsolescence. Naturally, people will sometimes want to modify the style of clothing, decor, etc., and in a cool society they do it when the existing stuff wears out or needs redoing. In the superheated society, new fashions are forced on the public, usually by appealing to status-aims, or to sexual insecurities. Apart from the waste of materials when clothes or furniture are jettisoned while still in good shape, considerable manpower is tied up in promoting such changes.

2 *Trivia* For $120 you can now buy a machine which will tell you which tie to wear, when you have fed it the colour of your suit and shirt. For a good deal more, you can get a version which will scan your suit and shirt with a television camera, so you don't even have to tell it. Effete as I am, I still feel able to choose my own tie. A recent book lists many other examples of such futile novelties, from paper nappies for budgeri-

gars to mink belly-button-brushes. (My own favourite is the executive sand-tray, offered to airline passengers at the special price of $14·50. You place this rosewood tray, containing 'tranquil sand' on your desk, and relieve executive stress, from time to time, by tracing patterns in the sand with a plastic comb. If our society can't survive without executive sand-trays, it had better give up.)

3 *Advertising and Display* When advertising tells us of the existence of a product we need details of, or did not know existed, or even of a price or style change, it fills a social need. When it seeks to bludgeon us into buying one brand rather than another by sheer repetition, and when it tampers with our unconscious life by associating major values with the product, it is not merely wasteful but actually harmful.

The same goes for much display, promotion and public-relations work. Starting out as a worthwhile function, they balloon into something which at the best is a poor use of resources, at the worst is actually harmful.

4 *Pollution, Ill-health, Accidents* Another type of technological wastage comes from our defective costing: we see the cost of cleaning the sulphur dioxide out of the smoke of power-stations and factories, but overlook the cost to society of the ill-health which results. According to a recent calculation, if the pollution of air could be reduced by one half in the USA, the saving simply in terms of days of work lost through sickness and earlier death would be at least $2,000 million a year. This makes no allowance for the smaller capital investment in medical services and none for such possible indirect effects as greater output, nor for social effects such as the less frequent washing and painting of houses, public buildings, bridges and other structures (sulphur dioxide has a severe effect on stone-work, which begins to crumble and eventually has to be replaced). The savings here might come to as much again. Thus if the air could be made 50 per cent cleaner for $4,000 million a year, it would be worth doing, for nothing has been allowed for the grief and suffering associated with higher rates of disease and premature death. It is-extraordinary that calculations of this kind are seldom made, and made the bases of policy.

Other kinds of ill-health have social causes too, notably industrial and traffic accidents. The manpower which goes to caring for (or burying) the victims of car crashes is part of the price we pay for having a car. This would strike us more forcibly if we paid a 'crash tax' at the time of purchase, instead of losing the charge among insurance policies, state taxes, health service charges, etc.

5 *Substitutes, Distinctions and Obsessions* Much of our so-called 'productive' effort represents an attempt to restore to life just those satisfactions

which technological society has taken out. The transport which takes people to the country from the town at the weekend is only necessary because technology concentrated people in the city to begin with. In a similar manner, we put back into white bread the wheat-germ which we have extracted, and then charge the consumer more for what ought to be cheaper, since he pays twice—once for taking the wheat-germ out and once for putting it back in again. A visitor from Mars would, I imagine, peal with laughter at the sight of a rowing machine, which provides the town-dweller with some of the exercise he needs in the most boring manner, when in a better-planned world he could enjoy all the satisfactions of actually rowing.

Gambling, a vast industry today, thrives on the need for stimulus, the need for a purpose, the desire to escape from a hopeless and frustrating situation. In most primitive tribes gambling is unknown. Much the same is true of pornography and prostitution. In healthy societies they are unwanted.

Our society searches for distractions from its boredom, and many so-called entertainments and novelties contribute about as much to happiness as would taking a sleeping pill, though they cost much more. A symphony concert is one thing: Muzak in the lift is another.

6 *Crime* Crimes against property, including vandalism, are also rare in primitive societies, while in ours they grow steadily. Often they do not simply transfer wealth from one person to another; they destroy wealth (as when silver objects are melted down, or in the case of industrial sabotage) while the cost of crime-prevention in general and the cost of trying and imprisoning the offenders represents another vast social cost, i.e. a diversion of manpower.

7 *Non-Jobs* A major category would be work done unnecessarily or incompetently. 'Senator Philip Hart of Michigan concluded that every year consumers pay between 174 and 231 billion dollars for which they get nothing. This includes eight or ten billion dollars a year for automobile repairs which were improperly done, not necessary, or not done at all; thirty million dollars for ineffective combination drugs now being ordered off the market; and one billion dollars for automobile insurance which duplicates protection that consumers already have.' One of Ralph Nader's staff recently cited this statement, but everyone knows of instances in their own experience.

8 *The Search for Status* A short paragraph but a big subject. The extent to which some people engage in conspicuous consumption has been documented by so many writers from Thorsten Veblen to Vance Packard that discussion here would be tedious. In a society which provided functional status, i.e. prestige dependent upon known ability,

much of the search for status badges would become pointless and would drop away.

To all this we could add the vast cost of armaments and 'military preparedness' which almost certainly exceeds real needs, even in our strife-torn world. The belief that more is better and newest is best dominates the minds of generals and admirals, just like other people. (But in Japan you do not try to defeat a strong enemy by opposing him with equal strength: you use your skill to turn his own strength to his disadvantage.) Throw in the cost of 'national adventures' like the space race and the supersonic transport, and the cost of sheer mismanagement (the US Army's orbiting laboratory cost $1·2 billion and never got off the ground) and what do you have?

I doubt if as much as 50 per cent of the productive effort of the USA actually goes to making things which really contribute to the material standard of living in any meaningful interpretation of the term. In Europe, the figure would be a bit lower. So—if we eliminate all this waste motion—we would have three choices. Either we could work half the hours, without loss of living standards; or we could live at twice the standard; or we could use the effort thus freed to re-jig work so as to make it more appealing, to clean up the slums, the water and the air; to cover the costs of decentralization and population limitation; and in general set about constructing a rational society. Or, of course, we could settle for some combination of all three benefits.

(I am assuming, for the moment, that we can make the transfer without causing unemployment. Our present economic system of course is incapable of balancing the effort-budget effectively. I shall discuss the economic aspect in the next chapter.)

Whether this appeals to us or not, it seems likely that in less than fifty years time, resource exhaustion plus the demands of third-world countries for a share in material affluence, reinforced by the necessity of limiting pollution, will not only have put a ceiling on affluence but will have begun to squeeze out the inessentials from our dropsical society.

V. *Education and Reflection*

After the student revolt in Paris of May 1968, a twenty-seven-year-old law student, Julien G., resuming his studies after sixteen months of compulsory military service, told an interviewer: 'Suddenly in the midst of these events I thought: "Look, for eight years I have been receiving an advanced education, and really I've done nothing but pass exams, imbibe a culture, and absorb photocopies and technical *fiches*; now, having reached the threshhold of adult life, I no longer know why I am acting or what I am going to do; I am no longer capable of reflecting on the subjects which I have read and re-read—as a student of political sciences, Marxism, revolution, struggle." I find myself looking at words which I am incapable of analysing, and I say to myself that everything that I have been taught is no longer any use to me.'

What an appalling indictment of the educational system—and unfortunately one which would be echoed by students in Britain, America and many other countries. How can such a thing be?

Education, as has been pointed out by Professor Mitscherlich among others, has three aspects: cognitive education (learning how to think), effective education (learning how to feel), and social education (learning about life). Education today is almost entirely cognitive education: the acquisition of facts and factual systems (theories) together with the latest fad, learning how to recombine facts, dignified with the label of 'creativity-training'. Much of this kind of education is oriented towards earning a living—it teaches the cognitive components of an adult skill, such as practising as an engineer, an economist or a doctor. Such skills are, of course, necessary. But in a human sense they are trivial.

It is far more important that people should grow up able to love and to be loved. Professor Ashley Montagu is brilliantly illuminating on this subject, and Chapter 12 of his *The Direction of Human Development* should be obligatory reading in teachers' colleges. Why, he asks, should we have had to rediscover by scientific experiment in the twentieth century that love is essential to human development, when in every society the fact is enshrined in religious and philosophical teachings, such as the Sermon on the Mount? 'The answer,' he suggests, 'is that we have been miseducated out of the capacity to be lovers of our fellow human beings, and that we have on the other hand been confusedly trained to keep our eye on the main chance . . . We have tended to live by false values, and to transmit these values to the young.' Montagu quotes a us Navy psychiatrist, Dr James Clark Moloney, as stating that on the island of Okinawa, he never saw a spoiled, self-centred, fearful child. 'The wealth of affection that exists between the adults and the children in an aboriginal tribe has to be seen to be believed . . . The little folk sat round our fire at all times of the day, yet in spite of the apparent lack of discipline by the parents, they were not the slightest trouble, any request that we made being obeyed with perfect good humour. There were sweets, sugar and all sorts of dainties in open cupboards, only a few feet from where they used to sit, yet no child touched them.'

It is well established that, if a child has not formed a loving relationship with its parents by the ninth month of life, it is unlikely ever to do so, and will remain emotionally incompetent for ever after. However, since the importance of love is now accepted as a 'scientific fact' and no longer regarded as 'sentiment' we may hope that by the time Utopia is established most parents will consciously attempt to provide the conditions for its development, and society will teach adolescents not to romanticize it, nor cynically to downgrade it.

What seems to me much more serious a problem is our present failure to teach young people how to cope with life. We teach them nothing about themselves, or their identities—and little enough about how to maintain their bodies in a healthy state, let alone their psyches. They learn nothing about the psychological differences between individuals, and between the sexes. We should tell them about do-people and be-people, about mother-identified and father-identified people, about tough and tender people, and the values these types of people espouse.

Then again, we should teach them about the social contract: about the nature of democracy (which is not about 'counting heads' as so many people suppose, but about protecting the position of minorities) and about ethics. We should teach them how the economic machine functions, not in a spirit of presenting a pre-ordained and perfectly functioning mechanism, but also not minimizing the difficulties of devising something better. (Today many young professors criticize existing institutions in terms which suggest it is only self-interest or lack of imagination which prevents the immediate introduction of something far superior.) We should teach them to distinguish a class system from a status system, and both from a caste system, instead of undermining the force of functional status by playing on the resentments of the under-privileged. We should teach them the pros and cons of change.

But above all we should teach people how to try to be happy. The Utopian citizen will, I think, be more sophisticated than we are: he will know much more concretely what really gives him satisfaction and what only provides a temporary lift. He will know what he can readily do without. He will spend money more wisely—not in the primitive sense of knowing whether Brand A is a better buy than Brand B, but in the larger sense of knowing whether he is catering to a neurotic need, and how far he should subordinate short-term pleasures to long-term satisfactions. He will also assess his demands against the true social costs, and decide whether or not to go ahead, instead of merely asking whether he has enough money or credit.

He will understand more of the nature of culture, and the complexities of language: he will recognize nonsense questions and circular definitions, and will have some idea of the nature of cause and effect.

Finally, students need time to reflect. When a comrade told Julien G., 'You don't take time out to listen to yourself,' he at once realized that this was a true observation, and that modern society actually prevents one from reflecting.

In some of these respects we shall simply be returning to an older conception of education. For though the education of two centuries ago was overloaded with dogma, it did also try to inculcate values—whereas today it seems to be the object of education to show the meaninglessness of values. Furthermore, it attempted to provide some historical perspective.

In Utopia, much of this teaching will not be verbal, but will be effected by exposing people to teaching experiences. During the Second World War, a number of children who were so poorly socialized that they could not be billeted on foster parents were placed in a country house known as Barns, near Edinburgh, in the charge of an imaginative young teacher. He announced that there were only two rules: they might not set the place on fire, nor swim in the river without supervision. For a while anarchy reigned, but the children soon became exasperated by total freedom and elected a dictator. When he proved too dictatorial, they substituted an oligarchy, then modified this to a democracy. In this way they learned by hard experience that democracy, though far from perfect, is better than the alternatives. It will be by experiences of this kind that the Utopian child will learn. (In the case of the Barns venture the experiment was speedily closed down by the education authorities, on the grounds that the children were not completing the specified number of hours of school-instruction, even though these formerly unteachable children were now showing rapid, if uneven, academic advance.)

I suspect it is the case that individuals have a built-in developmental programme, which should govern the pattern of their education: you cannot teach a child simple movements until it is ready to learn them, as Arnold Gesell has shown in his great longitudinal studies of children. When it is time to learn about balancing, they will demand to walk along walls, and not before. Higher learning is probably similarly programmed. Thus it is basically true that the child must programme his own education, as students today demand. But it is also the case that children learn to ignore their built-in programmes. Thus it has been shown that young children tend to select the foods which meet their biological needs, but, as their palates become sophisticated begin to choose the meretricious sweet or attractive-looking foods.

Thus, in an overall view, students are not equipped to specify what they should be learning. I suspect also that certain combinations are unsuitable, and that facts should be acquired in a certain sequence. Our contemporary 'smørgasbord education' (as it has been termed) defies these natural laws. It is an irony that it is often Marxist students who demand student control of education: for in the early days of the Russian experiment, all class discipline was abolished, and for just the same anti-authoritarian 'man is born good' reasons that prevail today. The system proved such a frightful failure that it had to be abolished and the pendulum swung to the other extreme. Current Russian education is more rigid, more closely supervised, more disciplined, than anything a Western student ever dreamed of.

To the extent that education must always be, in part, factual, it is important that the facts be both accurate and representative. 'It ain't what you know as causes the trouble,' as Artemus Ward said, 'it's what you know that ain't so.' Today we treat isolated facts as if they were magically valid, in themselves—rather as if they were magic spells.

Unhappily few teachers have any conception of the total nature of education. They are almost entirely concerned with technical improvements in cognitive education and 'thinking how to think'. Students, too, need to be given an idea of the overall purposes of education—need to see what school provides as simply an 'assist' to their self-education, a privilege to take advantage of, not an exercise to be gone through blindly, at the end of which one is, somehow 'educated' and need learn nothing more.

VI. *The Way Ahead*

The move towards Utopia may start, I suspect, not in America but in Europe, and perhaps in the Scandinavian countries or even in Great Britain. It is true that in America there are already many small experiments in existence; but there is also an inspissated opposition. America is a country of extremes, and if the New Liners are further forward than in Europe, the Old Liners are further back. While the USA is often the leader in technological change, in social change she is often fifty years behind Europe. (Obvious examples are social insurance and a free health service.)

On the other hand, in the demographically crowded countries of Europe the task of decentralization is harder, since there is relatively little space to decentralize into. (As against this, values have not decayed so far: materialism is still a dirty word.) As already noted, decentralization is particularly difficult for Britain, Denmark, Holland and Belgium —perhaps also for Switzerland, where so much land is mountainous. (Norway, on the other hand, has many islands.) It would be easy in Sweden, Spain, Italy or even France, and of these Sweden may be the first to attempt to build a paraprimitive society.

The change is unlikely to come by revolution—for revolutions always end by establishing monolithic, dictatorial, patrist societies. If the change comes at all it will be gradually. Already there are signs, like the new interest in 'job enrichment' and the recognition that high-rise buildings surrounded by grass plots are a social disaster. We seem to be modifying our attitudes to child-upbringing, to the treatment of delinquents; we are even beginning to look critically at the economic system, and to question our belief in the possibility of endless growth.

And if the first step to any reform is education, then we have already begun.

If a working model could be set up, and it began to show improved performance in respect of crime, mental health, labour turnover and similar statistical measures, as against control communities, this would help convince people. But such a project would have to be on a large scale to prove anything. It would have to be in some degree self-supporting, capable of supporting a university and school system, of manufacturing heavy machinery as well as marketable goods, capable of sustaining health care and of maintaining relations with the main sources of power in the host community. A small community, parasitic on existing society for its power-tools and penicillin, would convince no one. At the same time, an experiment which was too consciously an experiment would prove little. The participants would lose their spontaneity under the constant scrutiny and criticism of the outside world. At the same time, government recognition and support would probably be needed. Perhaps the first step is for some far-sighted foundation to finance a study into how such an experiment could best be instituted.

Subsequently, perhaps, 'islands' of paraprimitivism could be established within the old culture, to which people could 'emigrate' when the mood took them. Moreover, this would enable people to test the temperature of the water. If it proved agreeable, people would flock in increasing numbers to the paraprimitive communities, which might have to protect themselves against the influx of people wishing to benefit from their advantages, but not sharing their values or willing to support their unwritten codes.

As I shall argue in the next chapter, a paraprimitive society would have to operate with a different kind of economic system from our own but, even before we go into details, we can see the kind of difficulties which would arise.

In our existing society, it is already the case that a firm which wishes to act in a socially responsible manner (say, by cleaning its effluent) puts itself in a weak competitive position against the firm which is less responsible. Again, small production runs are less economic than long production runs, when there are heavy fixed costs. How can the small factory in the small community defend itself against the advantages of size, where they genuinely exist? The paraprimitive community might thus have to tax all imports, and subsidize all exports, in order to survive. This is why government support will be necessary. If only some small state like Luxembourg, already sovereign, would commit itself to such an experiment!

Failing a 'dry run' of this kind, the change will have to come by inches, dependent on the imagination and goodwill of a few far-sighted people, and supported by a public demand for a more humane way of life.

The transition to a paraprimitive society will be especially difficult in those countries, like Britain, where a considerable reduction in the size of population is needed before decentralization can be effectively introduced.

This has several implications. The birth of fewer babies leads to a phase where there are fewer adults of working age, but they still have to support a population of elderly people derived from the days when the population target was higher. Thus there is an abnormally heavy economic load on the worker (somewhat offset by the smaller number of children during the period of contraction, but not after the new target level has been achieved).

Probably more serious is the depressing effect on trade and industry. In a period of expansion, a man may start a firm for making (let us say) bedsteads. Even if he has overestimated the demand, as the population gets larger the demand for beds gets larger. Time rectifies his misjudgment. In a period of contraction, on the other hand, those people who are already making beds find their sales falling, and some will have to abandon this way of earning their living. But while it is fun to start a new enterprise it is not fun to operate at a loss and finally go bankrupt. Furthermore, in a period of declining sales, lenders become unwilling to advance capital and gloom prevails, so that even projects for which there is room find it hard to get launched. Above all, the employee in the declining firm has fewer opportunities of advancement, and may even be dismissed.

It is human nature to hang on to one's enterprise in such circumstances, even when reason says it should be closed down, so such contractions go more sluggishly than expansions. Back in the days when many people thought the population of Western countries was due to fall of its own accord, a Cambridge economist, Professor W. B. Reddaway, wrote an excellent analysis, *The Economics of a Declining Population*. Unfortunately, he was about thirty years ahead of the market; it ought now to be reprinted.

It also follows that much capital equipment, including housing, roads, etc., will become superfluous. And this would also be the case even if no contraction occurred, but simply decentralization and regrouping of industry. Some conception of the problem can be gained by imagining the population of London, New York or any other large city reduced to a half or even two-thirds the present figure. Obviously there would be rows of empty houses, landlords would be unwilling to repair and redecorate those that were still in occupation; there would be secondary problems of looting, vagrant occupation, etc. The same would be true of shops and offices. All distribution companies, for gas, water, electricity and telephone, would be maintaining main pipes and cables for a decreasing number of users. Reservoirs, power-stations, phone-exchanges and gas-holders would become supernumerary. Obviously some phased withdrawal would have to be planned, but this would not be easy, because the distribution areas would not coincide. Analogous problems would arise as regards police-stations, local authorities, schools and so on. Worst-hit of all would probably be underground transport, with its tremendous fixed investment in tunnels, signalling apparatus and the like. (In contrast, surface transport could be reduced and re-routed relatively easily.)

Fortunately, the movement for environmental protection and a growing awareness of the world population problem are pushing even the slow-moving British government in the direction of developing a population policy and considering the question of optimum populations. So the means of bringing about contraction of population without economic malfunction will probably be worked out, whether Britain moves towards paraprimitivism or not. And since there are many countries where overpopulation is not a problem, these are not radical arguments against paraprimitivism.

VII. *Could We Adapt?*

I have been careful to describe the paraprimitive society as what Western (and indeed Eastern) man would aim at if he had any sense. This does not mean that I am optimistic about it actually happening. While it is encouraging that there is an active minority in the USA and Germany and elsewhere which is attempting something of the kind by establishing communes, some at least of which aim at a paraprimitive life, it must be recognized that they are, so far, parasitic growths. They depend on the majority continuing to produce the penicillin and the power-tools, the plastic domes and the fuel, not to mention the transport systems, upon which the commune depends. Unless and until heavy industry, advanced technology and higher education (especially the training of doctors, surgeons and medical personnel) are integrated into a para-primitive community, its absolute viability has not been demonstrated and the community survives only on sufferance.

I do not doubt the possibility: I merely say that the communes prove no more than the existence of a vision and a hope.

There seems no immediate likelihood that the silent majority, either in Europe or the USA, will spontaneously change its values. At present, it is solidly sold on the 'consumer-package'—meaning the currently attainable mix of deep-freeze and colour television, three-bedroom homes and second cars. Will the next generation prove wiser? Slightly, no doubt, but only slightly. Besides, there is an underlying problem.

The individual who is determined to escape from it all, to follow his own whim, is not in general the person who is going to drive himself through a seven- to ten-year course in medicine, say, or even a course in the hard realities of structural engineering. It calls for a different type of personality.

Nor does it seem probable that the revolutionaries, supposing they should succeed in their aims, will attempt anything remotely like this plan.

In addition to all this, there are strong vested interests in the existing system: I mean not only the whole financial–industrial complex, in the sense in which the term 'vested interests' is normally applied, but all those who have acquired special skills, have developed appetites which the existing system helps to satisfy, the teachers and administrators and warriors whose personal lives have inevitably been tailored for so long to the existing pattern, whether they approve of it or not. And I do not exclude myself. The trade unions also have powerful interests in maintaining the existing system.

If we had a lot of time, in a number of generations we might produce a shift; but we may not have so much time. The only thing which I can imagine bringing about a rapid change is a successful demonstration—a pilot-model in which people could, so to speak, try paraprimitivism for size, iron out the problems and decide whether it suited them.

The only alternative to reversing the trend of society is to try to adapt ourselves to it. Is such adaptation possible?

The short answer, I believe, is 'No'. If we become more and more frustrated and suicidal, we can resort to technical fixes, like taking euphoriant pills. We can limit our aggression with other pills, or find substitutes, just as we try to substitute for normal exercise by using a rowing-machine or exerciser. But there is no real sense in which we can adapt to boredom, frustration and lack of purpose. A society whose members are increasingly unfulfilled must inevitably become more and more unstable and history shows that they are taken over by dictators or turn to war, or both. Therefore, we *must* rethink.

The forces which prevent us breaking away from this disastrous trend, where they are not psychological ones, are economic. Those who would like to move towards paraprimitivism are handicapped by economic necessity, and communities which retain something of the primitive are steadily disrupted by the superior economic strength of modernized communities. In the next chapter, therefore, we must look at the economic foundations of our society. Why is private profit often synonymous with public loss?

9

The Rat Race

I. *Introduction*

'It is progressively harder for industry to discover new needs to fill . . .
It is no longer possible to say whether producing industries exist in
order to satisfy consumer needs or whether consumers, goaded by ever
more persuasive advertising, exist as appendages to a system of industrial production.'

These are not the words of some angry student or Marxist theoreti-
cian: they come from Professor Donald Schon, an industrial consultant
who has undertaken important assignments for the American government and for business, an ex-Director of the Office of Technical Services for the US Department of Commerce, no less. If even men like
Schon consider that man exists for industry, not industry for man, is it
any wonder that kids like Shannon Dixon feel themselves in the grip of
impersonal forces? And of course it is not just the momentum of the
industrial machine itself which is alarming: it is the changes in the way
we live—the creation of a technomaniac society—which are produced
by this inversion of priorities. The rat race has become a rat rap from
which we do not know how to escape.

As if to underline all I have been saying, I read in today's paper of a
plan to re-erect the Crystal Palace—the great glass-and-iron building
which housed the Great Exhibition of 1856—in Texas, *indoors*!

And of course it is even more ludicrous that, while industry has to
stimulate appetites in order to dispose of its goods, schools are understaffed, housing is inadequate, mental health is neglected and so on.
Clearly the money which goes to buy unwanted goods must somehow
be shifted from the bank accounts of those who spend it on trivia to the
bank accounts of those who run schools, mental health clinics and the
rest. (Professor Galbraith posed this problem in his famous *The
Affluent Society*.)

It is sometimes objected that, if industry ceased to manufacture trivia
and to promote consumption by advertising, fashion-changes, appeals
to status and so forth, unemployment would result. Indeed, this erroneous argument has seriously been advanced by the advertising industry
in its own defence. But unemployment does not result from a change of
economic aim. When cars replaced horses, there were fewer jobs for

grooms and coach-builders, more for chauffeurs and car-builders. Grooms were no doubt unemployed at first, until they read the signs and learnt to be chauffeurs or bus-drivers. Similarly, if we want fewer gadgets and fashion changes, but more houses and psychiatric social workers, there will be some transitional unemployment until people switch to the new openings. Provided the change of aim is not too rapid, the stress remains small. Such structural changes happen constantly. What causes mass unemployment is something quite different: declines in buying power over the whole system, due to people saving too much of their income and spending too little.* As we get richer this tends to occur more and more.

While the industrial machine, for so long seen as the West's proud achievement, seems to be becoming an end in itself, a Moloch swallowing up men, its reputation has been further undermined by ever-growing evidence of dishonesty, sharp practice and disregard of public interest. In *The Doomsday Book* I told how the dangers of breathing asbestos dust have been known for over half a century. Yet, as I write, one manufacturer is arraigned for serious and repeated neglect of the not very stringent safety regulations in the UK (asbestos levels more than 600 times the permitted amounts were found) and similar stories of anti-social behaviour are reported almost daily. In the USA, Ralph Nader has made a reputation by exposing such derelictions. The *Wall Street Journal* recently reported that retail stores give short weight to the tune of somewhere between 1·5 and 10 billion dollars a year. The US Department of Defence is overcharged by household moving companies for moving the possessions of service-men by five million dollars a year falsifying the declared weight of each load by an average of 625 lb. The catalogue is endless.

Small wonder that many New Liners are turning their backs on industry, and on what is commonly called 'the rat race'. This striking term is worth a moment's consideration. I read it as expressing the savage competitive struggle both between firms and within them. It is the external struggle which leads firms, and those within them, to connive in operations which are ethically dubious or even plain dirty; internally, the term refers to the struggle for personal advancement within firms, leading to toadyism, attempts to eliminate or do down rivals in the promotion stakes, etc. By extension, it refers to the struggle for social status generally, with its conspicuous spending, snobbery, toadyism, empty personal relations and so forth. Indeed, the social struggle is often little more than an adjunct to the business struggle.

As everyone knows, the rat race reflects the intensity of competition which occurs in an economic system in which one man's gain is another man's loss: what we may loosely call the system of private profit. If this

* The full story is complicated. I described it in *Economics for the Exasperated*.

is true—and I am going to suggest that the reality is more complicated —then obviously we need to change the system, for it is evident that the paraprimitive society, or indeed any reasonably Utopian society, is incompatible with the primacy of the mad race for profits. Not only could a paraprimitive society not operate on such a basis itself but it would find it hard to survive within the context of a wider society operating in this way. For, to adapt Gresham's Law, bad behaviour drives out good. The paraprimitive society would be under constant pressure to lower its standards in order to 'compete'.

What then is the alternative? For many of the disenchanted New Liners the answer is simple: Marxism, meaning by this some variant of the theme of state-owned corporations linked by an artificially determined system of prices. In the USA, of course, the issue of private enterprise versus public ownership arouses such strong feelings that detached consideration becomes impossible. I therefore hasten to say that I regard state ownership as no less unsuitable for the primitive society than private enterprise. Living in a country which has both, I see that it works rather well when the product is absolutely standard and the only changes are in the volume of demand—as in the case of electricity and gas. It works less well in industries which are more complex (such as posts and telephones) except where strong competition exists (as in air transport). It fails totally where rapid response to complex and changing demands exists, and no one in his right mind would want to see the restaurant business, publishing or the clothing industry run by a state board. It has struggled along in Russia because the basic needs have been for roads, power and housing, etc. It will run into increasing trouble as standards of living rise. A mixture of the two has advantages: it got the Americans to the moon first.

Unfortunately, public corporations are even more apt to treat the consumer as a convenience and not as the object of the operation than are private concerns, as experience testifies. In Britain public corporations (like State Boards in Communist countries), while having an excellent record as regards such matters as working conditions, quality and safety, have treated consumers high-handedly on many occasions, have too often ignored amenity considerations, and tend to exhibit delusions of grandeur. Moreover, experience shows that when the ambitious man cannot vie for money he vies for prestige and power instead. Bureaucrats are famed for 'empire-building' as well as for preferring inaction to action. The bureaucrat settles for an easy life, and industrial efficiency, or responsiveness to needs, declines intolerably.

If, then neither public ownership nor our present system of private ownership offer a solution, is there any alternative? I believe there is. For our present system of private ownership is not the only version possible. Indeed, it is not a system but an amalgam of devices, each of which could be modified. After all, there are primitive societies in which goods are bought and sold, but which do not proceed to the competitive extremes found in our own system. These extremes arise because individuals are prepared to perform certain actions, such as selling potentially dangerous goods. The question at issue is just as much a personal and moral one as it is an economic one. It is also a social one, since the degree and effectiveness of public pressures on such individuals can vary.

Without presuming to draw up an economic blueprint, let us look more closely at both the human and the organizational aspects of the profit system.

II. *Mixed Motives*

Simplifying a little, we might say that there are two rival theories of economic behaviour, which I will call the Theory of Mixed Motives and the Theory of Pure Profit.

The Theory of Pure Profit was invented by Adam Smith and Malthus in the eighteenth century, and cast into its clearest form by David Ricardo, a successful nineteenth-century stockbroker. It was never true, but is still taught religiously to students of economics. It declares that people, with a few contemptible exceptions, buy and sell, lend, develop land, save and so on, entirely and exclusively on the basis of calculations as to the most financially profitable outcome. Thus a manufacturer will charge the highest price for his goods that he thinks he can get away with, and pay the lowest wages which will attract the type of labour he needs. The saver will put his money where it will earn the highest interest, the employee will work wherever he can earn most, and so forth. The fact, which even economists cannot quite ignore, that some people obviously do not behave in this manner is treated as exceptional, and such people are dismissed as 'sentimental' or 'impractical'.

But the truth of the matter is that in almost every society of which we have knowledge, and even to a considerable extent in modern Western society, people tend to take almost all their decisions (including those dubbed 'economic') in the light of *all* the factors in the situation, and not just the economic ones. Thus we hear people say: 'I let her have it cheap because she was an old-age pensioner.' 'I sold all my South African holdings because I disapprove of the racial policy in South Africa.' 'I could make more money selling insurance, but I prefer to do this.' 'I have left all my property to the National Trust, so that it will not fall into the hands of the developers.' 'It was an absurd price, but it took my fancy.' And so on.

I am not referring at this moment to the purchases we make for indirect reasons, such as the attempt to win status by owning a large car: in such a case we have, in a sense, 'bought' the status, or tried to do so, on a calculus of cool self-interest. Nor am I talking of the ill-judged things we do when we are tired, or hypnotized by advertising—such as the bar of chocolate that we buy on impulse as we pay our bill at the supermarket, because the money is in our hand. I am talking of the things we do for generous or social reasons, in which we accept economic loss (or reduced gain) because we are concerned for other people, or for wider interests. The employer who keeps on an old employee though there is little he can do to help is recognizing a personal relationship, or the employer who takes on a man who has been in prison, taking a risk himself in order to give the man another chance, is allowing 'sentimental' considerations to outweigh 'self-interest'. The employee who accepts a salary cut when the firm is in trouble is (assuming he could get work elsewhere) displaying an emotional involvement in the firm which has no place in the Malthusian system.

Economists sometimes try to bring such behaviour into their system by such arguments as: the man who finds a sinecure for an old employee is simply 'buying' an easy conscience for himself; the person who takes a low-paid job in social service when he or she could earn more in commerce is thereby obtaining 'satisfaction' and the loss of salary can be regarded as the price of purchasing that satisfaction. But this is mere word-juggling: it is rephrasing a generous act to appear as a selfish act. This may be convenient for economists, but it does not alter the reality.

Finally, there are gifts. Economists have never been able to fit them into their cynical system.

The fact is that there are *no* purely economic acts. All actions have relevance in moral and emotional spheres. Economics, as still taught today, is an anthropological travesty. Unfortunately, more and more people, particularly in their business activities and decisions, attempt to behave as 'economic men' and are encouraged to do so by economic theory, and by the institutions which have been set up to facilitate 'economicized' transactions. Many modern economic institutions have the effect, whether intended or not, of preventing face-to-face contact between buyer and seller, so that emotional considerations are ruled out; the data which might otherwise modify a purely selfish judgment are excluded. We have been trying to make the Theory of Pure Profit come true. We have substituted mechanical, inhuman transactions for human ones. This is the nub of it.

One of the ways in which the multiple nature of 'economic' actions is obscured is by use of the phrase 'the profit motive'—a masterpiece of ambiguity. The phrase may mean that there must be a margin between income and outgo. Obviously a shoemaker cannot stay in business if he sells shoes for the cost of the raw materials. He must make 'a profit'. But this means no more than that he should charge his own labour in as a cost. If he does this, he could be said *not* to be operating at a profit.

But there is all the difference in the world between saying that a man should receive *some* remuneration for his labour—or for the loan of his money—and saying that he should maximize that remuneration regardless of all other considerations. George Bourne, whose books about country life in the last century as seen by a country craftsman have fallen into undue neglect, tells how a blacksmith would refuse higher payment than he asked, saying that he knew what the work was worth and did not wish to be overpaid. Shades of Adam Smith! Such an attitude goes back to the Middle Ages, when the question of the 'just price' was much debated. In those days of powerful monopolistic guilds, it would have been possible to exploit the public unmercifully, in the way that many trade unions attempt to do now. While there was endless argument as to what was the just price in any particular case, the notion of a price which would be fair to buyer and to seller was universally understood. The notion of charging what the market would bear was universally condemned. This was the tradition, supported by the church, which the economists of the Age of Reason finally shattered.

(As will I hope be clear, I am not here concerned with the pros and cons of having some people remunerated on a fixed scale—wages and salaries—and others by a fluctuating sum—profit. This I shall discuss later.)

It is the progressive 'economicizing' of business decisions which leads to our present impasse, in which other values are neglected in favour of those things and services which can be bought and sold. A system which only reacts to prices necessarily favours those things on which prices can be put. The results are often so disastrous that we make attempts to re-insert non-economic values into the system by finding ways of attaching prices to them. We do this when we fine a firm for polluting the environment, or for failing to protect the safety of its employees. Unfortunately, such attempts are slow, clumsy and only partially successful. Thousands of coal-miners were killed and injured unnecessarily before adequate safety regulations were introduced. Pollution caused and still causes enormous damage which we are only now beginning to economicize by imposing the costs of pollution prevention on the polluters. We have still to get around to the idea that giving the employee a psychologically satisfying job instead of frustrating him and reducing him to a robot is a thing to be worked into the system.

Economists are accustomed to refer to costs which the entrepreneur doesn't have to bear as 'externalities'. Thus it is an externality if the employee develops cancer after leaving the employ of a chemical firm or an asbestos maker; it is an externality that he puts on the road a very slow truck which wastes the time of other motorists; it is an externality if he pollutes water or atmosphere. It could be said that today we are engaged in an attempt to convert externalities to internalities, in order to prop up the sagging structure of Ricardian economics.

But while we attempt on the one hand to prop up the system, we push it over with the other. The current tendency for teams of accountants to take over firms which have not been making 'satisfactory' profits, and to render them into successes by ruthlessly cutting costs and exploiting markets, i.e. by the kind of behaviour Ricardo said was natural, is a good instance of the trend. The growth of large complexes or 'empires' of holding companies, subsidiaries and subsidiaries of subsidiaries, is a trend with a similar effect. The small-scale independent employer could, and often did, dilute his economic behaviour by 'sentimental' considerations: perhaps he refrained from building a new plant where it would spoil a view, or built it to higher architectural standards than were absolutely necessary; perhaps he tidied up his scrap-yards and car-parks; perhaps he even gave an unsolicited bonus or wage-increase. Taken over by another company, and judged solely on his ability to show an acceptable return on the capital invested by the owning firm, his freedom to act in a 'sentimental' (one could even say Christian) manner is curtailed.

It is true that the very large company is conscious of its public relations, and performs a number of mildly public-spirited acts in order that it shall wear the appearance of a benevolent private employer, and for this reason very large companies often have a better record than the less-satisfactory small companies. But when it comes to an issue which really affects profits, the sheep's clothing falls off, revealing the Ricardian wolf beneath. The determination of copper-mining companies to exploit mineral wealth in national parks is a recent British example. Another was the passing of an Act of Parliament, under pressure from industrial interests, to permit an ecologically valuable valley to be flooded. Issues of this magnitude are nowadays settled by governments, since it has become clear that Ricardian economics is too biased a method, but unfortunately governments tend to favour Ricardian solutions too.

The pyramiding of companies also facilitates the squeezing out of 'sentimental' or moral considerations by virtue of the fact that it destroys the system of personal and social pressures to which I referred in Chapter 3. The entrepreneur who lives in a small town runs the risk of being pilloried if he acts in too obviously anti-social a manner. He may become *persona non grata* with people he admires or wishes to influence; his family may suffer and bring pressure to bear upon him. He may be criticized in the local press. The subsidiary run from a remote city escapes such pressure. The man responsible for the unpopular decision is probably not even known by name or sight to those affected, and the local manager can always be replaced by another.

Closely associated with the Theory of Pure Profit is the Theory of the Price Mechanism, which is supposed to explain why the pursuit of Pure Profit leads to the best of all possible worlds for everyone.

III. *Myths of the Price-mechanism*

So much has already been written about the deficiencies of the price-mechanism—I wrote about it at length in *Economics for the Exasperated* quarter of a century ago, and I was by no means the first—that it is quite extraordinary that it can be touted as a cure-all.* So it seems necessary to summarize as tersely as possible some of the main defects of this supposedly omnipotent device.

In theory, the price-mechanism (as many readers will know) works as follows: when a manufacturer offers a supply of goods which people want, they will compete to get it, outbidding one another until the weaker buyers drop out and the demand begins to match the supply. The fact that the price has risen gives the maker a larger profit, encouraging him to increase the supply, and encouraging other manufacturers to enter the field; as the supply increases and exceeds demand, the sellers are forced to drop the price to bring in more buyers. This they do until the price has fallen almost to the cost of manufacture—or to the cost of the least efficient manufacturer, who now drops out of the running. Thus the supply is now trimmed back to match demand.

Thus the system is supposed to prevent excessive profits—for the enhanced profits earned by the first-comers provide them with the capital with which to expand output—and to ensure that goods are supplied at a price only just enough above cost to ensure that manufacturers come forward.

Such is the theory. In practice there are a dozen or more reasons why it does not function like this, some of which are crucially important.

1 *'Unsaleables'* Perhaps the most fundamental is that people require many things which cannot be put on offer at a price, and in competition with alternatives. Among these, as even nineteenth-century economists confusedly recognized, are the government, the police and armed forces, roads and street lighting and cleaning, and many other things which the public consumes jointly. Recently we have come to realize that we cannot buy, or express our desire for, clean air, pure water, less noise and environmental preservation generally. Indeed we cannot express our

* For a more up-to-date account, see Prof. E. J. Mishan, *Growth: the price we pay* (Staples Press, 1969), especially Chapters 12 and 13.

desire for a better social environment, in the sense considered in this book, by offering a price: we cannot buy a paraprimitive society.

2 *Wise Buyers* The theory also assumes a wholly rational and super-naturally knowledgeable buyer, who is never taken in by poor quality, who thinks ahead, and is never cozened by emotional appeals or playing on his weaknesses and insecurity. But it is obvious that a purchaser cannot tell whether there is mercury or cadmium in the fish he buys, or whether the obscurer parts of his car or television set have been properly made. Perhaps infinitely wise buyers would evoke museums and art collections, as well as providing for their old age. In practice, museums and indeed schools have to be provided by another method, and pension schemes are initiated by industry and government as well as in response to private demand. This brings us to another point.

3 *Income Distribution* The theory assumes that income will not be so unevenly distributed that the poorest cannot afford education, medical care and provision for old age. The unreality of this needs no comment.

As history shows, when labour is more plentiful than jobs, the price of labour can be forced down to subsistence levels, or lower. This led to the abolition of a free market in labour and the substitution of labour monopolies or near-monopolies, known as unions. In consequence, comparably with manufacturer's monopolies, they can force the price of labour up, especially where the manufacturer has costly equipment which he cannot afford to keep idle, long-term contracts which he must continue to service, and where he cannot build a buffer-stock. The most notable instance is the airlines, which explains why airline pilots contrive to earn disproportionately large salaries.

4 *Perfect Market* The theory assumes that all goods are sold in perfect market conditions. There are dozens of exceptions to this. People do not necessarily buy goods as a series of disconnected transactions: some purchases depend on others. If you buy a television set, a car or a gas-stove, you are bound to buy spares if it goes wrong. The maker can charge much more than the market price for these spares, since to refuse them would mean the sacrifice of your costly investment. The same thing is true of gramophone records, recording tapes and so on, most of which are sold at highly arbitrary prices.

Canada, to everyone's embarrassment, is about to become the world's largest producer of sulphur. She already has 6 million tons stock-piled, and the figure is expected to reach 50 million tons by 1980. No one knows quite where to put it. This has happened because sulphur appears as a by-product in the purification of natural gas—and Canada uses a lot of natural gas. As a result, the price of sulphur has dropped from $37·50 per ton in mid-1968 to $6·41 per ton in July 1971. There are plenty of other instances of this coupling of two products for which the demand is unequal—for instance, lead and silver are mined jointly. But of course the biggest crack in the myth of the perfect market is the fact that industry constantly works to create monopoly positions—or, more subtly, positions which are virtually monopolistic without seeming so. By the use of trade agreements, protective patents, and in many subtler ways, large firms manage to take the edge off competition, even where anti-monopoly legislation exists. For details of how monopolistic power is used, see Joseph C. Goulden's hair-raising account of A.T. & T., *Monopoly*.

In any case, public utilities are inevitably monopolistic in nature.

5 *Utility* For example, the supply of water to houses cannot be offered on a basis of rivalry between different manufacturers or suppliers. Much the same is true of gas, electricity, telephone service, the road system and so on. From the first, it was necessary to treat such public utilities on a different basis. Inevitably, the supplier is in a monopolistic position, and has to be restrained from exploiting it. (In the case of gas and electricity, there is an element of competition, it is true, but it is slight, for one cannot run a television set on gas.)

Again, a public transport service may be operated as a utility, in the sense that a service may be provided late at night, or in under-populated areas, even at a loss, on the grounds that the buyer does not want simply to buy so many journeys as to have a service available. The public is assumed to be happy to pay more than the cost on some journeys, in order to be assured of a service which would otherwise not be available, because unremunerative at other times. If the field is opened to competition, some operators will skim off the cream in the rush periods, leaving the utility to operate the loss-making runs. In such cases, we abandon competition, as in the case of London Transport. Thus, it is absurd to abolish certain railway services simply because, taken in isolation, they do not cover their costs. Obviously the railway system as a whole must break even, or show a profit, but it is inherent in its monopolistic position as a public utility that it should operate some unremunerative services. The same is true of airlines, postal deliveries and so on. These economic facts have been fully understood since the nineteenth century, if not much longer; it is truly incredible that the right can still advance naïve cost arguments.

6 *Time-lags* The theory of the price-mechanism omitted to explore the time-factor: how long does it take for a manufacturer to respond to a change in demand? It overlooks the possibility of such tricks as suddenly lowering quality, making a large profit until the public wakes up to what has happened, and selling out to a mug just before the profits

slump—a ploy often worked in the restaurant business. It also failed to foresee such gambits as introducing a new model and refusing to supply replacement parts for the old, compelling the buyer to scrap perfectly satisfactory equipment prematurely.

7 *Agriculture* Another activity which fits poorly into the price-mechanism model is agriculture in all its forms. The supply of grain, say, may be excessive one year thanks to favourable weather and may be deficient in another, irrespective of whether the farmer is trying to increase output, or the reverse. Hence farm-price support programmes, buffer stocks and the like.

8 *Unincreasables* The price-mechanism fails conspicuously to function in respect of land. Manufacturers cannot come forward with more land, obviously, so the theory is modified to say that less and less suitable and valuable land is brought into use, as the demand expands. But one piece of land cannot be substituted for another, as one car or one suit of clothes can. If a city is expanding or a road being built, certain specific plots are required and no others. Thus the owners are in a monopolistic position. When I was in Sydney some years ago, there was much talk of an immigrant who was demanding £130,000 for a farm he had bought not many years before for £10,000, since the city wanted the land. He got his price; but other countries resort to compulsory purchase at an arbitrary figure in such cases. That is, the price-mechanism is abandoned. The converse situation arises when a mining or oil-refining company wishes to drill on farmland, say: it can offer a price which has no relation to farmland prices and thus take land, which may be particularly suitable for farming, for another use.

There are also things of which the supply cannot be increased, such as beautiful scenery, old buildings and works of art from the past. The futility of trying to apply the price-mechanism to such things is shown, for instance, by the Roskill Commission's attempt to value the churches which would be destroyed by London's third airport, on the basis of their insurance value. Since a reconstructed church or a copied painting is not equivalent to the original, even insurance based on such costs is no clue to the benefit the public derives from them, or the loss it would suffer by their destruction. Conversely, the astronomic prices paid for outstanding works of art arises from their uniqueness, the owner being, as it were, a monopolist.

9 *Costly and Unique Items* The theory of the price-mechanism also breaks down where excessively costly items, requiring long periods of technical development are involved, of which the supreme example at the present time is the supersonic transport. Manufacturers cannot chance their

arm and hope there will be buyers. Governments decide to fund the development costs for reasons which may not be economic at all, such as the military applications. (Similar arguments apply to going to the moon.) The question we need to ask in such a case is: could the money be spent better in another way? Or as the economists say: are the social benefits equal to the opportunity costs? Now it is easy to think of things more important to society than hurrying people across the Atlantic an hour or two faster (even if we ignore the amenity disadvantages or 'bads' associated with supersonic flight.) The price-mechanism totally fails to cope with this choice, because it supposes the existence of one man, or a small committee, making the choice for personal reasons, when it is actually made by 'the government', influenced by a complex system of pressure groups and interests.

In Britain today, *over half* the total expenditures are made not by individuals or even firms, but by public officials of one sort or another. So this is not an exceptional situation we are talking about. The price mechanism also fails to cover astronomical telescopes and other costly scientific equipment, made on a 'one-off' basis, and many kinds of research, notably medical research.

The argument could be lengthened, but enough has been said to show that the price mechanism is far from being the miraculous arbiter of right-wing dogma. At almost every point, it has to be regulated and modified.

On close inspection, these criticisms can be seen to expose two distinct defects in the system, from which a third follows. First, it does not evoke, or cause the provision of, certain kinds of goods and service. Second, it does not prevent the production of 'bads' or disservices. Hence, it does not distribute scarce resources so as to maximize human satisfaction. In theory, people will pay most for what they want most— but if 'bads' are ignored, if monopoly or near-monopoly exists, and if buyers are irrational, if some 'goods' are not marketable, and so on and so forth, prices cease to bear much relationship to pleasure.

In earlier days, it was not the market price but the just price, which formed the keystone of economic relationships. The just price was conceived as the cost of manufacture plus a profit which enabled the manufacturer to live at the traditionally expected standard. There was thus a just price for shoes, say, which applied even in monopoly conditions. It is on record that, during the last war, French peasants offered glasses of water to thirsty soldiers at high prices, though water was not short as such. They were exploiting their monopoly position rather than making use of the just price. Their action was generally condemned. Manufacturers in a position of temporary monopoly can often do much the same, without being detected.

A sane society would work its way back towards the just price.

The price mechanism, in any case, is only concerned with the distribution of marketable goods and services. But men require many things in life—and I have discussed most of them, such as a sense of identity, long-term security, contact with nature, or the power of self-determination—none of which are dependent on goods, even if, in a goods-oriented society, we try to use goods to help us achieve these ends. The false belief that the supply of goods is the core of what it is about has been embedded in economics since its birth. Professor Galbraith points out that when the first economists wrote, shortage of goods *was* the problem: but the ideas we formed in the days of poverty are poor guides in an affluent society.

IV. *Industrial Empires*

The innovation which has fostered this dehumanization of behaviour more than any other is the emergence of the limited liability joint-stock company. By a series of legal decisions, following a remarkable piece of legislation in 1862, Britain created an extraordinary legal fiction: it proved such a bonanza that the rest of the Western world soon imitated the British lead. Today, we are so used to it that few people see what a disaster it has proved.

As things now stand, the joint-stock company has most of the legal attributes of a human being without the usual disadvantages. It can buy and sell, sue and be sued, own property, pay taxes, receive rents and in general perform all the economic functions previously performed only by people. But, unlike human beings, it is immortal as well as invisible. Since it never dies, it never pays death duties. Thus while the accumulations of money made by individuals are steadily dispersed by death duties, those of industry are not. In this way, industry acquired the power formerly held by the landowners. Properly managed companies can go on for ever: thus new vested interests were created, just as undesirable as those they replaced, or more so.

Furthermore, like a malignant tumour, the joint-stock company has a built-in tendency to grow, and grow, and grow. Healthy tissue ceases to grow when it has reached the size dictated by the body's requirements. Not so the joint-stock company, which never ceases to set aside part of its profits for expansion, if it can.

But, even stranger, joint-stock companies can legally do something civilized man can no longer do: they can own other entities like themselves. This gives them the power of creating vast networks of industrial power, the modern analogue of slave-ownership. The owning company can starve or kill its subsidiaries, and take the whole surplus earned by their labour for itself. At first this led to the industrial empire, which brought together firms with interlinked interests, such as coal, steel and refractories or various kinds of chemicals. Now we have the industrial complex, which combines activities as diverse as publishing and truck-making, and cannot even plead that it achieves technical co-ordination in justification of its existence.

It is sometimes claimed that such empires bring the benefits of skilled management to companies which were badly run before; in practice, all that most top managements ask is that the subsidiaries shall turn in a reasonable percentage on the capital employed. If they do so, management leaves well alone; if not, they have a shake-up. They know too well that large centralized organizations are inefficient, and are very happy to leave the subsidiaries their independence provided they can cream off the profits. Such empires can also be used to create conditions which are tantamount to monopoly, without appearing to be. Prices can be 'fiddled', as one company within the group trades with another, which may also have tax advantages. Products which appear to be in competition may not be. Thus the two best-known American outboard engines are made by the same manufacturers and are virtually identical. The dealers for each are in competition—thus the manufacturer uses the spur of competition on the distributor while escaping it himself.

The industrial empire makes for standardization and limits choice, since it can exclude choices it does not care to make, while its economic strength enables it to crush the small firm which seeks to fill the gap. Moreover, such empires are self-perpetuating and immortal, since by spreading risks over a large number of activities, the chance of serious failure is eliminated. (And when they do look like failing, governments have to step in and save them.) They are far too complex for shareholders to supervise in any real sense. They are truly empires—or, rather, states within the state. Instead of industry being integrated with the community it serves, it is simply integrated with itself. They are a sort of meta-capitalism.

One of the commonest arguments in favour of the system of private enterprise is that it widens the range of choice to the maximum. This is untrue wherever monopoly, concealed or otherwise, exists. More importantly, it is untrue even in an open market, once we widen the range of our attention to include not merely the goods and services supplied but also the incidental 'bads' and disservices which go along with them. Where the environment is quiet, a man has the choice of quiet or music or noise; where it is noisy, he has no choice. Similarly, where the air is polluted, he has no choice but breathe it.

These company complexes not only operate by Ricardian, i.e. inhuman, economics, but have the strongest possible vested interest in maintaining the system. But even when independent, the joint-stock company has an actual obligation to its shareholders, to exploit every opportunity of profit-making in the Ricardian sense. This is the bind which commits our system irrevocably to materialism. The conclusion is as inevitable as it will be unpopular: a first step towards a more humane society is to modify the law governing such organizations, a law which now goes far beyond its original purpose of making it easier to raise capital by limiting the risk of individual participants.

Numerous arguments against such an outrageous proposal will be advanced. Most of them will take the line: 'Without the joint-stock company our civilization could never have reached the standard of material productivity which it has attained and which is the envy of less advanced nations.' Precisely. It was a very good device for material progress. Now that material progress is ceasing to be the only or even the main criterion, in some countries, it is not a good device any more.

Not only the joint-stock company but also institutions associated with it, such as the stock markets through which its assets are exchanged, would be radically affected by such a change of policy. One would need an additional chapter to consider the financial institutions—banks, insurance companies, monetary funds, etc.—which also function in a Ricardian manner in support of the system. What is more, government departments, statutory bodies, local authorities and nationalized industries are all behaving in an increasingly Ricardian manner. The bureaucrat who receives an application for a job from someone who turns out to have a criminal record will be disinclined to hire him because if the trust he shows is betrayed, his superiors will say: 'You should never have taken a man with such a record into the public service.' Whereas if his trust proves justified, he will receive no reward for his philanthropy. The generous action which the individual can readily take is effectively excluded for the official in a large organization, and public bodies are worse in this respect than private ones—instead of better, as one could have hoped. Bureaucratization is essentially the reduction of human and humane decisions to impersonal ones. Lastly, there are signs that we are beginning to look at the economic organization in a new way in yet one more field.

V. *The Rewards of Virtue*

In the classic conception, a firm is owned by its shareholders, whose money is used to buy the buildings and equipment. The shareholders appoint a manager (or appoint directors who appoint a manager) and can dismiss him if not satisfied. They instruct him, it is widely assumed, to make the largest possible profit; minor infractions of the law are condoned, provided they don't go so far as to bring real retribution. The same applies to infractions of the moral law. In short, a firm is viewed as property and comes under property laws.

This is an over-simplification, not unlike the Theory of Pure Profit. The truth is that a firm has several aspects. It is, primarily, an institution which serves the community, just as much as are the fishing canoes of the South Sea islanders. It is, in part, an institution which serves those who work in it. And it is in part, but only in part, an institution which rewards those who provide capital for it. I believe that we have moved a good deal of the way from the view of the firm as private property to the view of the firm as public convenience. If so, the question arises who should appoint the management? The obvious answer is: representatives of the consuming public, representatives of the employees and representatives of the shareholders, all three; perhaps also representatives of the local community, since not only people-as-consumers but also people-as-citizens are affected by its presence.

It is significant that such ideas are beginning to be debated even in rather orthodox circles. Thus Robert Townsend, a former president of Avis Rent-a-Car and the author of *Up the Organization*, has criticized the self-perpetuating nature of most large concerns, pointing out that it is a mere pretence that the stockholders select the directors: generally the chief executive's list is returned unopposed. As T. K. Quinn, a Vice-President of General Electric (the American one) has noted: 'The directors were in every case elected by the officers. We had, then, in effect, a huge economic state governed by non-elected, self-perpetuating officers and directors—the direct opposite of the democratic method.'

Says Townsend: 'I am not convinced that the outgoing chief executive is the right man to pick his successor. This smacks of the old plantation-owner myth.' And he adds: 'Who could make a better choice? The employees could.' In France there are a number of 'communities of work' one of which I studied some years ago, situated near Valence. It made wrist-watch cases and was known as Boimondau. Here, as in other such work communities, the chief executive was elected and had all the usual powers, except that he submitted his plans for the future to all the employees (*and* their wives) at periodical mass meetings. If they did not agree, and he was adamant, he had the power to go ahead on a vote of confidence, though up to the time of my visit the situation had never arisen. However, the system of workers' control ignores the interests of the community at large, and history records cases of co-operatives which sought to maximize their profits without consideration for non-members.

Townsend also proposed the idea of a 'public director' suggesting that all companies with more than a billion dollars of assets should be required to have a sort of Ombudsman of this kind on the board. He would have a budget of a million dollars and be able to hire scientists, lawyers, engineers and accountants to 'develop answers to the questions the company wasn't asking but should be asking'.

I expect to see more proposals of this kind. In Britain, public corporations (i.e. nationalized industry) have accepted trade-union representatives on their boards, but have bitterly resisted consumer representation, and have done all they could to make the Consumer Councils, set up to put the consumer's viewpoint, meaningless. The Conservative government has disbanded the general Consumer's Council. Since Conservative governments always lean against current trends, this is quite a good omen.

Reconsideration will turn next, I think, to the curious system of differential reward embedded in the profit-system. Employees are guaranteed a fixed annual sum, more or less, but have little security of tenure. Owners have security of tenure, but get a sum which may vary from zero to very large indeed, i.e. the net profits. But as soon as we change our thinking so that those who lend capital are seen simply as providing *one* of the factors of production (the others being materials, labour and know-how) there ceases to be a strong reason to reward them in such a peculiar way. Under existing arrangements, the prospect of a large profit is needed to offset the possibility of a loss. But if capital is provided by investment trusts, so that success and failure is averaged out, this argument disappears. In any case, very large diversified firms, with their eggs in many baskets, are already insulated from risk—no one seriously expects Dupont or Imperial Chemical Industries or I. G. Farben to go broke.

Britain's nationalized industries are instructed by Parliament to so arrange prices that they break even 'taking one year with another'. Except that they put money aside for expansion, no doubt Dupont and ICI do much the same. The small private enterprise is a different kettle of fish. The search for market openings, and the immense amount of work and thought which go into launching a new enterprise, can hardly be evoked unless the prospect of large gains is present to offset the possibility of losing everything.* (Large firms, in contrast, take few risks, preferring to buy up processes into which small firms have poured effort as soon as they promise to become profitable.)

Today, when egalitarianism is all the rage, it is common to hear proposals that everyone should receive an equal income. Such a proposal is not only impractical but actually out of line with human psychological needs. It is impractical because motivation would decline, so that the total sum available to be distributed as incomes would decline, while new openings and processes would not be exploited

---

* The system of payment-by-profits is often given credit for the powerful way in which it motivates private enterprisers. It might therefore be pointed out that the system fails to motivate employees, hence strikes, absenteeism, unnecessarily high scrap-rates and other disadvantages which go far to offset the above-mentioned advantage.

vigorously. But more important is the fact that people want to earn more next year than this—they want to make progress. In wage negotiations, unions place great stress on tying pay to seniority as well as to merit. Moreover, responsibilities vary, both domestic responsibilities and those within the firm. In Boimondau, wages were allocated according to a points system, points being given both for the type of work done, size of family supported and for social contributions outside work.*

VI. *The End of Economics*

The kind of shift I have been trying to suggest, then, is not concerned with private versus public ownership, with profits, as such, or with capital. It is a distinction between making profit the *sole* criterion of action and making it only one consideration among several. It is not a question of private or public ownership of capital, so much as one of how much power, how much risk are to be linked with capital. In short, I am looking towards a de-economicizing of economics, if you will pardon such a barbarous word, the substitution of human for purely monetary assessments.

But there remains a role for the professional economists. Much of the difficulty of making this switch comes from the inability of our economic indicators to measure real satisfactions, or even what should be simpler, the real costs of production. It is as if we claimed to have improved a man's nutrition by enabling him to live on caviare and chocolate creams. In terms of the money spent in feeding him, he appears to be better off. In nutritional terms, obviously, he is worse off, and before long signs of protein shortage and vitamin deficiency will begin to appear. Our society shows these tell-tale signs of psycho-dietary deficiency, even as we consume the glittering trivia with which it presents us.

The various suggestions I have canvassed must be read in conjunction with one another, even though they are unlikely to be introduced at the same rate. The kind of economic system emerging we might call a polylithic one, in contrast to the monolithic socialist system—a *congéries* of small, independent, private but socially controlled units, coupled with systems of supervision which could detect anti-social practices, and integrated into the local community much more than now.

In the small community, anti-social behaviour on the part of a local firm readily tends to become known, but at present there is seldom an

---

* In Glacier Metals, a British firm making ball-bearings, the entire staff worked out a scale of reward based on the weight of responsibility carried, the managing director included. See E. Jacques, *Measurement of Responsibility* (Tavistock Press, 1956).

authority to which the citizen can appeal for action, except when it is a trade-union matter. (The unions show how powerful such supervision can become, however.) If 'better people' and 'social pressures' are two legs of the tripod, the third is 'legal limitations'. At present, our laws are very inadequate—I suppose in all Western countries without exception. It is only recently that the laws of most countries have been modified so as to limit effectively the sale of worthless or harmful medicines. At the moment we are—very slowly—modifying the laws governing industry's freedom to pollute—after a good century of pollution. Many other areas remain unlegislated, and supervisory bodies tend to become tools of industry, rather than watchdogs.

(Thus, the British Chief Inspector of Factories, Mr W. J. C. Plumb, who retired in 1970, is quoted as saying: 'The Inspectorate has never aimed at, and has certainly never achieved a rigorous enforcement of the Act.' The Inspectorate even reported 'defending the company from criticism and the possibility of prosecution' in the case of Central Asbestos Co., against whom a total of £86,469 in personal damages was awarded in 1970, for cases of asbestosis caused by breach of the safety regulations. Earlier, the company was fined £170!)

Professor Mishan makes the important point that economic activities always take place within a legal framework defining what is permissible. For instance, if slavery were legal, a manufacturer could obtain his labour for no more than the cost of buying or capturing slaves and maintaining them at the subsistence level, as was once done. He no longer has that freedom. He was once free to employ small children and to ignore the safety of employees. He was once free to dump his effluents in rivers or the air; free to sell adulterated or dangerous food and drugs; and much else. He is now losing these freedoms also. It is entirely up to society to say what constraints it will put upon the economic activities of its members. Since technology has made it easier for the industrialist to cause public harm, controls necessarily become more severe and more numerous. But they lag behind, and many regulations need strengthening and applying more rigorously.

It is arguable that local communities should be free to apply such standards as they see fit. There is an analogy with states' rights in the USA, where the state of Michigan has attempted to set stricter standards of radiological protection than are established by the Federal government. There is a danger, if such controls are left solely to local bodies, that some may be corrupted into setting unduly lax limits, but this can be avoided by making Federal standards into a floor below which local authorities may not go, though they may aim higher if they wish.

To sum up, then, the present system is biased in favour of goods as against other desirables; it neglects bads; it provides motives for anti-social and inhumane behaviour because it is mechanical and inhumane itself. The way to correct it is not to substitute vast monolithic publicly owned boards and corporations, which are equally open to inhumanity and distorted valuations. It is to substitute decisions made by that marvellous instrument the human brain, which alone can weigh all the factors, ponderable and imponderable, in a situation. And a 'personalized' economics can only be built from small-scale, face-to-face contacts: a 'polylithic' instead of a monolithic system.

While society seems to be moving steadily in the direction of modifying the system of self-centred private enterprise by centralized controls of one kind or the other, the idea of a change of course to a decentralized polylithic system will naturally arouse bitter opposition, because it strikes at the roots of power and seeks to disperse it, instead of simply setting one power against another. And this opposition will come not only from business but also from the unions, since they are in the large-scale organization racket too.

Yet these modifications would not seem so unthinkable if we were not all exposed to a continuous barrage of mindless propaganda about the virtues, nay, the perfection, of the existing system. It would be maturer to say: this is not a very good system, but we can improve it. To defend it blindly is the surest way of undermining it.

Now let us examine the even more fundamental questions of human morality and behaviour.

Citizens of Utopia

I. *Introduction*

THE Zuñi Indians of New Mexico are known for their peaceful, un-competitive way of life. Forty years ago, the annual report of the Bureau of American Ethnology summed it up: 'In all social relations, whether within the family or outside, the most honoured personality traits are a pleasing address, a yielding disposition, and a generous heart. All the sterner virtues—initiative, ambition, an uncompromising sense of honour and justice, intense personal loyalties—not only are not admired but are heartily deplored. The woman who cleaves to her husband through misfortune and family quarrels, the man who speaks his mind where flattery would be much more comfortable, the man, above all, who thirsts for power or knowledge, who wishes to be, as they scorn-fully phrase it, "a leader of his people", receives nothing but censure and will very likely be persecuted for sorcery.'

Contrast with this a judgment of the American character made in 1888: 'They are a commercial people, whose point of view is primarily that of persons accustomed to reckon profit and loss. Their impulse is to apply a direct practical test to men and measures, to assume that the men who have got on fastest are the smartest men, and that a scheme which seems to pay well deserves to be supported.' In a survey of the values of some 500 American men and women, made in the mid-thirties, the six traits rated highest were, in descending order: Honesty, Depend-ability, Self-control, Co-operation, Courage and Initiative. The six rated lowest were: Courtesy, Good sportsmanship, Open-mindedness, Reverence, Obedience and Thrift.

What is the origin of such wide differences? In the Marquesas Islands of the Pacific, the children generally have several mothers. This comes about because, when a man marries a girl, he is held to have married her sisters also—a custom which exists, with variations, in many other parts of the world. Consequently, a child who demands attention or comforting from its biological mother, but is refused because she is busy or preoccupied, simply goes to one of its other mothers. It is not surprising therefore that the adult Marquesans are strangers to romantic love on the Western model. To them the notion of 'the only girl in the world for me' seems absurd. Their outlook in such matters is more nearly expressed by the saying 'There are plenty of good fish in the sea.'

The point of the story is not simply that childhood experience sets the pattern for adult attitudes. It is also that a whole group of people may display certain similarities of attitude because customs which are general in their society, and unquestioned, affect the experience of children. It is not simply a question of how parents choose to 'bring up' their children, though this is part of the mechanism; the whole physical and social environment of the child plays its part. A child brought up in a high-rise block of flats has a different set of experiences from one brought up on a farm. An only child has a different kind of childhood from one who is part of a family of twelve. Hence, the growth of urbanization and small families changes the personality of those affected.

To build an Utopian society we need to produce Utopian citizens. And even if we aim at something less ambitious than Utopia, it is still the case that we are limited by the defects of human behaviour. Anti-social behaviour of any kind inevitably diminishes satisfaction. Power-hungry or money-grabbing people will simply pervert any Utopia in which they might find themselves, finding ways to exploit the trust and good nature of others for personal gain—as has so often been seen when white traders have come to well-adjusted pre-technical societies in the South Seas and elsewhere. Violent and vicious men will create insecurity for all—and since bad behaviour drives out good, before long all will have been forced to join the battle. In the Utopia described by William Morris, no one was ambitious or acquisitive, curmudgeonly or arrogant; all were helpful and civilized. No one deposited litter, vandal-ized gardens or took drugs. Morris thought this would come about with the demise of capitalism. It has been the great delusion of Socialists that social misbehaviour was solely the result of poverty and exploita-tion: that when these were eliminated, man's natural goodness would manifest itself. This we can now plainly see to be untrue. So the crucial question becomes: can we raise the level of human behaviour, and, if so, how? Man is not naturally good, just as he is not naturally bad. Both patterns are learned ones. The failure of socialism is due to its depen-dence on the assumption of goodness, as that of capitalism is due to its dependence on the assumption of badness. The new doctrine which will eventually replace both can only be built on understanding the pro-cesses which determine human personality.

For some strange reason, people find the idea of influencing person-ality very hard to accept. They know countless instances of individual children whose behaviour has been influenced by their childhood—for example, the only son spoiled by a doting mother. But they find it hard to generalize from these cases or to see how unintentional lessons are taught to children.

Experiences which influence a person permanently may be called constitutive experiences, and it is these which we have to explore. It is one's earliest experiences, usually, which are constitutive, and often they are repressed from consciousness, but continue to work their effect, especially if later experiences seem to reinforce them. People are quick to generalize: a person who eats mushrooms for the first time and is subsequently ill is likely to keep off mushrooms ever after—and if this happens twice is almost certain to do so. Thus first experiences are usually constitutive; hence the first months of life, when the baby is having its first experiences of affection or rejection, of comfort or discomfort, of being cared for or neglected, are above all constitutive and set up attitudes which persist throughout life. The aggressiveness and chip-on-the-shoulder attitudes which are all too familiar spring from long-forgotten early disappointments.

It was towards the end of the Second World War that Abram Kardiner, a German-born psychoanalyst, put forward the fruitful idea that differences in methods of upbringing might account for the basic behavioural differences between members of different societies: differences which had been thrown into focus by the work of anthropologists like Ruth Benedict and Margaret Mead. Ruth Benedict, who died in 1948, was one of the first people to treat cultures as integrated wholes: she pointed out that some of the tribes she studied were highly spontaneous, which she called the Dionysian pattern, while others took a more restrained or balanced position, which she called Apollonian. Kardiner's insight was that each society must tend to favour particular methods of child-upbringing, and that this must therefore tend to set a stamp upon the adult personality of the majority of members of that society. Thus one could account for such differences. This common element he called the basic personality structure, though he was careful to point out that every individual will have experiences which are *not* dictated by beliefs about the treatment of infants, and so his personality will contain elements over and above the basic personality. (There are also hereditary factors, of course.)

When I came across this idea in 1947, it burst on me like a bombshell that here was the only radical method of bringing about cultural change. If we can persuade people to alter methods of upbringing we can shift value systems, limit aggressiveness and much else. Obviously, attempts to influence children in desired social directions have been made from time immemorial. What was new was the realization that certain very early experiences which had been taken for granted were of crucial importance. Matters of discipline and actual instruction, which can hardly start before the age of three years and which are often left even later, only build on a psychic foundation which has already been laid for good or ill.

When I wrote about the implications of Kardiner's idea for our own society in 1946 and 1947, barely half a dozen societies had been studied in the light of this theory, and much of what I said was necessarily speculative. Since that time, however, more than seventy cultures have been studied. Indeed, we have more information about how people actually bring up their children in some 'primitive' societies than we have about our own. Besides this, the actual psychic mechanisms at work are more fully understood, thanks to continuous research by Western child-psychologists. All this has revealed that the way in which child-rearing practices affect personality is more complex and interwoven than was at first appreciated. For instance, Kardiner and some of those who took up his ideas thought that where infants were closely swaddled, or confined in birch-bark tubes, as in some Indian tribes, or otherwise prevented from moving their limbs, a considerable degree of aggression would result from the frustration. It turns out, however, that many infants seem to find great security in this situation, which presumably resembles in some way the conditions in the womb. Much depends on the age to which this is prolonged.

The psychoanalytically-oriented workers who pursued these leads were also much preoccupied with such matters as the earliness and severity of weaning and house-training, which were believed to affect dependency, acquisitiveness and other adult attitudes. It turned out that the picture was far more complicated than had been realized (e.g. an infant can be fed pap from birth as well as receiving the breast, and this can continue to a relatively late age: is he then to be described as weaned early or late?). In any case, these factors were of much less importance than had been thought.

Margaret Mead, whose studies of child-upbringing in New Guinea, Samoa and elsewhere are famous, has demonstrated in detail how societies vary widely in the treatment of children, in many respects. In one the baby is carried on the mother's back, always in close contact, skin to skin; in another, it is placed in a rough basket without a soft lining and left alone. It may be taught chiefly by words, as with us, or by physical manipulation, as in Bali. It may be pressed to achieve maturity, as in the USA, or held back, as with the young Samburu males.

I shall not attempt to analyse the process in this kind of detail, but shall simply urge the reader to study Margaret Mead's *Male and Female* and her other books. For our present purpose it is enough to consider three questions. How are values formed—with special reference to patrism and matrism, and hard- and soft-ego? What causes delinquent, in the sense of selfish and unco-operative, behaviour? What is the cause of violence and aggression? These seem to be the issues most relevant to our immediate problems. In addition, I shall say something about mental health generally, for clearly a society of depressives, schizophrenics and obsessives would be far from Utopian.

The central question is: does it seem likely that we could, by changing childhood environments, effect a change in society for the better? What are the limits of the possible? Inevitably there are influences we cannot hope to control. There are hereditary elements in character—Professor Eysenck declares that the tendency to neurosis, no less, is inherited. There is a good deal of recent work tending to show that the later development of children is affected by stresses on the mother during pregnancy, ranging from those due to cigarette smoking, investigative X-rays and drugs to loud noises, emotional upsets and other psychological factors. Birth itself is a shock, sometimes a severe one. There are indications that quite a few children suffer a mild degree of brain-damage from oxygen shortage at birth. Again, a child may lose one or both parents early in life, by illness or accident.

It follows that in no conceivable society could we ensure that every child started life without trauma. But it is unquestionably the case that we could by taking thought greatly reduce the traumas suffered, both before and after birth. And we could, even more easily, change the circumstances and methods of upbringing which form the basis and biases of personality. Let us start with the question of values.

II. *Changing Value Systems*

It seems almost certain that we can and do influence the values which the next generation will hold by the methods we use to bring up our children.

I have already suggested that matrism results from absence of the father. Biller, in his valuable book, *Father, Child and Sex Role*, has summarized the evidence for maintaining this, which is quite extensive.

The process by which a child models itself on its father was called by Freud 'introjection', but one does not have to be a Freudian to accept its existence. American learning-theorists incorporated this process in their teachings, since, whatever the explanation, it undoubtedly occurs. The evidence is firm that it takes place chiefly between the ages of two and three and is largely complete by the age of five. It is therefore the absence of the father during this rather limited period which is important. It is very difficult to change the self-conception formed at this age by later exposure.

In the USA, the father is absent in 10 per cent of all families. But total absence is not the only condition for preventing the child from modelling itself on its father. If the father returns home from work after the child has gone to bed (as is not unlikely at the age of two to three) or if he is away in the armed forces or on a job which keeps him from home a great deal, the process is liable to fail. The evidence also shows that introjection occurs best when the father actively nurtures the child, tucking it into bed, giving it its bottle, perhaps, and generally manifesting as a supportive figure. Again, *it is necessary that the father be masculine in behaviour* if the son is to develop masculine attributes. Moreover, the father must not only be dominant but must allow the son opportunities to exercise dominance. A totally repressive or highly critical father is likely to be rejected. Much also depends on the mother, who may constantly belittle the father and take the major decisions herself—a matriarchal pattern found especially in some lower-class milieux, notably among black people. At the other extreme, a very severe and repressive father may be rejected by the child: introjection is based on love, which is why the supportive father is most easily introjected.

Introjection of the father is also inhibited by the presence of a very masculine mother, especially if she discourages the son's masculine tendencies, as is likely to be the case. Equally, the over-protective mother weakens masculinity, especially when she adopts a veiled sexual attitude to her son, making him into a substitute for an absent father. (Cf. the case of Inburn, cited in Chapter 7.) This is a common background to homosexuality. Over-protection seems to be especially important at two ages: about nine months and again about two to three years. The over-protective mother is rare in the lower classes, probably because she is likely to be too busy earning a living to have time for much protectiveness.

Incidentally, it has been noted that, when the mother works, the children tend to draw a weaker distinction between the role of the sexes —doubtless because the distinction actually is weaker. But since over-generalization occurs, the attitude grows from one generation to the next, which may help to account for the current assimilation of the two sexes, so widely remarked on.

It must be added that the son's perception of his father at the age of three or so is a very inaccurate one, in adult terms. The father inevitably appears as a stronger and more decisive figure than he really is, so that impressions of authority can be derived from easy-going fathers.

Study of various groups of children exposed to such conditions shows that, in addition to adopting matrist values, they exhibit anxiety and are more prone to psychological problems; they are more likely to engage in crime; their marriages are more likely to end in divorce; and their IQs may be lower. In addition, more surprisingly, such children tend to show greater verbal and conceptual power and less mathematical ability than normally parented children. Since verbal ability (and synthesis) are commonly regarded as female characteristics, and since mathematical ability (and analysis) are regarded as masculine, this seems a particularly interesting confirmation of the thesis that parental exposures of the kind we have been discussing really do affect personality in a detailed manner.

Of course, there is room for dispute how far the characteristics we regard as feminine are inevitably feminine in some profound sense, and how far they are the consequences of a social convention. Perhaps girls behave like girls simply because they are taught to do so. I am not concerned with that issue here, and use the terms 'masculine' and 'feminine' in the commonly understood sense, without implying approval or disapproval.* It is, however, well established that inadequate fathering—either by a weak and incompetent parent or by a puritanical and possessive one—tends to result in Lesbianism. Fathers who devalue girls, and those who wish them to be like sons, cause similar problems. Such girls experience difficulties in school, and in marriage.

Enough has been said to show that the process at work involves many factors, and there are others I have not mentioned. For instance, what father-substitutes are available to the child? Where the father is wholly absent, does the mother re-create him in the child's mind? ('Just like your daddy.') Does she encourage masculinity? (Thus where fathers contradict their wives and seek to mould their daughters differently, the daughter is liable to develop severe schizophrenia.) No research has been done, unfortunately, to discover what proportion of sons are deprived of paternal influence at the crucial age of two onwards, but it is reasonable to think it could be a majority, in the United States, bearing in mind that the father who spends most of Sunday on the couch with a pack of beer, watching television, is virtually an 'absent father' in the context being considered.

Anthropological studies confirm these, largely American, findings.

Nothing like the same wealth of evidence is available in relation to soft- and hard-ego attitudes, but Professor Eysenck has some suggestive data concerning the perhaps rather narrower tough/tender dichotomy which he has observed, and which corresponds to extraversion/introversion. He cites evidence that homes where little affection is shown (and where affection is thought to be unimportant) tend to produce the 'tough' pattern, while affectionate homes (in which weaning is carried out gently) produce the 'tender' pattern.

However, Eysenck himself thinks the origins are hereditary. This is in keeping with his general behaviourist position, and he explains the phenomenon in Pavlovian terms. Perhaps both physiological and psychological factors are involved, for one experimental study claims to show that heredity accounts for 70 to 80 per cent of the effect. Further research is badly needed.

* Cross-cultural studies show considerable agreement about sex roles, and indeed preferences, in a range of societies differing widely in other respects.

III. 'Beat Him When He Sneezes'

No society can function unless its members display a certain readiness to co-operate—to suppress personal preferences and advantage in the interests of all. The Utopian society calls for a particularly well-developed conscience, quite apart from the question of what values are regarded as important.

The formation of conscience has been the subject of innumerable psychological studies. The core of the process is the child's identification with its parents and consequent tendency to model itself on them, and to adopt their standards, a process which, as we have seen, takes place between three and five years of age. (The standards formed at this time are later modified by imitation of other admired figures, and by thought and observation of the behaviour of others.) But the distinguishing feature is the development of a sense of 'oughtness' or moral obligation, quite distinct from fear of being caught and punished. In adult life, we find individuals who refrain from actions they know to be forbidden when they anticipate being caught and punished but who commit such actions unhesitatingly when they think themselves safe. The conscientious person, of course, observes his internalized standards even when no one else is watching.

Since identification is the process by which standards are internalized, it follows that contact with parents, and an affectionate relationship with them, is essential. For boys, particularly, it is the father who is important. (Also relevant are the standards the parents practice, and those they preach; and the kind of rewards and punishments they employ.) It follows that the same processes which make for patrism also make for conscience, and those which make for matrism make for lack of conscience. Indeed, this is just a special case of the dichotomy between self-control and spontaneity. Bacon, Child and Barry, studying a variety of cultures, showed that societies with low 'father-availability' have a higher rate of crime than average. Thus the extreme patrist is conscience-ridden to the point of absurdity, the smallest departure from the rules being a source of guilt; self-control finally becomes an end in itself, and loss of self-control a moral failing. In contrast, the extreme matrist lacks conscience altogether. The abandonment of sexual regulations is followed by the loosing of overt aggression, as was vividly demonstrated by the millenarians, and this abandonment of self-control finally comes to be regarded as a virtue in itself. As in the case of values, the sane course is to aim between these two extremes, accepting a certain amount of guilt-feeling as the price of sociality. To be 'free of guilt' is as undesirable as to be 'guilt-ridden'.

The special importance of the father's influence in conscience-formation arises because the position of the male child is different from that of the female, in that he has to transfer his attention from his first love-object, his mother, to his father in order to model himself on the latter. In any case, fathers appear as figures of authority in most cultures, including our own, and therefore as the final source of morality. Studies of delinquent boys show clearly that it is not 'broken homes' which give rise to anti-social behaviour, but rather lack of affectionate relationships with parents, and especially the father.*

Far the most important of such studies, because of its thoroughness, is the so-called Cambridge Somerville Youth Study, begun in the thirties. More than 360 boys were studied in their homes, and their parents also observed; then they were followed through to manhood. Indeed, they are still being checked on periodically. Though the study has failed to reach many of its ambitious goals, it has certainly shed a flood of light on the way in which the family environment is related to delinquency and crime. By 1959 all the boys had passed the age of twenty and it was possible to issue a report analysing the differences between those who had come before the courts—and 40 per cent of all those studied had done so—and those who had not. (Since only state criminal records were available, boys who committed crimes outside the state, and those who avoided detection, escaped classification as delinquents. The effect of this would naturally be to water down the differences, so that the case may well be even stronger than appears.)

It emerged clearly that level of intelligence, physical condition and 'social' factors like poor housing were not related to subsequent delinquency; the home atmosphere decisively was. There were few criminals in cohesive homes; rather more from homes that were quarrelsome but affectionate; broken homes gave rise to violence and alcoholism, but not to delinquency. It was homes which were both torn by strife and neglectful of the children which gave rise to the great majority of crimes and to early juvenile delinquency.

Where the father was warm, even if passive (gentle, thoughtful, rather than authoritarian or active) the sons were rarely criminally disposed. Where the father was absent, neglectful or cruel, there was much. Psychologists have often over-stressed the role of the mother: as this study dramatically shows, the role of the father is, for boys, even more important. To some extent, the study showed, a warm mother offsets the effect of a cruel or neglectful father, while a warm father offsets a cold mother.

* The term 'delinquency' is not a precise one, since young people may be brought to court for actions motivated in various ways, e.g. a burglary may be carried out as an act of daring or to alleviate boredom, rather than to acquire goods illegally. And some illegal acts, e.g. possession of marihuana, are not felt to be wrong by those found guilty of them. I use the term for lack of a better, but with reservations of this kind.

The mother's personality is also of fundamental importance, but in a rather specific way which could not have been easily predicted. The most unsatisfactory type of mother was the one who 'just wanted to be left in peace': her sons were likely to have a high crime-rate, especially sex crimes. Cruel, absent and neglectful mothers also tended to produce criminal sons, and these were less likely to reform after a period of delinquency when the mother had been neglectful.

Again, Bandura and Walters, two child psychologists, made a particular study of aggressive delinquent boys and found them critical and resentful of fathers but retaining a good deal of respect and affection for mothers, despite the fact that they felt rejected by both. The dangerous combination seemed to be a rejecting or withdrawn father coupled with a mother who discouraged the child from depending on her and even encouraged aggression. ('Stand up for yourself.') There is a vicious circle here because the boy who has failed to introject the father will hang about his mother's apron-strings, and she will feel obliged to discourage his dependency. The situation is worsened if the mother disparages the father in front of the child. Equally, a father who disparages his son makes it hard for the son to identify with him. These workers noted that punitive discipline made matters worse. (It should be borne in mind that I am here only considering boys. A passive father has a bad effect on girls, as regards delinquency, whereas a passive mother has little effect on them.)*

It also emerges from the Cambridge study that boys tend to imitate their fathers when the mother is neglectful: we can interpret this as an attempt to win their mother's love by making themselves her love-object.

The type of discipline employed was also important. But even more important than the kind of discipline was consistency in applying it. The child who is punished one day and let off, or even praised, for the same act the next day, is inclined to feel it is worth taking a chance. For every type of crime—sex, property, violence, traffic offences, etc.— there was a background of inconsistent discipline and these were the delinquents least likely to reform. Lax, but consistent, discipline was associated with violence, sex crimes and crimes against property. Strict discipline, whether it consisted of punishment or withdrawal of love, tended (as one might expect) to prevent crime. Also significant is the distinction between withdrawal of love and punishment by loss of privileges.

Discipline of a punitive kind (according to Stephenson, an English

* Phyllis Greenacre notes that the 'conscienceless psychopath' who blandly exploits others—lying, borrowing money, etc., but usually avoiding actually breaking the law—has a remote, preoccupied, fear-inspiring father and a self-indulgent, pleasure-loving, pretty mother who is contemptuous of the father. They are primarily interested in themselves and have a poor relationship with the child. (*Trauma, Growth and Personality* (Hogarth Press, 1953).) See also A. Aichhorn, *Wayward Youth* (1935), for similar observations.

investigator) causes the child to doubt whether he is accepted. And boys resent discipline from the mother. The use of psychological discipline by the father is the most effective pressure. Stephenson also found acceptance by both parents very important for conscience-formation. He sums up thus: 'What the mother is like is of greater importance than what the father is like and what the father says is of more weight than what the mother says.'

Two American workers, Neil and William Smelser, studied 253 boys and their families over a five-year period and came to similar conclusions, which they summed up as follows: 'The son is extremely likely to become criminal unless (*a*) both parents are loving and the mother is non-deviant, or (*b*) parental discipline is consistent and one parent is loving. Twenty-four of the twenty-five boys whose fathers were criminal, and whose backgrounds evidenced neither of these mitigating circumstances, had criminal records as adults.'

But they make two other interesting points. The old adage 'like father, like son' needs qualification, at least when one is thinking about criminality. Children imitate their father's criminality only when other environmental conditions (rejection, maternal deviance, erratic discipline) tend to produce an unstable, aggressive personality. Secondly, it is often said that children only follow their parents' values if the latter's actions reinforce what they teach: but the Smelsers found that—if discipline was consistent—sons followed the expressed values, not the behaviour, of a criminal parent.

Finally, Smelser and Smelser make the striking point that the much-touted egalitarian family, in which father and mother carry equal weight, is in fact the worst environment. 'Boys tend to be more responsible when the father rather than the mother is a major authority figure [here they confirm what Stephenson found] girls are more dependable when the mother is the major authority figure . . . In short, boys thrive in a patriarchal context, girls in a matriarchal . . .' (Thus they confirm what I have sought to show, the high status of men in a patriarchal or patrist society, the high status of women in a matriarchal or matrist one.)

They then cast this finding into a form more directly relevant to the problems of our own society, in which the young are accused of lacking initiative and ignoring obligations. 'To state the issue in a more provocative form, our data suggest that the democratic family, which for so many years has been held up and aspired to as a model by professionals and enlightened laymen, tends to produce young people who "do not take initiative", "look to others for direction and decision" and "cannot be counted on to fulfil obligations".' (The three judgments quoted are from an article by Professor U. Bronfenbrenner.)

Where does all this leave us? In the most general terms, it is very clear that if we want to change the pattern of society we must start in the family. Unfortunately, one cannot create loving parents by telling them this is what they ought to do. There are some things one can influence: whether the father gives time to his children, how far he leaves discipline to the mother, whether that discipline is consistent, and so on. But even this is difficult to achieve in just those families where it is most necessary.

Having discussed delinquency in terms of disturbed personality, I must digress to say that delinquent actions may have other causes, or a mixture of causes. Some delinquents seem dominated by a need for stimulus and excitement, and this may have a physiological origin: Professor Eysenck has argued, on the basis of experiment, that this 'stimulus-hunger' is hereditary. Again, some delinquents perceive the world incorrectly because they have brain damage. Certainly a component in delinquent behaviour is the desire to prove one's courage and skill. Our society fails to provide the institutionalized tests of bravery, endurance and skill which almost every primitive society offers to its adolescent boys, and which enable them to prove that they have attained manhood, both to others and to themselves. There is also the conformist who joins a gang and naturally conforms to its values while he belongs. As an adult, he conforms equally firmly to society's norms and becomes known as an unusually law-abiding citizen.

Reformers have often argued that poor social conditions are a cause of delinquency. They can contribute to delinquency in at least three ways, but they do not determine it. Paul Goodman has argued passionately, in *Growing Up Absurd*, that the young slum-dweller feels intensely frustrated. Society does not offer him a meaningful and satisfying role to play. The gap between his standard of living and the one he sees on television and elsewhere is wide. And for sundry reasons poor families may be more liable to domestic strife than wealthier ones.* These are not hares I wish to pursue here, since my subject is not delinquency as such but personality formation. I mention them only to avoid giving too one-sided an impression.

IV. *An Ordered World*

The motive which drives the child to imitate its father is love and the desire to be loved: withdrawal of affection by the parent is the eventual penalty of failure to conform. But parents, of course, have other weapons: they can reward with privileges and punish by withdrawing privileges or inflicting pain. The behaviourist psychologist believes that

* Several studies disclose that persons of the lower class have less effective consciences than persons of the middle class—hence, among other things, the rise in car accident rates as car-ownership spreads down the social scale in the UK. (See, for instance, B. M. Spinley *The Deprived and the Privileged* (Routledge and Kegan Paul, 1953).) As we should expect, she notes that this goes with hostility to authority, and feminine identification.

learning, including social learning, can be studied adequately in terms of reward and punishment, meaning deliberately intended rewards and punishments; they underrate the importance of the spontaneous satisfaction of 'being like daddy' and the spontaneous dismay at seeing a parent's sorrow or disappointment.

A full treatment of the subject of personality formation would therefore involve studying the various types of reward and punishment used by parents, and later by others in authority. The variations are numerous: thus it makes a difference if punishment is given immediately after the offence, or after a delay or period of uncertainty. Is restitution required to be made, or does the punishment itself return the offender to grace? Is reward used in preference to punishment, or the reverse? What kind of punishment: loss of privilege, withdrawal of affection or infliction of pain? How consistent is the discipline? Does the father or the mother administer it, or both? Aronfreed, in his *Conduct and Conscience*, has listed many other factors besides these.

Various theories of how parents should behave are now current. Some say only rewards should be used—but how does one reward truth-telling in a child who always tells the truth? Others say: use neither, but let the situation itself provide the discipline. Does one then let the child poke hairpins into electric outlets until it gets a possibly fatal shock? The simplicities of training rats with shocks and food pellets cannot be so easily transferred to the human situation. The issue, I suggest, is wrongly conceived. The important fact is that a child needs to live in an ordered world. We have come to understand the child's need for affection pretty well, and have learned to treat its anal and sexual activities as natural rather than wicked, but the child's need for a context of order is still very little comprehended. Adults too, expect certain things to go according to the rules. They become quite irritable if trains do not arrive on time, if shops do not open at the expected hour, if the electric power supply suddenly fails, and so on. The child's demands are similar, if simpler. He expects meals to arrive at the usual times, mother to be available when things go wrong, to be able to sleep comfortably when tired. However, in the kind of families which Betty Spinley studied, such expectations are disappointed. The child cannot even expect to see the same father as last week, or to find mother or a meal when he returns from school. So he learns the lesson that nothing is dependable. Understandably, this makes him perpetually anxious.

At the turn of the century, Madame Montessori, the great teacher, pointed out that a child is anxious to discover the rules, both literally and figuratively. It tests the strength of materials, it discovers that hot objects burn you, and investigates what is necessary for a door to stay closed. It also investigates the rules. 'Mother will slap me if I take sweets without permission' is a discovery quite analogous with 'The stove will burn me if I touch it.' Provided it does not read lack of affection into the mother's reaction, the child treats the two events pragmatically. As Montessori pointed out, a child will gradually increase the range or force of its behaviour in an attempt to discover at what point a prohibition will be issued. It simply tests the limits of the situation. A good part of what adults misconstrue as 'naughtiness' is simply exploration of this kind. It follows that if the limits are set in different places at different times, it does not know how to act. If mother treats behaviour as 'cute' or amusing on one occasion, and prohibits or punishes it on another, this leaves the child in doubt what to do. If this happens much, it raises doubts in its mind about other prohibitions and instructions. Perhaps suddenly this behaviour will prove wrong too? There is a mass of evidence to show that inconsistent treatment is far more harmful to the development of the child than consistent severity.

The disorganized home, where there are no regular mealtimes or bedtimes, where parents cannot be relied upon to be there, or to behave consistently when they are there, and where obligations and responsibilities are undefined, is profoundly disturbing. Children from such a background cannot fit themselves into the pattern of school, with its timetables and fixed rules. Later, they have difficulty in fitting themselves into a work situation, and into life itself. Clearly, they will also be unable to fit themselves into any conceivable Utopia. Technological society becomes more and more ordered; the growth of population also makes narrower regulations necessary. (You don't have to have traffic lights on a rarely used intersection.) Adaptation to an ordered world is more than ever necessary. But the family situation is increasingly disordered.

V. *Don't Adjust Your Mind*

The words 'Don't adjust your mind; the fault is in reality' have been inscribed by students in public places in many countries. They express the adolescent's justifiable disenchantment with the world as he finds it, and his determination not to abandon the ideal of a better world. I entirely agree with this attitude: it is just what this book is about.

But they are sometimes applied in a different context, in which I would take just the opposite view. It is argued that the whole process by which the child is 'socialized', i.e. taught to behave in a socially acceptable manner, has the effect of ensuring that it accepts the status quo, and thus makes progress (still more, revolution) impossible. Therefore, it is concluded, the child should not be socialized but should be allowed to follow its own inclinations.*

* As the words 'socialized' and 'socialization' are more often used in a political sense, I wish to stress that I am here using them purely in the sense of 'civilizing'. I am not talking about socialized education or the communist view of the family

The defect of this argument is that it oversimplifies. Socialization is a simple word for a complex group of processes. First, there is the development of a sense of 'oughtness'; second, the child learns the absolute criteria by which 'oughtness' is applied, (e.g. honesty); thirdly, it acquires value systems (e.g. spontaneity/control); lastly, it learns about conventions, institutions, norms and other social paraphernalia. It is this last group which is most in need of revision. Here I would agree, we tend to teach people that what is, is right: and I would strongly support the introduction of a more constructively critical kind of education. But it is throwing out the baby with the bathwater to abolish socialization because you do not like it. The sense of 'oughtness', or some sense of social obligation, is essential in any society, and if we throw this out, we shall not get acceptance and support of better institutions either. The second item concerns absolute values, such as honesty or kindness. These too are essential in a better world. (Certainly, some parents may fail to teach kindness, or honesty, and to that extent the socialization process is open to criticism and improvement.) The third group, as I sought to show in earlier chapters, is not 'taught'— one acquires a feeling for spontaneity or control from experiences which are unplanned—though it is true that, later on, parents and others will preach the desirability of one or the other. In short, the socialization process is open to error, but is nevertheless essential.

The attack on the socialization process has been made in its most virulent form by Dr R. D. Laing, author of *The Divided Self* and other books, and his disciple David Cooper, author of *The Death of the Family*. It is worth looking briefly at this formulation because it exposes the error very clearly. Laing and Cooper see that the process of introjection depends on the parent being loving; therefore, they condemn parental affection; thus Cooper writes of 'the brutalizing assaults of loving parents' against which the child sensibly defends itself by withdrawal. Not only parental affection but the family itself must therefore be abolished. This is in my view rubbish. A child brought up without affection or family support would be highly disturbed, personally miserable and unable to co-operate with others in any kind of human society.

Laing also maintains that the child should be taught no rules of behaviour. Thus he quotes Jules Henry: 'If all through school the young are provoked to question the Ten Commandments, the sanctity of revealed religion, the foundations of a patriotism, the profit-motive, the two-party system, monogamy, the laws of incest, and so on . . .' then there would be, says Laing, 'such creativity that society would not know where to turn'. And he adds, 'Children do not give up their innate imagination, curiosity, dreaminess easily. You have to love them to do that.' Now I am all for questioning the two-party system and anything else. But the conclusion that this kind of education would lead to a flowering of creativity is simply untrue. The greatest creative minds in history were all people who had been taught the codes of their society. The young today who question everything are rarely either creative or happy.

Since Laing's prescription would produce psychotics, he is then driven to maintain that the mad are sane, and the sane mad. But the man who believes that his pelvis is made of glass, or that he is Napoleon, or that he is being influenced by radio from another planet, is objectively mad: there are no two ways about it.

The core of Laing's position is that man is good: remove the deforming pressures or society and his natural goodness will overflow in creativity and love. This is just as untenable as the Puritan view that man is inherently bad and will find his own way to perdition. As I have shown, the belief that man is inherently good is the delusion of the matrist. The dichotomy is false; the fact is, man is neither bad nor good. The words are inapplicable. He has impulses which can equally serve bad ends or good ends. He looks after Number One, because if he did not he would not survive, but if he becomes a monster of selfishness, he handicaps others from surviving, which is bad. The impulse itself is neutral. 'Bad' and 'good' are subjective assessments, as Laing must well know.

In his biographical excursion *The Bird of Paradise* Laing describes how appalled he was, as a medical student, by seeing a small boy die in great pain from a tumour, by the birth of a hydrocephalic child, who also died, and other experiences. He describes how he went into a pub carrying the remains of the malformed infant in a bag and was tempted to show it to all and sundry. It angered him that they should be calm when he was in a turmoil. But most of us, and doctors especially, have to face the horrors of existence at one time or another.

An entirely different but equally dangerous position is taken by Professor B. F. Skinner, the behaviourist psychologist, for whom is named the Skinner Box, in which rats are subjected to electric shocks or rewarded with food, as a means of understanding human behaviour. For Skinner, man is neither bad nor good; he is simply a bundle of conditioned reflexes and behaves in this way or that simply because he has been taught by reward or punishment to do so. Hence he concludes that children should be conditioned rigorously to be good citizens from birth onward, whereupon all our problems would disappear. In his widely read Utopian novel, *Walden II* (the title echoes Thoreau's classic *Walden*) he gives some indication of how this 'behavioural engineering' as he terms it, is to be managed.

For instance, children arriving back at the community tired and

hungry after a long walk and expecting supper find it is time for a
lesson in self-control. 'They must stand for five minutes in front of
steaming bowls of soup. . . . Any groaning or complaining is treated as
a wrong answer.' The children, in Skinner's version, make a joke of it
and sing a song to pass the time. Later, the experience is repeated, but
this time they are not allowed to sing or joke, but must keep silence.
Then half are allowed to start eating, while the rest must wait a further
five minutes. This is supposed to eliminate envy, as well as teaching
self-control. The director explains: 'We set up a system of gradually
increasing annoyances and frustrations against a background of
complete serenity.' This he describes as 'a simple and sensible programme'.

Surely it is hopelessly naïve as to believe that such a system
would work. Experimental rats, we may suppose, are limited by the
world of their Skinner Box, and have little inkling of the experimenter
as the deviser of their world. But human beings are famous for
asking themselves questions beginning with the word 'Why . . .?' I fear
Walden II would either produce robots or find itself with a revolution on
its hands. Skinner allows nothing for hereditary factors; nothing for
personal disaster—say, the death of a parent while the child is young. He
knows no sense of the individual: for him one parent is no different from
another. He might never have heard that adopted children experience
psychological difficulties.

But it is not the efficacy of the means which Skinner proposes that
concerns me so much as the ends. He is totally confident that he knows
what patterns to indoctrinate, what kind of people he wants. This
strikes me as scientific arrogance.

Underlying all this is an issue of major importance, relevant also to
my own arguments. Are human beings born with a built-in plan of
development, or are they blank slates on which anything can be written
as Skinner assumes?

A plant or an animal has a built-in programme. It can become so
large, and take on a specific shape. We can stunt it, by withholding food,
or confining it in a small space, but, however much food we give, we
cannot induce it to grow larger than it normally would, nor can
we induce an oak to bear chestnuts. (Though genetic interference
may become possible before long.) Does man have a psychological
developmental programme as well as a physical one? Is he, so to say,
autonomous or simply the product of circumstances? Studies in child
development make it certain that at least *some* features of behaviour
are preprogrammed. New abilities develop in a well-defined sequence.*

Now, if man has a built-in programme, all we have to do is to provide

---

* Animal studies are also illuminating. Thus studies of bird-song show that some

optimum conditions and he will reach perfection without further help. (This is known as a normative view, since it implies there is an ideal pattern to which individuals conform in varying degrees.) In this case, we do not have to worry about ethical responsibility, or even about techniques. We just let nature take its course. If man is infinitely malleable, however, we are plunged into the Skinnerian dilemma. Freedom and dignity vanish.

For my part, I have no doubt that both factors are present. We do have to provide optimum environments, but we do also have to teach the detailed patterns when the developmental programme calls for such instruction. We are neither gods, as Skinner, nor onlookers, as Laing would have us believe. As ever, life proves to be more complicated than we supposed.

I have discussed value formation and the development of conscience at some length, because of their critical importance, but the discussion has had an academic air: I have failed to bring out how wildly disorganized is the home environment of a good percentage of the children in Western countries. Let us take a look at the position in Britain, which is probably not as bad as the worst nor as good as the best.

VI. *Children In Distress*

Almost invariably, parents feel completely confident of their ability and bitterly resent advice or criticism. Yet they differ widely in their practices, so they cannot all be right. Frequently, they are demonstrably wrong. For instance, Dorothy Burlingame and Anna Freud have shown that infants in the age range $1\frac{1}{2}$ years to $2\frac{1}{2}$ years cannot stand more than one day's separation from their mother without showing visibly regressive effects. Yet mothers who leave a child of this age with a nurse or a friend for ten days or more, while they go off on holiday, are not uncommon. Again, it is at least thirty years since it was shown conclusively that inconsistent treatment of a child is more damaging than severity. Yet parents who forbid behaviour one day, and overlook it as 'cute' another, are widespread. I choose these examples because they are particularly obvious: there are many more recondite ones.

Many people are surprised to learn how widely parental methods vary in the severity and type of punishment used, in their tolerance of aggression, sexual interests and the age at which they expect the child to achieve certain standards, e.g. bowel control.

We have far too little factual information to go on, but some useful

---

features of the song are learned from other birds, while others are produced even by birds brought up in isolation from their own species.

studies have been done, mostly in the USA, such as that by Sears, McCoby and Levin of the Laboratory of Human Development at Harvard University. They studied 379 mothers in two suburban areas, one mainly middle-class, one mainly working-class, in Massachusetts. They found that nearly half of them house-trained their children before the age of six months, whereas other mothers allowed eighteen months or more. The children who were least emotionally disturbed were those trained at six to nine months: 18 per cent were upset, as against 35 per cent of those trained before the age of six months. When the methods used to train were severe, 55 per cent of the children were disturbed. In other words, the biggest group of mothers was producing the highest proportion of disturbed children by their methods.

These mothers also varied widely in the extent to which they tolerated aggression to parents or to other children; 38 per cent believed that neither verbal nor physical aggression should be permitted towards parents in any circumstances, and another 24 per cent felt nearly as strongly, i.e. about two-thirds were non-permissive. Eleven per cent were quite permissive or completely permissive. A similar contrast was found with regard to sex.

What emerged strongly from this study was the coherence of the parents' personality with the methods of upbringing favoured. The parent who lacked warmth to the child and was anxious about sexual matters in her own life, was the parent who punished most, who restricted sex and aggression most, who asked more in achievement from the child and who was most likely to produce an emotionally disturbed child. (Though individual children varied widely in their sensitivity to such treatment.) Conversely, the calm, warm parent was more permissive, expected less and was more likely to end up with an emotionally stable child.

The other striking conclusion was that the working-class parents were considerably more likely to be of the cold, punitive type than middle-class parents. (However, other studies suggest that there are striking differences within classes: the upper section of the working class tending to be severe, the lower section permissive; while in the upper class the reverse is true. There may well be differences between different countries, and between rural and urban populations, in this matter also.)

Variations such as these are common even in relatively well-ordered families. The situation is obviously far worse in the highly disordered families which are all too common in the anomic conditions of large cities in Western society.

Sir Alec Clegg, the Chief Education officer for the West Riding of Yorkshire, and Barbara Megson, a former teacher now in his office, have done an admirable study of such children under the title *Children in Distress.* I shall quote from it here, because the conditions they describe can be found in most Western countries.

'Homes which are under intense stress may do more harm to the child than homes which are poverty-stricken or squalid . . . There is the child of the father who drinks to excess, or is a bully, or is in and out of gaol; there is the child of the mother who is neurotic or deranged or feckless to the point of neglect; the child of parents who never work or who quarrel or who seldom speak to each other; the child from the home given over to overt malpractices; the child who has by law been given to the virtuous mother, though it is the reprehensible father whom she loves; the home with conflicting loyalties; the home where there is prolonged illness; and, perhaps worst of all, the home which offers the child neither love nor security.'

To give concreteness to the word 'harm' in the above list, the authors describe a number of cases, of which I shall quote only one at length: 'When the boy was younger he was tormented by his father. The boy had a pet mouse which was the centre of his life and the father frightened the boy by saying he would kill it. After leaving the family for a time the father would return and terrify the boy with the threat of taking him from his mother. In consequence of this the boy is a nervous wreck. He cannot look anyone in the face, he twists his fingers and hands together as though in constant anguish, and is excessively frightened of any situation—for example, he began the term a week late, he is frightened of the metalwork room, he is frightened of being separated from his one friend, and if there is a lesson he does not like he doesn't sleep at night and is sick.'

According to a British report, some 15 per cent of all children need special care and attention at school as a result of stress at home; and D. H. Stott, the British educational sociologist, has made investigations which suggest that boys are more often disturbed than girls. But this is certainly not the full array of personality derangement; there are plenty of children who do adequately, sometimes even brilliantly, at school who show character disturbances in adult life. The casebooks of psychoanalysts are full of such material. Clegg and Megson, of course, as education officers, are predominantly concerned with those cases which present a problem at school, and do not deal with the wider implications.

The cruelty and stupidity of some parents passes credibility. One can perhaps understand the reaction of the father who is driven crazy by his child crying and hits it so hard that he fractures its skull, even while condemning his behaviour. At least the reaction is comprehensible. But what is one to make of the father who refuses to let his child have (free) treatment for a speech defect? Or what about the two children who threatened to run away and were visited in their appalling home by a welfare officer, to whom they explained that they wanted to go because 'Dad's always on to us.' It turned out that the children collected coal from the waste heaps in a mining village and sold it to an old widow for five shillings a sack. Dad was 'on to them' because he wanted them to charge her six shillings. 'But we don't think its fair to charge old Mrs C—— six bob 'cos she can't afford it, and he keeps getting on to us, so we want to leave home. We share the money between us and we think it is enough.'

Clegg and Megson specially note what they called 'the work-shy father' who lives on public assistance and odd jobs, most of the money going on drink and gambling, and the children being underfed and badly clothed. It is not simply that the father will not work: his whole personality is disorganized and feckless, and he is incapable of carrying through any sustained project at home either. Commonly these men have dogs, Alsatians or greyhounds, which are fed on meat. There are, also, of course, equally feckless mothers, who neglect their children while they attend bingo halls or drink in the pub. One teacher tells how the children of such a mother follow the teacher round the school, hanging about in doorways or creeping back into the classroom or cloakroom and huddling in a corner. 'This could be because father has been whisked off to prison, brothers and sisters have disappeared "into care"—or just simply because there is no real family unit in the beginning to give them a sense of belonging . . . These children often wander about all day, during the holidays, knocking at doors to try to find someone to take them in. In the end, of course, nobody will, because once they do the children stay with them from early morning until late at night and nobody even bothers to find out where they are, what they are doing, or whether they are lost, injured or dead.'

Poverty is not the cause of these conditions, though it may make them less tolerable, as Clegg and Megson emphasize. In some very poor homes one finds secure and cheerful, though dirty and disorganized, children. The most noticeable factor is the far higher incidence of such children in industrial as against rural areas—13 per cent in the former, 2·5 per cent in the latter, in the case of two areas studied by these writers. (They also note that rural children from bad homes are more likely to be aggressive, urban children timid and withdrawn.)

It seems to be the case that these totally incoherent families are on the increase, at least in Britain. Thus between 1955 and 1966, British official records show that there was an 85 per cent increase in children abandoned; children deserted by the mother, leaving the father unable to manage, went up by 100 per cent; illegitimate children for whom the mother could not provide by 200 per cent; children with parents in prison by nearly 50 per cent; children in thoroughly bad homes by 166 per cent; and children committed to care because of their own offences by 76 per cent. These figures only include children who could be traced. Meanwhile the number of illegitimate live births went up by 377 per cent for girls of fifteen and by 293, 248 and 222 per cent for the three year-groups sixteen to eighteen.

Clegg and Megson list a number of steps which they believe the public authorities should take, mostly intended to offset the effect of poor home conditions. But the existence of such homes they treat as a datum. The question I pose is a different one: how did the parents get that way? Almost certainly because they, in their own childhood, were wrongly handled. As has been said, the best way to make a boy neurotic is to give him a neurotic father, and for neurotic we can substitute many specific character defects, such as 'shiftless'. How then can we break out of the vicious circle?

Given facts like these, there can be little wonder if the adult population contains many disturbed individuals, some depressed, others incapable of affection, some obsessive or sexually hung-up, others antisocial or delinquent. Little wonder if we are faced with problems of alcoholism, suicide and mental instability. And the situation appears to be getting worse. Living standards may be rising, but social disorganization is increasing.

What is extraordinary is that so little is done about it. The cost of the social pathology is incalculable. If we add the cost of crime to the cost of mental ill-health, and allow something for industrial disputes, drop-outs from the educational system and other incidental effects, it becomes clear that this is, simply in financial terms, the overriding social problem. We need to mount a major attack on many fronts ranging from improving housing conditions to the education of parents in how to bring up children. We also need to provide psychiatric help and support as freely as we provide care for those physically ill. At present such help as is given to the socially disoriented is chiefly voluntary, and is inadequate. We only care for the mentally disturbed when they become a danger to others or to themselves in a material sense. Yet, as Alex Comfort has pointed out, attempts to deal with the problem of mental health evoke almost paranoid opposition.

We also need to do much more research, and to disseminate the results of what is known more widely. Budgets for research in mental health are a tiny fraction of budgets for research in physical ill-health (in Britain about one-tenth) although the number of beds occupied by mental patients is as large—to say nothing of those, far more numerous, who are not hospitalized, but are still liabilities to society. Mental prophylaxis would have to be the main plank in the new political platform which replaces Conservatism and Socialism. It is the overriding need of our society.

But I am suggesting much more than an operation in mental health.

I am proposing that we attempt to modify the basic personality structures of our various societies. Or rather, I am saying that unless it is feasible to do so, all hopes of creating a better world are illusory. If today, small groups are setting out to try to create a new life-style, it is because chance has modified their personalities in such a way that they want such a life-style. They will never convince those whose personalities are different that they should follow suit. And unless the training they give their own children is appropriate, their communities will lose their appeal and decay or disintegrate. Personality formation is the pressure-point for social change.

To try to change society by modifying the personality-structure of the next generation—a process which may have to be continued for subsequent generations—is inevitably a long-term programme. The impatient young are unwilling to wait for reforms and will no doubt reject it. Even more serious, there are those who may use knowledge about personality formation to create a tame and conformist citizenry. Communists already attempt to do this, and approvingly quote the Jesuit dictum: Give me the first five years and I will answer for the rest.

The question of how we are to ensure the wise use of man's growing knowledge of the springs of behaviour is therefore the most crucial question of our time. The political and educational issues to which I now turn are only meaningful if we constantly remind ourselves of this context.

The New Anarchism

I. *Right and Left*

In Western countries, there is a growing alienation of the public from politics. More and more people begin to feel that governments are blind to the issues which most concern them, or that they are incapable of dealing with them. The mushrooming of pressure groups—amenity societies, student protest movements, scientists for social responsibility, conservationists, abortion law reform bodies, women's liberationists, to say nothing of ethnic and nationalist associations, and so on—is evidence that government is failing to listen to the voice of the people, or, if listening, is failing to indicate that it has heard and understood. A striking example of this lack of contact occurred in Britain, when a site was selected for a third London airport after a survey of great sophistication costing £2½ million. Once announced, there was a tremendous public reaction against the spoliation of a fine piece of countryside within easy reach of London, much used by townspeople for recreation and by commuters from the city, and the project was swept away on a tide of indignation. Thus the government might have saved the country £2½ million if it had thought to make a far cheaper survey of what the public was prepared to tolerate first. As this instance shows, governments make quite different assessments of the relative importance of technological convenience as against amenity, from those made by those they govern.

Anthony Wedgwood Benn, who held ministerial offices under the Labour government in Britain, has recently written: 'Parliamentary democracy and the party system have in recent years been criticized not only for their inability to solve some of our problems but also for their failure to reflect others adequately . . . It is not only some members of the public who are disenchanted. There are people inside active politics, of whom I am one, who have long begun to feel uneasy, and to believe that the alienation of Parliament from the people constituted a genuine cause for concern.' Britain is not the only country where such doubts are being felt.

Parties of the right and parties of the left (I use these terms so that what I have to say will apply in every Western country, leaving the reader to substitute Conservative, Socialist or whatever variant on these terms he is accustomed to) agree on one thing: material wealth is the object of the exercise. Even Marxists and Maoists are at one with the Tories and Republicans in wishing to increase the gross national product as rapidly as possible. Wedgwood Benn, who is trying to understand the declining popularity of the Labour party in Britain, points to the fact that the central feature of all political argument in Britain since the war has been economic performance, and it has been assumed without question that a government that could ensure full employment, stable prices and a balance of payments surplus had 'got it made'. Defeated governments blamed their defeat on their failure to achieve these economic ends. But, Wedgwood Benn suggests, perhaps these are not the key issues? Since it is the core of my argument that people are deeply and increasingly concerned about the frustration of non-economic needs, and, since the pressure groups I have mentioned are all concerned with non-economic demands, I don't doubt he is right.

The analysis I made in the first part of this book enables us to see very clearly what is happening. Basically, we see a political battle between two types of hard-ego mentality, patrist version and the matrist version, when the battle the public is interested in is the battle between soft-ego and hard-ego mentalities. As the reader will probably recall, the patrist believes in preserving the status quo, believes in a hierarchical social system, is repressive as to sex and morals, thinks things are getting worse. The matrist is permissive, egalitarian, more interested in food and welfare than in sexual morals, and believes things are getting better. The hard-egoist believes in the struggle for success between independent individuals, the soft-egoist in a sense of community, in being rather than doing.

When we come to apply these concepts to actual political parties, naturally the position is not so clear-cut, for historical reasons. Thus in Britain, the hard-egoists gradually ousted the patrists from power around the beginning of the century, but the label Conservative (which obviously implies patrist) has been retained to disguise the fact that, like the Republicans in the usa, it is now a business (or 'success') party. Again, the British Labour party has a solid core of working-class patrists, whose minds are closed to new ideas, and are conventional as to morals, but who vote for Labour because they want a larger slice of the cake for themselves. They have nothing but scorn for the 'middle-class intellectuals' in the party management, with their soppy matrist ideas. In the ego-scale they are extremely hard-ego. 'I'm all right, Jack,' is a phrase coined to indicate the absence of group solidarity they display*. So far have they drifted from matrism.

---

* When a factory is short of orders, and the men are asked to spread the work in order to avoid redundancies, they often decline point-blank, as a shop-steward recently told me.

Many sociologists have commented on the reactionary attitudes of the lower-middle class, both in the UK and in the USA, where the 'hard-hat' has become notorious for his intolerant attitudes.*

It might seem a contradiction that the position we regard as the extreme left, namely communism, has become authoritarian. The original plans of the communists were, however, for an extreme equality and an extreme diffusion of power: every factory, farm and village was to be run by a council (known as a soviet) and the 'soviet union' was simply a union of regional soviets, in their turn unions of soviets at lower levels. But, as generally happens, revolutions started by matrists are taken over by patrists. Spontaneity and discussion are less effective in the crunch than discipline and a hierarchic command system, which is why armies are run in this manner. Patrists took over the new-born communist system and soon dematricized it.

Basically, the hard-ego success-oriented man (whether he be called Conservative or Republican) is against the big father-figure of the state, which tells you what to do, and on whom you depend. He is a man who has revolted from family dependency and obedience. He has also turned his back, by so doing, on the family group, and elected to stand on his own two feet. Thus he is against state intervention in business (Dad telling you how to do it) and still more against state ownership. He is against the share-and-share-alike of the family, where all the children get the same food and privileges and share the same communal services. It is not so much that he is *for* the price mechanism as that he is *against* 'paternalism', as he so revealingly calls it. The price mechanism leaves him free to make his own decisions, but if some other device could be found which would likewise leave him free, he would probably go along with that too. The price-mechanism does not, repeat not, guarantee patrist society; it does guarantee a hard-ego or success society.

Conversely, the Left does not object at all to the State, which it sees as a beneficent mother, not a tyrannical father. And it does feel that all should share alike, that all are equal, and that all depend equally on the maternalist state. These things seem natural, not objectionable. Mother knows what's best. Hence the passion of the Left for passing regulatory legislation and setting up statutory and supervisory bodies—the social equivalents of Nursie and the maids. (The conception is quite a bourgeois one.) But Nursie is apt to become a petty tyrant, and often regards her mistress as out of touch with nursery reality. She does not care to see the children grow up and challenge her decisions; she is in any case more apt to issue prohibitions than to make positive suggestions

* Thus, asked whether criminals ought to be flogged or worse, 46·3 per cent of lower class in the USA, 36·5 per cent of middle class and 8 per cent of upper class respondents said 'yes'. For the statement 'What young people need is strong discipline' the corresponding percentages were: 63·6, 49·1 and 8 per cent.

about what to do. The Radical ideal is beginning to look pretty old-fashioned.

Thus, while both Right and Left differ wildly on the patrist/matrist scale, on the hard/soft scale they are virtually identical: they both believe in 'success'. Consequently, the soft-egoists, who do not believe in 'success', are disenfranchised. The politics of the future, it is becoming clear, will be split on the hard/soft scale, with the materialists and individualists locked in combat with the immaterialist and group-minded lot. (The first thing the latter must do is find themselves a label: there is probably a bright future for an Immaterialist party.)

Politics is concerned both with ends and with means. And it seems to be part of human nature that the means often become more important to people than the ends they were devised to attain. They become ends in themselves. Thus we need to examine the means advocated by both Right and Left, especially in the economic sphere, since material production is their primary goal. The Right, as everyone knows, favours private ownership of industry plus the operation of the price mechanism. The Left favours public ownership and does not hesitate to use regulation to achieve the desired end whenever the price mechanism appears inadequate. It is interesting to ask whether their faith is justified.

II. *Ends and Means*

Since they differ so little about fundamental aims, much of the party struggle has to be derived from differences as to means, and specifically whether 'private enterprise' or 'public ownership' is the more efficient means of producing goods and providing services. In the USA of course, as in the USSR, commitment to one or other is whole-hearted, as least on the surface; tacitly, the USA accepts the need for public authorities to handle all activities not expected to be profitable, just as the USSR permits a certain amount of private enterprise where communism would be obviously ineffective. In most European countries, and especially Britain, the dispute as to means is more open.

The truth of the matter is that both these systems are lamentably inefficient: but in their desire to defend them, supporters praise them to the skies. It would be more realistic and mature to recognize that there is, on balance, little to choose between them (except, of course, for those individuals who make a good thing out of one or the other) and that we should try much harder to improve them or even look around for something different.

In Chapter 9 I described at some length why the price-mechanism, the key myth of the right, cannot possibly produce a rational employment of resources. Now let us turn the microscope on the key myth of the left, which is, in the phrase of H. G. Wells, the existence of a 'competent receiver'.

Believing that the private entrepreneur exploits the consumer, whenever he is able, for his own profit—and that he often makes excessive profits in doing so, thanks to quasi-monopolistic situations—the socialist proposes to put business activities, especially industrial-productive ones, in the hands of persons paid fixed salaries, responsible to an independent committee or to the government itself, and not to shareholders. The delusion consists in the belief that there is an adequate supply of technically competent, public-spirited and energetic individuals, sitting idle on the sidelines, all ready to come forward, step into the shoes of the bosses, and run the newly nationalized activity in the desired manner. Since there is, in reality, no such reservoir of skill, when industries are nationalized they continue in the main, to be run by the same people as before. In Britain, one of the coal-miners' chief complaints after vesting day was that the old pit managers were still in their offices issuing orders as if nothing had happened. They had expected them all to be swept away overnight.

The most senior positions are, indeed, often given to men from outside the industry—in Britain, during the post-war nationalizations, they were often given to retired soldiers, apparently on the assumption that they knew about large hierarchical organizations. Unfortunately, they knew almost nothing about wooing the public: on the whole, private soldiers have to take what they're given. (Many of the early difficulties of British Railways arose from this cavalier attitude to transport systems.)

Of course, in time a new management élite can be recruited and trained; the availability of men with technical experience is not a fundamental problem. The fundamental problem is one of attitude. Will the salaried administrator try as hard as the entrepreneur whose profits are keyed to his efforts? It is true that in industry, too, junior managers are salaried, but they have both hopes of rapid promotion and perhaps an eventual place on the board, with shares in the company, to spur them on. In civil-service-type structures, promotion comes to be increasingly by seniority, rather than on the basis of exceptional ability or application. It is a commonplace that the civil servant is reluctant to take decisions: if he is wrong, he will be blamed, whereas if he is right he will not receive promotion or a salary increase, because salaries are scaled. The civil-service-type structure, of which the British (and most other) post-offices are examples, can just about cope with a static situation, but is very weak at adapting to change, and even weaker at pursuing vagaries of public taste. For many years the postal services changed little in character: the technical innovations of recent years have revealed the rigidity and lack of adaptability of this kind of structure. Thus the British Post Office still employs, in its telephone exchanges, mechanical selectors long after progressive services have changed to the so-called 'crossbar' system, which is already, in its turn, becoming obsolete, and being replaced by the new electronic exchanges. The British Post Office is now making low-key efforts to adopt the crossbar system—a system already technically obsolete before it has even been adopted. Presumably it will not begin to think about the electronic exchange until that too is obsolete.*

Because of these limitations, socialists now prefer, as a rule, to put publicly owned activities in the hands of public corporations, which are made responsible to a minister, and are instructed to break even financially, 'taking one year with another'.

Such corporations, run very much on commercial lines, certainly prove more efficient, but British experience indicates that precisely for this reason they also commit many of the sins, common in private industry, which nationalization was supposed to eliminate, and because of their monopolistic position are even harder to control. Britain's Central Electricity Board is notorious for the many attempts it has made to run high-tension cables through Green Belts, National Parks and other areas of exceptional national beauty. It has fought cases against local groups formed to protect the environment with as much ferocity as private industry, and has not scrupled to attempt to push plans through in secrecy or to crush opposition by legalistic devices.

Again, when the steel industry was wholly nationalized, it sought to erect buildings, designed entirely by technical engineers, of such hideous character that the consulting architects refused to give their approval to the plans, and long struggles occurred, as embittered as any with the most reactionary private concern, to obtain some concession to the public interest in amenity.

A major failure in socialist thinking is represented by the assumption that such boards could be made accountable to the public simply by making them answerable to a minister, and by occasional debate in the House of Commons. Members of Parliament are not, for the most part, sufficiently informed about the problems of coal, steel, gas, electricity, railways, road transport, air transport, postal services, computer services, etc., to detect unerringly management deficiencies before they have grown serious. How could they possibly be? And how can they acquire a new block of know-how overnight, each time a new nationalization is carried through? The failure of the British scheme to grow

* It is true that the GPO was starved of capital by a system of annual budgeting, which prevented it from looking ahead. But had a parallel situation arisen in industry, dramatic efforts would have been made to change the method of budgeting. Until quite recently, the Post Office accepted this limitation and it was eventually changed more by outside than by inside efforts.

groundnuts (peanuts) in Africa should have provided the warning: it failed because of management errors, but this only became clear after the failure had become catastrophic. (The us Army's orbiting laboratory, which never got off the ground, is another example.)

We may summarize the defects of bureaucracy as follows: (1) bureaucrats are no more likely to be technically competent than businessmen; (2) bureaucrats, denied the pursuit of financial gain, turn to the pursuit of promotion by conformity to established views, and to the pursuit of status by empire-building; (3) bureaucracies cannot cope with the myriad individual decisions made by the entire population they control and are forced to apply blanket rulings and to treat individuals as equivalent.

The fact is, the solutions offered by both Right and Left are very poor ones, and the best we can do is to use one or the other as circumstances seem to indicate. Where the product is uniform and the distribution inevitably monopolistic, as with electricity supply, public ownership works better, on the whole, than private. Where the product is far from uniform, because tastes vary widely (as with restaurants) private enterprise is preferable, even though this means that some restaurants will be insanitary or will overcharge. It is the fact that both Right and Left believe that they have espoused satisfactory solutions which makes their solutions so very unsatisfactory. We have to work hard controlling both to keep them from failure.

The best course seems to be to mix the two, stirring up the bureaucrat with a whiff of competition, and restraining the businessman with regulations. (It would be nice to have two—or more—bureaux of Inland Revenue, giving taxpayers the choice of which they made payment to, and linking the salaries of the revenuers to the numbers of people choosing the bureau to make payment to. Naturally, such a plan would promptly be condemned as 'wasteful duplication'—but it might not be wasteful at all. We do not regard the Ford Motor Company as 'wasteful duplication' of General Motors.)

What inhibits us from using ingenuity to improve the social effectiveness of either system is our infatuation with the principle. Coupled with it goes the deep-seated wish to centralize. The junior passes decisions up the hierarchy so as to avoid responsibility, the top man feels that the decisions will not be taken correctly if he does not take them himself. This may even be true, but skilled managers know that such a course leads to overloading and so to more inefficiency than if the decision had been decentralized. Politicians do not realize this, and continuously erode the power of local authorities and of regulatory bodies.

It seems, then, that the 'competent receiver' is no more a talisman than is the price mechanism. Why, then, are the citizenry so obsessed by these myths? The answer is important. Each, in its way, represents an attempt *to avoid the need for taking decisions*, and hence incurring the responsibility for faulty decisions. If, under private enterprise, a firm goes bankrupt, we do not have to ask: is it socially desirable that this should happen? We just say: 'He couldn't compete.' (The basic inadequacy of this arrangement is revealed when obviously important concerns go bankrupt, as recently happened in Britain in the case of Rolls-Royce and Clyde Shipbuilders; in such cases, we have to face facts and take a decision whether or not to rescue them.)

The Left solution recognizes the weakness of this method but tries to minimize personal responsibility by selecting a small number of persons and giving them a book of rules to make decisions by—we call them bureaucrats. The next step will be to use computers which have been fed with all the rules, and the bureaucrat will escape responsibility by pleading: 'My computer told me to.' Computers will in some ways be an advance on bureaucrats, since they will be able to handle more detailed systems of rules, and hence provide more often for exceptional cases. On the other hand, they will also produce even more absurd results when situations arise which have not been allowed for in the rule book, to say nothing of the inevitable mechanical and programming faults.

Both systems abdicate humanity. Only the human brain can assess every situation in human terms, weighing the emotional and sentimental elements in the situation. We cannot, except at the price of inhumanity, delegate decision-making to machines or machine-like specialists. Instead, we have to diffuse it and decentralize it throughout the whole population. Only this is democracy.

However, the growing loss of confidence in government does not arise only from its obsolete ideas about ends and means. The institution itself is under fire.

III. *Loss of Confidence*

The growing dissatisfaction with central government as such springs from two main causes. The first is the immature and irresponsible behaviour of some members of government, not to mention plain stupidity and prejudice. When members of the House of Commons, 'the mother of Parliaments', attack one another physically or engage in vulgar abuse, they undermine the prestige of the entire institution. Members of Parliament (in any country) tend to feel themselves members of a club; they often forget that the retort which seems so effective at the time will look cheap when reported in the press next day. Besides this, they often expose their ignorance by entering into debate on subjects which they have not studied. (Thus, in Britain, members have often criticized public corporations for not doing things which the Acts constituting them forbid them to do, Acts passed by those same members.)

Worse than irresponsibility and ignorance is chicanery, a term I select to indicate behaviour which is downright unethical, especially behaviour which prevents the democratic process itself. The history of politics is one long series of devious political manoeuvres. Thus when members crowd into the chamber by pre-arrangement to force through a measure which, in open debate would have been defeated, or when measures are counted out on technicalities, the professional parliamentarian rubs his hands with glee at a successful manoeuvre. From the viewpoint of the public, such intriguing is merely despicable and serves to confirm their low opinion of the morality and disinterestedness of their representatives.

Elected representatives—and I have met many—are convinced that they are highly regarded by the public, and felt to be doing a solid job. They would be appalled to know how low they are rated in many quarters. Ralph Borsodi, in his *Prosperity and Security*, said that successful politicians are either cats or peacocks. Those I have met have almost all been peacocks—rather bedraggled peacocks at that.

The second reason for loss of confidence is subtler: it can be summed up as the belief that governments—and the bureaucracies which serve them—exist 'to do things to people'. In other words, the average representative has given no thought to the underlying principles of democratic government, or to the nature of the function he has been chosen to perform.

Parliaments are not executive bodies. Representatives attend them to express the views of those they represent and to learn what the executive proposes and to carry back to their electors the reasons adduced by the executive to justify its proposals. But power is selective, and Parliaments everywhere have sought to take on executive functions, with considerable success. Furthermore, in their thirst for power they have steadily eroded the process of local and subordinate authorities: that is, they have centralized power. They have also passed laws bestowing new powers on themselves, contrary to established law (e.g. compulsory acquisition of land, arbitrary arrest, formation of secret police or police branches). The main function of an upper chamber is to prevent the representative body from becoming too arrogant. Naturally lower houses seek to muzzle, or castrate or abolish upper houses.

The function of governments is not to 'do things to people' but to consult with the people concerning what they wish to be done, to enlist their approval and support for schemes which may be desirable, and to reconcile (not just to overrule) divided opinions, where they exist. Governments should be agents and mediators, primarily, not 'authorities'.

Quite to the contrary in practice, they work out their plans in secrecy. (In Britain, public officials are actually sworn to secrecy under the Official Secrets Act: they should, of course, be sworn to keep nothing secret.) Proposals are constantly sprung on the public as *faits accomplis*. The time allowed for the mobilization of public attitudes to such plans is often deliberately made impossibly short. Commissions of enquiry, *may*, but are not obliged to, consider such views—or if obliged to consider them, are not compelled to heed them. A whole body of law, subtly formed to keep the public in its place, has been slowly formulated.

One of the myths by which governments seek to justify their un-democratic behaviour is that of 'the mandate'. They claim, that is, that because they have been elected, they are thereby charged, without further discussion, to put into effect every proposal which may have been included in their electoral statement of intentions.*

In reality, many will have voted for them because they approved one or two key items in their proposals—there could well be other proposals which were highly unacceptable to a majority of their own supporters. Others will have voted for them merely because they thought the proposals of their opponents were even more doubtful. Frequently, people will have voted for the man rather than the policy of his party, in any case. The 'mandate' is a lot of poppycock, and it is adduced simply to justify omitting the process of consultation which is what democracy is really about, and which more humble men would undertake instinctively.†

The fact is, too many politicians and bureaucrats are not merely arrogant and dictatorial in themselves, but they also underrate the voter, or citizen. They think of him as ignorant, prejudiced or apathetic. But today citizens are better informed and more thoughtful than ever before, and many of them are increasingly irked by their inability to put their views forward. Many people have said to me: 'I do not ask for power. I do not expect that my views will necessarily prevail, but I do want to feel that they have at least been given serious consideration. If after considering everyone's views, the government (local authority, or governmental department) still feels it right to go ahead, then I will accept that.'

Thus, it is not powerlessness which irks the citizen (as is often said)

* For the purposes of this short discussion it has not been possible to distinguish as carefully as I should have liked between parliament, parties, individual representatives, and executives or 'governments', chiefly because the structures are slightly different in every country and I have tried to write in terms which are universally applicable. This also applies to bureaucracies.

† As Anthony Wedgwood Benn has observed, there may eventually be severe handicaps for a party which wins the election without winning the argument.

so much as being disregarded as an individual. This is even more wounding.

Political history shows us, in the West, a steady devolution of power from the initial dictatorship of a divinely ordained monarch, to a vote which became more and more widely dispersed—first from property-owners to all males, then to women, then to adolescents. This process was supplemented by the development of other 'centres of power'—notably the trade unions—capable of influencing government decisions. The growth of overt pressure groups is a further step in this long process.

There is no reason to suppose it is going to stop at this point. Power will become more and more widely dispersed. The question presents itself whether perhaps parliaments are not on the way out. Is the election of representatives a valid solution any longer? They were formed at a time when the appointment of representatives was the only means by which public opinion could be communicated upwards. Today there are better methods, and others could be devised, by analogy with the various methods used to assess response to television programmes in the USA. The voter does not merely vote for a candidate in state elections, he also votes on specific proposals (for instance, should motor vehicle taxes be used to establish better public transport systems?).

Not only is parliament an inefficient device for sampling opinion but it is (especially in Britain) unbelievably archaic as a legislative machine. From the time wasted in trooping in and out of the chamber to record a vote, when this could be done in seconds electrically, or the much greater time wasted debating measures which are dropped at the end of the session, and the whole issue re-opened next time, the system is pathetic. (This is another reason for the scorn in which the parliaments are held, and the pride which members feel in 'the traditions of the house' simply appears ridiculous to most of those outside it.)

Parliamentarians also incline to the error of believing that the way to solve a problem is to pass a law. But laws are meaningless if they cannot be, or are not, enforced. Often, the decision whether to enforce a law or not—or how vigorously—is taken by police chiefs who are virtually immune from public pressures. (This has been the case with laws against noisy or smoke-producing vehicles in England, among many other examples.) And, as the case of Northern Ireland shows, even the combined efforts of police and army cannot enforce laws to which such a determined minority objects, whether rightly or wrongly. Government is only possible on a basis of consent, and more than consent, support. It is the first task of any member to elicit such support.

The truth is, people have a great deal of power in the final analysis, a fact which is only now becoming clear to them. The future will, I am sure, see either a successful transformation of government into a body capable of interpreting, reconciling and harnessing that power—or else anarchy, followed by dictatorship.

IV. *Political Closed Shops*

If, then, the aims of the two main political groupings do not command assent, if the means to these aims are ineffective, and if the parties themselves do not inspire confidence or respect, the situation is dire. To make things even worse, it is extremely difficult to dislodge the existing parties. In every country, to varying degrees, the existing parties have seen the desirability (from their own point of view) of not letting any other party horn in, and have taken steps of one kind or another to make it as difficult as possible. In the USA this has come about mainly thanks to the inordinate cost of standing for political office, and especially for President. Costs are enormously higher than they were twenty-five years ago, mainly because of the need to buy time on television.

In Britain, the principal obstacle is different. Its nature was made clear in the 1964 election, when the Liberal party polled only a few thousand votes less than the winning party but obtained only six seats out of 316 seats in the House of Commons, say 2 per cent. It is perfectly true that a Chamber which is made up of a large number of slightly differing groups, and in which no one group commands a majority, tends to become the scene of intrigue and shifting alliances, and cannot develop a decisive policy. But this can be prevented by use of the 'transferable vote' system. The present system has the effect of producing a political closed shop; as a result, the existing parties can lose touch without losing power. People may vote for them 'because the others are worse' or may vote for whichever party is out of power on the grounds that it may undo some of the harm brought about by the party which is in. Or they may sink into apathy, declining to vote at all.

Actually, citizens, though they seldom realize it, have one recourse: to spoil their voting papers. Political managers are quite sensitive to antipathy: they expect an enthusiast to vote *for* his party—a vote *against* a party is something else. I cannot see any political party ever having the courage to institute ballots which permit votes *against*, highly desirable though such a reform would be, but they cannot stop papers being spoiled, and if they were spoiled in a consistent manner— for instance, with a capital P for paraprimitive—the message would be clear enough.

However, to bring about a change involves not only a political reconstruction but a reconstruction of ideas. It is not that people are against paraprimitivism, but that they are doing things which are incompatible with it. Existing dogmas have to be broken down, or the new ideas get smothered, like a plant among weeds.

V. *Wrong-Think and Non-Think*

Ideas have an extraordinary persistence. We continue to repeat shibboleths for years, then suddenly wake up to the realization that what we are saying has long ceased to make sense. At the moment, the Western world is just beginning to have second thoughts about the doctrine of economic growth. 'More is better'—or is it? Soon that slogan will seem as obsolete as the divine right of kings. But until that moment of truth arrives, change is impossible: ideas block progress more effectively than steel doors. Such ideas I shall refer to, with a bow to George Orwell, as Wrong-Think.

But almost equally obstructive is something Orwell did not comment on, which I will call Non-Think. By this I mean the failure of some sound ideas to get off the ground. A current example is conservation. For half a century people have been preaching the importance of conservation, or 'protecting the ecosystem', to use the smarter, chromium-plated term. But only in the past two or three years has the idea become politically effective.

One could write a whole book about Wrong-Think and Non-Think, with an appendix on Double-Think: a compendium of the mental rigidities of our time. It would have a long chapter on class and status, I don't doubt, and another on the beliefs of the young—such as that no one over thirty ever felt compassion or made any effort to improve the social system.* There would be chapters on Marxism, behaviourism, reductionism and so on.

In the section on Non-Think, it would contain, I foresee, a chapter on the coming revolution in our attitude to mental health—using the word to cover everything from insanity to racial prejudice, from sexual obsessions to loss of zest. It is inconceivable to me that we should continue much longer to treat mental distress as a secondary small-scale problem, and to devote to it such a tiny fraction of our resources, in comparison with those we devote to physical health, and to even less important matters. But it is three-quarters of a century since Freud began to undermine our inhibitions about looking squarely at these disagreeable realities, and in the meanwhile the incidence of mental stress has increased, the stresses have become greater. That seems about the right time-lag for the politicians to begin to wake up to the problem.

* Professor Henry Winthrop has written a brilliant paper on this last point: 'The New Clash of the Generations', originally in *The Colorado Quarterly* (1968) **17**, 67–80, and reprinted in his *Psychological Aspects of Community* (MSS Educational Publishing Co., New York, 1971). It deserves to be more widely known.

After all, the frustrations and aggressions, the lack of social conscience, do breed very real social problems (do I hear the words 'Northern Ireland'?) which politicians then have to cope with if they can.

Of course, I can imagine the reaction. It has taken since 1919 to teach politicians economics; it will take until 2019 to teach them psychology. And by then they will be under pressure to learn about the social sciences. For this is the no less pressing task: to understand enough about our society to prevent it falling apart under the pressures technology is generating. Social health is interlocked with mental health.

In the chapter on social health in my imaginary opus there will be an important section on the transmission of culture. All that we are, we owe to what we learn from the past—as is demonstrated by these occasional feral children who are brought up by wolves, and remain like animals. Some parts of the culture (using the word in the anthropological sense of the totality of what we know, believe, and practise and not just in the sense of good manners or artistic awareness) are transmitted, of course, by the educational system. Others are, or should be, transmitted in the family, and these are transmitted poorly. Often the educational system attempts to fill the gap, with courses on cooking, or values, or etiquette—but this verbal and conceptual learning does not replace the learning-by-doing in the family situation. At present, we do not even know what is being transmitted and what is not.

What is worse, we entrust much of the transmission of values to commercial propaganda and advertising, which corrupts and devitalizes it. (As Professor David Braybrooke has indicated: 'Corporations do subvert American values very extensively, in important ways . . .')

Society also demonstrates what values it admires by how it gives its rewards. Our society rewards successful producers of goods and services lavishly, both in the sense that they receive lots of money and, in countries where titles and distinctions are given, as in Britain, in this way too. It is much less lavish to scholars, artists and creators. The US authorities, for instance, never employed their great architect Frank Lloyd Wright on any 'community' project, though he constantly badgered them to do so. As Paul Goodman observes, in recalling this fact, few of the great men of our time would get past a personnel officer if they applied for a job with a major corporation. Bertrand Russell (prison record? freethinker?), Gandhi (prison record? unacceptable attire?), Bernard Shaw (vegetarian crank? socialist?), Picasso (unstable domestic life?), Churchill (drinks?).

Worse than this, society does not reward virtue. Truthfulness, integrity, independence, public usefulness, are not rewarded—whereas their opposites only too often are. Says Goodman: 'There has ceased to be *any relation whatever* between personal honour and community or vocational service.' Far from rewarding the good citizen, it is often the case that the good citizen is dogged by unreal offences. A US senator disclosed how a boy with an excellent record was refused for the US Marines on the grounds of 'bad record'. It turned out he had once been fined for a parking offence, and at the relevant time the car was in the charge of someone else. Similarly, a person who has been fingerprinted as a suspect and then discharged may be dogged by this for ever, if it gets on his computer card.

I cite these cases only to make the general point that many of the causes of social dissatisfaction arise from social incoherence of a kind about which politicians do very little thinking. They may be willing to take up specific cases of injustice, when brought to their attention; they avoid considering the social factors which bring about such injustices. It is their business to do so.

If Non-Think is the main obstacle to progress, Double-Think is the brake on the wheel. The businessmen who extol the virtues of the price mechanism while steadily seeking to bring about monopoly, or the socialists who try to present universal problems, such as pollution, as being class issues, are guilty of a dishonesty not the less objectionable for being only semi-conscious.

VI. *A Political Platform*

Politicians are disastrously mistaken if they think that the growing restlessness of the electorate is nothing more than the educated citizen flexing his political muscles. The real issue is the failure of existing governments to perceive that the old objectives are moribund, and that a wholly new programme, keyed to the concepts of the quality of life and the opportunity for self-realization, is being called for, ever more insistently. The old patrist versus matrist issues are reaching the end of their active life; the as yet unformulated hard-ego versus soft-ego issues are the ones which are coming up.

How can we make group awareness and group responsibility effective in the conditions of modern life? How can we substitute a psychological growth society for an economic growth society? How can we restore community and a harmonious relationship with nature? How, in short can we reorder our relations with nature, time, deity, other men and ourselves? These are the questions. On them, new political alignments will form, new parties will emerge, new slogans will flourish.

A cautious Scottish minister, asked whether he saw any prospect of becoming a bishop, replied: 'It is pawssible but not prawbable.' In the same spirit, let me summarize what, if we were wholly rational, we should do.

1 We should try to restore to our lives the 'soft-ego' components which are currently neglected.

2 We should attempt to heal the split between patrists and matrists, loosening up the inhibited patrists while restraining the excessively uninhibited matrists.

3 We should try to restore the elements of mastery and self-determination to work and to life generally, while increasing the consistency of the environment.

4 We should try to restore community and a functional status system.

5 We should decentralize authority and power, including industrial and commercial power.

6 We should seek to restore a sense of identity and resist the coca-colonization of culture.

7 We should mark the transition from adolescence to adulthood by suitable tests and ceremonies.

8 We should restrict the unthinking application of technological innovations and seek to moderate the pace of change.

9 We should change the law governing joint-stock companies so as to prevent pyramiding and evasion of responsibility.

10 We should cut down the legislative activities of governments and enlarge their consultative, supervisory and mediatory activities.

11 We should deliver a major assault on mental ill-health, both clinical and sub-clinical.

12 We should make a major effort to improve the general standard of child-upbringing, while prosecuting further research on the aspects which are still puzzling.

The list could be lengthened easily enough, but I am merely trying to indicate the kind of programme implied by the discussions in preceding chapters.

It can be seen at once that this programme is wholly unlike that of any existing political party. If it won support at all, it would win it from members of all parties, leaving the other members of these parties to merge into a new opposition. For, as we have seen, both right and left are hard-ego materialists, and in proportion as we healed the split between matrist and patrist, the existing party differences would vanish. The danger would present itself of simply generating a new split on hard-ego/soft-ego lines. To avoid this would be the long-term political objective.

This programme would of course be condemned as reactionary both by Old Liners and by New Liners. The proposal that stricter methods of bringing up the young be introduced would be especially unpopular with the noisy young. The restriction of technology would be unpopular with scientists and technologists, the decentralization of business would be deeply unpopular with industry and commerce, the reintroduction of the just price would be unpopular with the financial institutions, the restriction of the power of government and bureaucracy would be implacably opposed by government and bureaucracy, while the pantheist element would cause a frisson of horror in the church. With the possible exception of the snake-worshipping orgiastic sects in Kentucky, it is difficult to see who would support it.

And yet, and yet . . . This is the programme towards which, however blindly, the world is moving. This is what the 'system break' is about. These are the issues which, piecemeal and in isolation from one another, are being slowly clarified. All I have done is to lay them all out on the table at once and to shine a very brilliant light on them, so that they appear unnaturally black and white.

The world is groping for a new work structure, a new economic structure, a new social structure and a new psychic structure.

VII. *The New Anarchism*

But even an Immaterialist party would shrivel away as the new dispersal of power progressed—a dispersal which we might christen 'the new anarchism'.

The natural political form for the soft-egoist is anarchism. Unfortunately this word has come to connote violence—especially the violent overthrow of governments—thanks to the bomb-throwing activities of father-rejectors who attached themselves to the movement around the beginning of the century. But anarchy does not mean 'no law', it simply means 'no ruler', and the central tenet of anarchism is that the general will of the group shall be discovered, and that members of the group, surrendering their independence, will accept that consensus. Anarchists differ about how the general will is to be discovered, and in general underrate the difficulty of the problem in any but the smallest communities. The fathers of the movement—men like Tolstoy—were peaceful and co-operative and tended to think that everyone else was, or would readily become, as co-operative as they.

The vision derives originally from Rousseau, who held that a properly brought-up person would be incapable of establishing a tyranny, and concluded that a commune could elect a committee which would effectively interpret the general will. Thus anarchy, properly interpreted, is true democracy. Where Rousseau and his disciples went wrong was in under-estimating the difficulty of bringing people up 'properly'.

The success society received intellectual underpinning from the theory of the 'survival of the fittest'. Kropotkin argued that, in fact, nature displayed many examples of mutual help, and concluded that societies based on mutuality were just as biologically sound as those based on competition. In historical terms, the emergence of the absolute state is reflected by the emergence of the absolute individual. States necessarily deal with people as individuals. Thus the decay of mutuality led inevitably to modern absolutism as well as to the alienated individual. Trying to reverse the trend, Kropotkin demanded 'less representation and more self-government'—a slogan which we could do worse than revive today.

Furthermore, the decentralized society was pluralist—that is, it had many power centres: each concerned with a specialized aspect of life—work, health, education and so on—but none having power over the society as a whole. Thus the centralized state broke down the pluralist society, and 'disenfranchised' the citizen, giving him only a vote in lieu of participation.

Kropotkin and, still more, Landauer were naïvely optimistic: they did not see that a co-operative community can be as selfish as regards its own collective interests as any individual, and never worked out methods of co-ordinating communities successfully. They were also—being Victorians—hypnotized by the productive aspect and tended to think in terms of communities organized primarily for productive work. History shows that such communities end by acting like capitalist concerns—as happened with the mining co-operatives in the Middle Ages.*

If any society could achieve a degree of anarchism, in the sense of pluralism, decentralization and so on—certain functions would still remain for a central government to carry out.

It has, I think, a number of functions, some as yet unrealized. First, as long as national states exist, it must represent the nation in dialogues with other nations. Second, it must handle genuinely national internal issues, and allocate that part of the nation's resources which is inevitably national—the defence and police forces, provisions for government itself, a bureau of standards and perhaps the administration of justice and health services.

But its main function will be that of consultant and mediator between the dispersed foci of power, whether locally centred or formed for *ad hoc* purposes. It must see that they are accountable for the proper use of their power and restrained from abusing it. It must protect individual rights and freedom of information. More than this, it must discover its role as the custodian of the national culture, values and identity—a role now almost entirely abnegated.

* Martin Buber recounts the historical development of these ideas, and their perversion by Marx and Lenin, in his superb *Paths in Utopia* (Beacon Press, 1960).

To ensure that decisions are taken at the right level is, from the organizational viewpoint, the key question in politics. Those at the top see the advantages of taking decisions at or near the top; those at the bottom would like to see them taken low down. Who is detached enough to determine the optimum level?

Finally, central government will have to play a part in the as yet unsolved problem of supervising international foci of power, both inter-governmental bodies and multi-national corporations. Until the day, still far remote, when a rational structure of political power at the supra-national level can be developed, the control of such bodies represents a major unsolved problem, and their power a potential public danger.

But the prospects of achieving a real decentralization of political power seem remote. The pendulum is swinging to an extreme, as usual.

Just as happened nearly a century ago, violence is beginning to invade the new anarchist movement. As Michael Lerner, of Yale University, points out, in an important review of this trend, we have come a long way from the Beatles' 'All you need is love'. The Steve Miller band sings: 'Let me tell you people I've found a new way, And I'm tired of all this talk about love . . .' Two characteristics of this development, he says, 'are the scale on which violence is undertaken and the view of the violent act of rebellion as somehow sacred'. He reports that Charles Manson, who is alleged to have ordered the murder of Sharon Tate and her friends, far from being condemned, has become 'a hero and symbol of revolt' for some groups. The popularity of karate is based on this admiration of violence, and Lerner says: 'Ritualistic murders and the explicitly sacred violence of karate are clear examples of the fact that this transformation of violence from profane to sacred does take place.'

Anarchy tends to drift into violence, I think, because the failure to form a super-ego provides no controls for the impulses of the id. Only the loving heart can dispense with super-ego control. A balance must be maintained.

Violence leads on to refusal to co-operate, as in the burning of draft cards, which takes the movement as far away from the Tolstoyan vision as it is possible to get. The in-group, which has a strong sense of internal community plus a strong sense of non-community, indeed opposition, in relation to other groups simply re-enacts, in a changed frame of reference, the nationalist pattern exemplified by Nazism. It is a very disturbing development.

However, Indian anarchism has remained peaceable in the form of the Sarvodaya movement, thanks perhaps to its essentially religious base.*

Is it possible to resume the Tolstoyan ideal of peaceful anarchism?

* Gandhi, the father of Sarvodaya (the welfare of all) used this term as the title of his translation of Ruskin's *Unto This Last*. See Geoffrey Ostergaard and M. Currell, *The Gentle Anarchists* (Clarendon Press, 1971).

A system which balances freedom and control is only possible when the persons in that system have balanced super-ego and id in themselves. Violence will pervert any intellectually derived system as long as people harbour violence in themselves. The real area of politics is in the mind. At the moment, we face the danger of a soft-ego philosophy as exaggerated and overdone as the success philosophy which it is beginning to replace. Once again, I insist, the mid-position, on both scales, is the one to aim at—not in the sense of a compromise between opposing parties but in the sense of personal psychological balance. Boring as it may be to repeat: the Greek philosophers were right when they asserted that moderation, balance and harmony are the basis of the good life.

The Technomaniacs

I. *Introduction*

'THE walls of the room were pulsating liquid crystal. The input was from optical fibres and lasers, all from a computer in Des Moines. The host asked his guests, "What will you have?" One said, "The Bahamas." Another said, "Hong Kong." And one other said, "Paris—in the spring." The host (perhaps Macbeth awaiting the ghost of Banquo) said, "We'll have them all. We'll start with Paris." He leaned forward and pushed a button. And, lo, they were there.'

I can just imagine the rest of the story. Two or three weeks more of showing off this glorified magic-lantern to his less successful friends, one frustrating evening at a more successful friend's house (where they can get to Mars too) and then disuse. A mass of delicate and ingenious devices, to make which rare elements have been torn from the earth, atoms split to provide the energy, pollutants poured into some sink or other and thousands of hours of human thought and effort—and for what? The toy of an hour. Nor is this all, for when Macbeth finally *goes* to Paris and the Bahamas, the shock of novelty will be gone. For a genuine experience he has substituted a pseudo-experience, and by cramming pseudo-experiences so close together that his power to react even to pseudo-experiences is blunted, he does not get much value even from them.

But the paragraph I have quoted is not from some second-rate piece of science-fiction, as you may have supposed. It is put forward in an industrial magazine, under the brave headline 'Telecommunications: one World Mind', in the genuine expectation of filling you with longing for the wonders of the future. For my part, I would not want the equipment as a gift, even if it were the product of a growth-process run wild. Such dreams are simply childish power-fantasies, which the technomaniacs wish to make real.

The technomaniacs are beginning to fight back against the soft-ego movement in support of their hard-ego values. Thus the Southwest Research Institute, in its publication *Tomorrow through Research* declares (under the pseudonym Ned Ludd): '*It is time to unmask the Neo-Luddites. We have a duty to strike a blow for technological liberty.*' In support of this appeal, it declares: 'It is time we realized we are daemonically driven to seek the truth . . . Socrates put it well when he said the un-examined life is not worth living. The simple life is not worth living either . . . Scientists, engineers and everyone should put a stop to nonsense.' The arrogance of this assertion, quite unsupported by any examination of facts, betrays how unscientific and how emotional the supposedly rational technologist can be.

An earlier issue of the same publication asserts: 'We are in an age of neo-Luddites who seek to smash the technological framework of the future because the machinery of our times is going too fast for their feeble minds.' But if people's minds are that feeble, then why expose them to intolerable strains? Technology is for people, not the reverse.

The chairman of a British Airline and a Marketing Institute put the same issue more reasonably when he said: 'If we really wish to return to a pastoral existence or build cuckoo-clocks rather than expand our technology and our communications and our technology as a whole, then let us at least say so, and some of us wasting our time in the [air-line] industry can learn the art of ploughing or some other activity.'

The technological enthusiasts promise us mile-high cities containing a million people, cities floating on the ocean (or even under it), cities roofed over with Perspex—anything but life with space, trees, animals and time to contemplate—as if they really feared nature and wished to shut it out. They are misnamed 'natural scientists' for they are really unnatural scientists.

When, like Philip Handler, the President of the National Academy of Sciences, they say, 'Science *is* capable of fulfilment of our dream,' we must reply, 'God forbid, for your dream is a nightmare, and fulfilment of it would be hell upon earth.'

This is how he describes 'the American dream': At some unspecified date in the future 'the bulk of humanity will be gathered in megalo-polises, dwelling in huge buildings surrounded by parklands, perhaps covered with domes within which the atmosphere will be maintained rather constant . . . Each individual will have a private, pocket two-way television instrument and immediate personal access to a computer serving as his news source, privately programmed educational medium, memory and personal communicator with the world at large—his bank, broker, government agents, shopping services, etc. . . . The bulk of the labor force, then, will engage in activities currently classified as services rather than production of goods . . . Most of us hold such a dream in common . . . The most important thing one can say about that dream is that it may well be feasible.'

That is precisely what many people are afraid of. Handler cannot know that most people have any such dream. Only extrovert school-boys are taken in by this sort of Wellsian future, an ideal which is half a century out of date.

Ironically, Dr Handler puts his finger on the real problem, for he continues: 'Biological and physical research can permit us to refashion ourselves and our world . . . There is really no question whether man can live with his technology. The real question is whether man can learn to live with himself.' The answer is: he *cannot* learn to live with himself in a technologically obsessed society, *therefore* we have to limit technology. Thus the real question is: can man learn to live with the technomaniac?

The technomaniacs also emphasize the short-term or obvious gains yielded by a technological advance, while keeping mum about the less immediate disadvantages, and advertising and 'the media' disseminate this propaganda. For instance, modern communications are praised because they bring us so much information; but an excess of information confuses, unbalances input and output, and puts an end to reflection. Today, few people have time to absorb all they hear and to incorporate it in their thinking and feeling. We could probably do with less information, not more.

This can only be called technomania. The curious thing about the technomaniac is that he does not confine his advocacy to what he knows about, as a scientist should, but rushes blithely in where angels fear to tread. For instance, L. W. Branscomb, director of the US National Bureau of Standards, in an article called 'Taming Technology', declares that technology has 'dispersed power' whereas, as every political scientist knows, it has concentrated power, enabling governments to rule much larger areas much more closely. 'Individual privacy, far from being threatened by technology, is increased by the cloak of anonymity provided in the urban community that is, itself, a product of technology.' In view of current fears about wire-tapping, data-banks, legal obligation to answer census and many other enquiries made by public authorities, the decreasing power of banks to keep clients' affairs secret, and the like, such a claim seems wildly inaccurate.

However, even this writer concedes that technology is producing change 'too fast and without effective opportunities to debate its effects and trade-offs', though he avoids the implication that such debate might lead to a brake being put on technology. Indeed, he considers technology is valuable 'precisely because it has brought change', as if change were an end in itself.

Even more dangerous is the willingness of some social scientists to pontificate on social matters, on the strength of their understanding of some limited sub-section of the field. An especially depressing example is provided by Professor David McClelland of Harvard University whose book *The Achieving Society* is concerned solely with how to press still further the competitive, materialistic pattern of the 'success society'. He argues that, since mobility of labour is a prime requirement, we must undermine the family and accept high divorce and remarriage rates. (The possibility that family life might be as valuable as productivity, or even more valuable, does not appear to cross his mind.)

We must free children 'from traditional adhesions like loyalty to one's parents, which in a modern society may serve only to prevent a free and efficient flow of labour in the market'. Interpersonal relationships are to be simply cash transactions, and he objects to selling an article at a lower price to a friend as being 'a market imperfection'. He prefers factory industry to cottage industry because it makes people easier to influence by the mass media. He favours wars, which he thinks may well have a marked effect on the desire for achievement by removing authoritarian fathers from the scene, and recommends that, failing wars, fathers should engage in seafaring or other activities which take them away from home. (I suspect he would find, in fact, that this would not invariably increase the urge for achievement— but the main evidence he produces in support of this assertion is that Telemachus grew up into an achievement-oriented son while Ulysses was away fighting! What it certainly would increase is the incidence of homosexuality.) Other methods for entrapping people in the success society which he proposes include reorganizing their fantasy life by exposing them from infancy to specially selected fairy-tales (*Jack and the Beanstalk*, presumably) and later to other Samuel Smiles-type literature. 'A country, or at least a significant proportion of its élite, has got to want economic achievement badly enough to give it priority over other desires,' he says, apparently unaware that the remark is two-edged.

As political and economic prejudices such views date back to Malthus. As recommendations in the twentieth century, they appal me.

It is obvious that any attempt to move society towards a more rational position is going to come up against entrenched opposition not merely from industrial and political vested interests, not merely from popular ignorance, prejudice or self-centredness, but actually from the intellectual élite whose primary job it is to infuse a little reason into the boiling brew of commitment.

Of course not every scientist is a technomaniac or a nineteenth-century Liberal. But scientists are, in general, over-committed to what I have called the 'hard-ego' position. Valuing knowledge and objectivity so highly, they underrate intuition, emotion and the oceanic feeling. Many of them fear the contents of their own unconscious and have cut themselves off from it.

Professor Thomas R. Blackburn, a chemist, has conceded that 'some undeniably dangerous attitudes do exist in science's present stance towards nature; and, to the extent that these attitudes exist, they represent dangers to the integrity of human freedom and of the terrestrial environment'. Though science claims to be 'ethically neutral', actual evils have arisen from it, and, as Blackburn says, the alienation of science and scientists from the rest of the culture is beyond question. The philosopher Alfred North Whitehead pointed out forty years ago, in his classic *Science and the Modern World*, that scientists, in using a simplified model of reality in order to bring the topic under intellectual control, lose sight of the philosophical foundations of their enterprise. Blackburn suggests that, just as scientists have become accustomed to treat light either as a wave-motion or as a stream of photons, and to the idea of complementarity generally, so they must now learn to combine the sensuous and the intellectual knowledge of nature in a common frame of reference. Complementarity warns us that these descriptions, which seem incomplete, are only partial; the frame of reference must be enlarged 'to include both models as alternative truths, however irreconcilable their abstract contradictions may be'.

A few scientists, to be fair, are on the side of the angels. Not all scientists are mesmerized by the idea that technology is all-powerful. Thus, the eminent British biologist, Professor C. H. Waddington, writing in the leading science periodical *Nature*, has asked: 'Can we really leave the present to a few technological fixes and the forces of the market?'

Perhaps more worrying is a certain shallow optimism on the part of certain sociologists who attempt to interpret the state of society. Thus David Riesman, whose *The Lonely Crowd* made many valid points, seems to me irrationally optimistic about the possibility of a growing sameness in the world in terms of development and styles of life. He considers that the disappearance of exotic regional differences (by which he means the contrasts between, say, Brighton and Bali or Miami and Marseilles) 'will only discomfit tourists provided that the differences . . . cannot be replaced by differences arising from the still unexplored potentialities of the human temperament, interest and curiosity'. I simply don't believe that to be true.

In short, it is not men who must adapt to the storms generated by science, but science and technology which must adapt to man. And that adaptation means more than a simple limitation of scientific activity. It means that the scientist must learn to moderate his materialistic and individualistic urges, and to incorporate in himself something of the Romantic. He must at least learn both to understand and to respect the intuitive and emotional aspects of being human.

II. *The Pace of Change*

Most of our frustrations spring from the intolerably high rate of social change, which results from the expansion of science and technology.

Indeed, Professor John Platt, of the Mental Health Research Institute at Ann Arbor, Michigan, would go further: 'There is only one crisis in the world. It is the crisis of transformation. The trouble is that it is now coming upon us as a storm of crisis problems from every direction.'

Not everyone appreciates the fantastic scale on which these changes have occurred. Our ability to control disease is perhaps a hundred times what it was a century ago, our energy resources a thousand times as great, our weapons a million times as strong, our speed of communication ten million times as rapid. The growth rate is exponential. The time required for a new invention to spread into general use shrinks exponentially. It took 150 years to diffuse the steam engine, 50 for the car, 25 for the radio-set, less than 15 for the transistor. At the same time, change has become more pervasive. Not one, but many fields are changing today. With a lifetime in which to adjust, problems are soluble; when the time comes down to fifteen years, the impact becomes insupportable. The technomaniacs fail to see that the human life-span is the unchanging yardstick in the situation.

The technomaniacs point enthusiastically to the benefits expected to accrue as a result of employing their devices—but even if these benefits are as desirable as they claim, which is doubtful, we still have to consider the costs of making the change. Every competent manager knows that you must get a certain life out of your equipment. There is a point up to which the waste in scrapping machine tools or other equipment is more than the benefit of installing improved equipment. (This is an active issue in telecommunications right now). The social costs of change which is rapid in relation to the human life-span are enormous. Sir Geoffrey Vickers has pointed out in his *Value Systems and Social Process*: 'We seem now to be approaching a point at which the changes generated within a single generation may render inept for the future the skills, institutions and the ideas which formed that generation's principal heritage.' To the objection that a man's skills may be obsolete when he is forty the technomaniac replies: 'Then he must be retrained.' He does not see that this is putting production above the man. In all probability the man does not want to go back to square one, giving up his status as a skilled workman and becoming an apprentice again. Why should he? The satisfactions of stability in his life may be more important to him than increased material wealth. I am not asserting that this is always or necessarily the case: I only point out that in a rational analysis the psychological and personal costs, the social cost of re-education, must be made part of the calculation. For it is much more than a question of retraining a workman in an industrial skill. We are talking about changes which render whole life patterns pointless, which disturb value systems, create alienation, make life boring or frustrating or not worth living, raise crime and suicide and alcoholism rates, and much more. In anthropological terms we are talking about disacculturation. We are doing to ourselves what we have already done to many primitive peoples, plunging them into a technological world for which their institutions and values were unfitted. It is well known that this breaks a primitive culture up, leads to loss of motivation, to alcoholism and eventual total anomia. The invisible costs of change are enormous.

It has recently been shown that change—a new job, marriage, divorce, a new home, the death of a parent, even change for the better—adversely affects health. In a path-breaking piece of research, which must eventually become a standard reference, Dr Thomas H. Holmes, with the aid of a young psychiatrist named Richard Rahe, at Washington School of Medicine, arrived at results 'so spectacular that at first we hesitated to publish them. We didn't release our initial findings until 1967.' Assigning points to major life-changes, they compiled a 'life changes score' for thousands of individuals and compared them with their medical histories. Al Toffler, in his *Future Shock*, summarizes their results like this: 'In every case, the correlation between change and illness has held. It has been established that "alterations in life-style" that require a great deal of adjustment and coping, correlate with illness—whether or not these changes are under the individual's own direct control, whether or not he sees them as undesirable. Furthermore, the higher the degree of life-change, the higher the risk that subsequent illness will be severe. So strong is this evidence that it is becoming possible, by studying life-change scores, actually to predict levels of illness in various populations.'

Forecasts were made for 3,000 navy men. Afterwards, Commander Ransom J. Arthur, of the US Navy's Medical Neuropsychiatric Research Unit at San Diego, reported: 'It is clear that there is a connection between the body's defences and the demands for change that society imposes.' It follows that no one need be surprised that Western society shows rising sickness rates combined with improved medical services. Toffler's important book recounts many other evidences of the damaging impact, psychological as well as physical, of change—and its wide success shows, I think, that many people already begin to suspect this.

As Vickers stresses, the stability of primitive societies depends on the fact that their way of life does not disturb the milieu or society itself. Stability in this sense, he believes, 'has diminished towards a vanishing point which I think is now in sight'.

We have been going through a phase of what Vickers calls 'free fall', in which we have enjoyed the products of technology without accepting the vast network of control and regulation which such a system implies. 'The content of our political system—the sum of relations which we aspire to regulate—has grown and is growing in volume, and the standards to be attained have risen and are rising. The action needed to attain and hold these standards requires more massive operations, supported by greater consensus over far longer periods of time than in the past. On the other hand, the situations which demand regulation arise and change with ever shorter warning and become ever less predictable, as the rate of change accelerates and the interacting variables multiply.'

But while the clamant need for regulation grows, the capacity of society to accept regulation declines. This partly because the situation is not physically experienced, like a famine or a drought, but is 'a mental construct, based on uncertain predictions' because individuals are cushioned from the immediate impact of the consequences of change by state action; because minorities oppose the needed response, for reasons of profit or of prejudice, and above all because the time available steadily contracts. There is, therefore, in Vickers' opinion 'a wild and growing disparity between the least regulation that the situation demands and the most that it permits'.

And he adds: 'We have no reason to suppose that political societies will prove to be regulable at any level which we would regard as acceptable. Many species have perished in ecological traps of their own devising. We may have already passed the point of no return on the road to some such abyss.'

There are subtler dangers, too: thus we see industry, desperate for technological 'edge' on foreign competitors, hiring whole sections of universities, for all practical purposes—and encouraged by government to do so—a thing by no means in the wider public interest. Scientists themselves sometimes work to entrap science in the rat race. Lord Rothschild's proposals for making research the servant of industry in Britain, though well adapted to government's desire to balance trade and help industry, are completely disastrous from a social viewpoint.

How far-reaching the implications of a technomaniac society, how little they are understood, can perhaps be demonstrated by an example, one of several which one could choose: because of the immense complexity and cost of modern technological operations, the market system is breaking down. Large firms form mergers to exploit atomic energy, space flight, telecommunications, aircraft manufacture, etc., and governments actually encourage such mergers. Governments also finance technology: 90 per cent of the research and development done by Boeing is financed by the State. Moreover, the new technological power centres can exert considerable pressure on governments. Thus the 'free-enterprise system' is breaking itself up by its own efforts, a point which does not seem to have occurred either to governments or to technomaniacs.

A popular delusion among the young is that these problems will solve themselves under a socialist or communist regime. In particular, it is assumed that the transitional unemployment can be avoided. Nothing could be further from the truth. The task of stimulating consumption of new goods in a world in which more and more people are asking for psychological nourishment is just as difficult in a state-controlled society as in a capitalist one, if not indeed more so. To own the means of production is irrelevant, when it is not production which satisfies the need. It is even dubious whether the socialist state can ensure full employment in these conditions.

This is not to say that we should aim at a static society, technologically or socially; what I assert is that there is an optimum rate of change. That optimum is related to the human life span, since a new generation accepts a new world. It follows, of course, that the young welcome change. They have few commitments, welcome a choice of openings and have seen so little change in their few years that it has not begun to hit them. As one gets older, change becomes more painful and one's own powers of adapting shrink. One cannot withdraw from one's emotional, intellectual or even one's economic commitments. One has more at stake: one's whole life perhaps.

If human satisfaction is our object, to determine the optimum rates of change (for there may be different rates in different fields) and to regulate these rates so that they approximate to the optimum, as far as may be possible, is a primary obligation. As Professor Dennis Gabor (Nobel prize-winner in physics and inventor of holography) has said: 'We are riding a tiger.'

One way of limiting the rate of change would be to limit the number of people entering scientific fields. Today there are probably five million people in the army of science, spending $40 to $50 billion a year. According to Olaf Helmer, the futurologist, formerly of the RAND Corporation (the American defence think-tank) the number will double by the end of the century.

In short, when 'Ned Ludd' says that the machinery of our times is going too fast for people's feeble minds, he is probably quite right. Could we adapt—for, if not, we must surely slow down?

'Adapt' is one of those conveniently vague words. One cannot 'adapt' to falling out of aircraft, to breathing sulphur dioxide or to eating mercury, lead and other heavy metals. The body's powers of adaptation are very limited, and there are penalties attached. A man can adapt to carrying loads of a hundredweight or so, at the cost of fusing his spinal discs, reducing his capacity for most other jobs and probably shortening his life. He can never adapt to carrying loads of, say, a ton or more. Naturally, in millions of years of evolution much greater adaptations can be made—marine animals learned to breathe air and live on land. But we are talking about what one could do in a lifetime or two, and that is very little. Therefore, there is really no choice. We must slow down.

Dr Donald Schon, an industrial and social consultant, who gave the BBC's Reith lectures in 1970, declares in one place: 'Change is enormously powerful . . . and anxiety-producing,' and in another, 'Change must become a way of life.' In other words, we must resign ourselves to being in a state of perpetual anxiety. Why should we?

Bertrand de Jouvenel, the French diplomat and economist whom I have quoted earlier, has put it admirably: 'There is to my mind some absurdity in the exhortation we hear to adjust to a technological society. Why should we? Is it not more reasonable to harness the process of innovation to procure a life rich in amenities and conducive to the flowering of human personalities?'

'Throughout our society,' Schon admits, 'we are experiencing the actual or threatened dissolution of stable organizations and institutions, anchors for personal identity and systems of values.' He regards this as inevitable. We must constantly relearn everything. Thus to sacrifice man to mechanism is in my view pure nihilism.

None of the foregoing means that wanted technical improvements should be blocked, as they often are by bodies with vested interests in customary methods. Thus Schon has outlined how the technically backward US building industry mounted opposition to a Federal plan to foster research, and succeeded in neutralizing it. Not only brick- and tile-makers, but unions and even building-code inspectors were united in wishing to resist the use of plastics, light metals and other new materials. The metatechnological society is not another name for self-interested conservatism.

III. *Permanent Impermanence?*

There is an important distinction, often overlooked, between making a specific change, from State A to State B, and a continuous process of change. In the first case the individual has to make a readjustment: this may be difficult or painful, but once it has been done, he can settle down again. This sort of change occurs when we move house, get married, emigrate, or when a marital partner dies, and on many other occasions. It is quite a different matter to live in a state of continuous change. We are required to adjust ourselves, if we can, to impermanence, to change as something which represents the norm. But man's capacity to make repeated readjustments is soon exhausted. If one changes one's home half a dozen times, it ceases to be a home and becomes a glorified hotel suite. Emotional investment cannot be made in it. The impulse to improve, or even to care for it, is vitiated by the knowledge that the effort will be wasted.

This is the adaptation we are asked to make today, to adapt not to *changes* but to impermanence as a way of life. This is deeply damaging. Man is not designed to live in a continuously and rapidly changing environment. The adaptations that he makes to cope with such a situation are highly undesirable; they guarantee him unhappiness and undermine the structure of society itself.

Some of the effects of continuous impermanence have been sketched —as long ago as 1949—by the great anthropologist, Margaret Mead. She was writing with the United States in mind, but pointed out that the situation would become increasingly general all over the world. She made three main points.

(1) In circumstances of continually shifting secondary culture contact, accompanied by rapid technological change, and frequent new migrations, no stable pattern can develop. The child reacts by developing a '*situational*' approach to life. (Erikson has called this a *tentative* attitude to life, perhaps a clearer term.) Situations are accepted: they are not expected to last. So the American freely joins new groups, avoids becoming deeply committed to forming strong attachments, and so can withdraw without too much pain when the situation changes. Nor does he expect these groups to have a homogenous character, for he knows they have been thrown together by chance rather than by a slow series of considered decisions, as would probably be the case in Europe and, still more, in pre-technological societies.

(2) Since one does not have the time to make thoroughgoing estimates of people, valuations tend to be based on simple *quantitive* measures. Thus in some American schools, there is 100 per cent turnover of pupils in a year: so school-grades or marks must be taken as indicative of ability; there is insufficient time to form personal assessments of everyone. Similarly, in adult life, the status of individuals is assessed by dollars or the number of column-inches of press publicity they receive. Restaurants are assessed by their size, luxury or the tone of their advertising. This is what accounts for the American preoccupation with such externals as size and with conspicuous status-symbols, such as large cars. (Dr Mead mentions that a similar change took place among the Plains Indians when their traditional culture, based on buffalo-hunting, was disrupted by white settlers. Status began to be based not on known skills but on simple counting.)

(3) The child's perception of the outer world becomes *atomized*. In a normal society, the child is presented with a set of experiences which are culturally interrelated and coherent. They embody the same basic values and guide his perception in a distinctive manner. If, however, they are unrelated, or atomized, it is much as if a child should be shown all the bones from a skeleton jumbled up, like the parts of a puzzle. Perhaps these, like the parts of his erector set, could be reassembled into any one

of a hundred different designs? (The parts of an erector set have no identity.) Similarly, the child's experience consists of bits 'each of which may be given temporary meaning in any one of a thousand patterns'.

This atomization affects the child's perception of the world in ways which are hard to grasp without taking specific examples. Thus, knowledge tends to be seen as a collection of facts, which may or may not prove useful in different circumstances—rather than as the organization and interpretation of facts to form a philosophy of life. Hence what has been called the 'snack-bar' pattern of American education, in which the scholar chooses items which seem to him likely to be interesting or useful, and no attempt is made to co-ordinate his input into a meaningful pattern. (So much so that students nowadays resent the suggestion that any such regulation of their input should even be attempted.) Or again, the development of aptitudes is seen simply in terms of the acquisition of skills, rather than as bases for a way of life. Indeed, human beings themselves are seen as infinitely interchangeable: one business associate is hardly distinguishable from another, one marital partner is much like another in the long run, so jobs and mates are exchanged with a lack of compunction previously unknown.

Margaret Mead suggests that the steady increase in schizophrenia is probably a consequence, or at least a symptom, of this state of mind. In schizophrenia all relationship with organized reality is relinquished, and the patient retreats into an inner world of subjective impressions. I would add that the current preoccupation with drugs, which also involves a retreat from painful reality into a subjective world, is a further indication of this.

In Chapter 7, moreover, I showed how the mere fact of change—plus the specific effect of certain types of change, such as increasing mobility—creates enormous difficulties for identity formation, as well as changing the nature of the identities which can be formed.*

The psychological and social costs of impermanence are, in short, so high as to outweigh the much-touted material advantages and the short-term benefits. This essential fact should be impressed upon those who so irresponsibly blow the trumpet for technomania.

IV. *The Sons and the Fathers*

The ultimate threat which the technomaniac society poses is that it makes man insignificant; he is not only a cypher, he becomes unneeded. Thus, however glorious the technological achievement, man, as man,

---

* People *must* find their self-respect in their adaptability, declares Donald Schon, without first investigating whether such a thing is possible, let alone desirable, in *Beyond the Stable State* (Temple Smith, 1971).

has no future. Tenuous and difficult to measure as the sense of insignificance is, it is nevertheless vital. Technology is at the root of modern existential despair, the feeling that life has no meaning.

This feeling is naturally strongest among the young, who feel that the world does not need them. This is why they insist that *they* are going to build a better world—because, so far, no-one has declared they are needed for such a programme. This explains why the youth revolt is strongest in the USA: it is the most technologically advanced country. And it explains why the field of education has been the scene of so much unrest—because it is education that prepares one for the task. This is why the young complain that their education is 'irrelevant'. As the yippy leader Jerry Rubin has bitterly said: 'The American economy no longer needs young whites and blacks. We are waste material.'

To take part in demonstrations, sit-ins and so forth, gives one a sense of being wanted, of having something to contribute. But as the child psychiatrist Bruno Bettelheim has pointed out in a brilliant article, the problem goes deeper. Youth has always had to struggle for recognition. Today we have introduced new factors to the situation. 'I think it is unnatural to keep a young person in dependence for some twenty years of school attendance,' he says. For those who are genuinely attracted by an academic life, a minority, this may be acceptable, but today we aim at giving a majority, if not all, a prolonged education. After sitting passively taking information in for so long, activism makes an agreeable change. (And, as he points out, the universities do not have enough experienced teachers to cope with the flood, so that teaching becomes anonymous, or is delegated to young assistants who are little more mature than the students with whose revolt they sympathize.)

But while the young are highly developed intellectually, they are unusually immature emotionally. Their intellect has been developed at the expense of their emotional life and some 'remain fixated at the level of the temper tantrum'. They are often unable to brook delay, think rationally or act responsibly. In the most extreme cases, those who tend to become militant leaders, there is a loss of ability to feel, combined with paranoid suspicion. These social isolates are drawn to extremism because it gives them a sense of belonging and provides a confirmation of their delusions, thus keeping them from losing touch entirely with reality.

It is not unnatural that students are, underneath, bedevilled by anxiety: anxiety about their ability to make good in a psychological sense, to prove themselves worth-while individuals in a society which offers too few opportunities to do so. This anxiety is naturally intensified by a programme of revolution without any plans for putting anything in the place of what is destroyed. Secretly, they fear the power they say they want.

Some of the student leaders, in addition, are, despite their protestations of social purpose, driven by hate. As one of them told Bettelheim: 'Instead of my true emptiness and hate, I could, in the Movement, claim that I loved Man. I could think I was constructive and not destructive.'

Very much in line with my own analysis in earlier chapters, Bettelheim considers that the driving-force of the student movement is the rejection of a weak father. It is the world of the parents which is rejected in all its aspects. All behaviour, even clothing and personal hygiene, are regulated more by the desire to annoy the older generation, rather than by any positive sense of what might be desirable in itself. And if students chant the praises of Mao Tse-Tung, it is because they want a strong father, not a weak one. It follows that the older generation should assert its values firmly, even if only so that the young can have the satisfaction of rejecting them. Reversing parental standards is a reasonable ploy, when life is meaningless.

And of all the standards which need asserting, the most important are those concerned with sex and violence. As Bettelheim argues '. . . many children today do not learn to repress aggression enough'. Having failed when younger to create super-ego controls (by introjecting a father-figure) they find themselves unable to cope with their own adolescent aggression. Again, societies which do not practise some degree of repression remain wholly primitive. 'Without a fair degree of sex repression, no latency period; without latency, no prolonged span of intellectual learning.' This does not mean that we should simply revert to traditional mores, however. Too often, the decision what to repress is based solely on the convenience of the adult. Furthermore, it is adult fascination with sex and violence which enables the students to achieve the impact they do. Students can always obtain press and television coverage by nudity, or other acts calculated to shock, out of all proportion to their number or the importance of their claims. Thus they exploit, shrewdly, adult weakness. The moral is not that they should be less shrewd, but that adults should be more mature.

As a matter of fact, many adults are privately envious of the freedom, especially the sexual freedom, of youth and, instead of taking an explicit moral position, seek to copy their juniors, who thus become the leaders of society, a trend which the news and advertising media reinforce with their constant display of youthful styles and stress on 'trendiness'. These remarks are by no means an 'attack' on youth: they simply attempt to diagnose an existent situation, with defects on both sides. We need, not a reversal of the trend, but a constructive middle position.

Before we can begin to envisage a better, let alone a paraprimitive, society, we must cope with the malaise of youth, both because it renders individuals unhappy and still more because constructive social change is only possible if the next generation can act positively and maturely, instead of being frozen into a posture of protest, based on emotional turmoil and laced with hatred.

This implies major changes in the family and in education, coupled with the creation of vastly better opportunities for youth to contribute its energies and enthusiasm to programmes of reform. It calls for the issue of genuine (not conventional) moral commands by adults and for the proclamation of positive (not merely prohibitive) aims. It is far from clear whether adults today are, in general, capable of meeting the demands which youth—and, through youth, society as a whole— thereby puts upon them.

Bettelheim omits to examine the most alarming feature of the attitude of many young (and some not so young) people today: the chip-on-the-shoulder element.* It is as if they had been cheated of their due, and this had bred a resentment of all those not so cheated. Some, of course, *have* been unfairly treated, socially and economically—notably racial minori-ties—but the same attitude is found in people who have been favoured, and certainly have much less to complain of than their parents. One must therefore look for another explanation.

The fact is, the world is disappointing and frustrating to all, and painful experience begins when one leaves the womb and encounters the cold air and the traditional slap. Some people learn to live with the limitations of existence, even though they may fight to reduce them. They do not let it throw them. Others never accept reality; they remain immature. Western society, I believe, is suffering from a much more widespread psychic immaturity than ever before.

This is just one manifestation of the failure to detach from the mother and accept the father that I described in the second chapter. From an excessive patrism, a large section of society has swung to an excessive matrism. Spontaneity, permissiveness, informality are good, but one can have too much of a good thing—even of liberty. Discipline, self-control, order are also important values. The total rejection of tradition, of authority, of convention and even of consideration for others are, quite simply, 'a bad thing'. Society needs these elements too.

And just as we need to integrate patrist and matrist elements in the personality, so do we in society. The central question is: how can we achieve major changes without sacrificing all regard for the past, and changing into a mindless revolution which may leave us worse off than before? We need totally to rethink and rejig social aims, the structure of government, the work pattern, education, child-upbringing and much else. To achieve such a change in the face of inertia and opposition we

---

* The importance of envy has been greatly neglected, except for the excellent study by Helmut Schoeck, *Envy: a theory of social behaviour* (Secker and Warburg, 1969).

have to press violently. So, like a man straining at a locked door, we may burst through and crash full length on the floor. Obviously, we need to reduce resistance to change rather than to increase the pressure for change.

Currently, society is split to an unusual degree between patrists and matrists, between hard- and soft-ego; those in the middle feel baffled and helpless, out of sympathy with the harshness and materialism of one side, but also out of sympathy with the sentimentality and unrealism of the other. 'Realists' and 'do-gooders' mutually despise each other. The man in the middle receives abuse and blows from both sides. This is a socially explosive situation. But it cannot be resolved merely by political and social means. The problem originates in the structure of personality, and the way it is distributed throughout society. If we continue to ignore the processes which form personality, the situation is more likely to deteriorate than to improve. The possibility is that a period of chaos will be followed by dictatorship. This is not to say that the social factors are unimportant.

V. *Plans of Action*

As the French sociologist Jacques Ellul has argued, technology is not concerned merely with machines, it is the study of techniques—of ways of doing things. In order to do things correctly, we must suppress our emotions and personal inclinations. A pilot who worries continually about the dangers of flying or the state of his bank balance will have to abandon being a pilot. Thus technology restricts our freedom and as it becomes more complex and more widespread it restricts our freedom in more and more ways.

But since we cannot afford to get rid of technology altogether, we must employ it with discretion. (Ellul speaks of 'transcending' it, but does not explain how, and says he does not know.)

The usual human response to such a problem is to turn to political action, whether it is to impose restrictions within the existing system or to replace the system. It is my thesis that a merely political response cannot be effective. We know that people maintain their attitudes with great persistence because they are rooted in their personalities. You can neither persuade nor legislate a hard-ego person into a soft-ego one, and to compel both to a middle position would be even more difficult. Violent revolutions simply impose rigid patrist patterns on the rest of society, and the pattern is a rigid one. I am looking for a Utopia which is flexible, which can evolve and adapt to changing circumstances. Such a Utopia is only possible on the basis of modifying personality. Then, in proportion to the extent to which people change their attitudes, political and social changes can also be made to confirm and support such shifts. Like a climber backing himself up a cleft—and I want to remind the reader of this image—you must advance first at one end and then at the other. To advance only at one end leads rapidly to a disaster. Of course, a change in basic personality structure is necessarily gradual, in the sense that it must take two or three generations to produce an effective change—though as we can see from the speed with which the eighteenth-century license turned into nineteenth-century Victorianism, and the speed with which this in turn gave way to permissiveness, dramatic changes can occur within about fifty years—say, two generations.

When violent revolutions introduce new institutional systems overnight, the next fifty years are spent bringing the personality structures of those who survive into line, and destroying those who resist this process, or prefer a different life-style. This is a Procrustean politics, which fits the guest to the bed, not the bed to the guest. It is a costly and inefficient procedure, and one which seems to leave society as materialist as before.

Today, political régimes which are seeking to impose a life-style unwanted by the population also seek to 're-educate' or 'brainwash' or recondition their citizens so that they come to accept the régime, and we must expect that such techniques will become steadily more effective. This raises fundamental questions: if a population has been conditioned to like what it is in fact being given, presumably it is happy, and a mock-Utopia of some kind has been created. (It is a strange thing that many of those who object to existing societies because they subtly indoctrinate their members to approve the status quo are in favour of Marxism, which indoctrinates its members even more thoroughly and more crudely. This is particularly true of the present régime in China, which uses advanced psychological techniques to prevent individual thinking and to promote group-mindedness.)

While social change is, in my view, primarily the reflection of personality change, I do not wish to underestimate the importance of social factors in slowing or spreading such changes. And while changed people will soon change institutions and express new values, this does not preclude us from improving the techniques for making such changes. How can we know, for instance, whether a given institution is doing as good a job as it might, or whether it is organized the right way? Does our educational system block or assist the expression of changed values? We do not have the essential basic data: how diverse are the values held by the existing population? How varied are standards of public behaviour, and is such variation class-based, age-based, region-based, religion-based or simply a matter of chance? And what degree of diversity in these matters is tolerable?

Still more general, we know little of the key psychological situations:

how much time *do* fathers spend with their sons, in various sections of society, for instance? On all these and many similar questions, each country should be doing intensive social research. In practice, little or nothing is being done and governments seem unaware of the need for information.

As Anthony Downs, President of Real Estate Research Corporation points out in a stimulating article, 'New Directions in Urban Research', there is a great shortage of ideas for new institutional forms. Our real problems, he sees, are social, not technological—but he overlooks the conclusion, that technology therefore cannot solve them. In the words of the comic strip character Pogo: 'We have met the enemy and he is us.' Pogo was referring only to racialism, but the remark has a much wider area of reference. This is the basic limitation of the 'technological fix' advocated by technomaniacs like Alvin Weinberg, director of the Oak Ridge National Laboratory (for nuclear research). To recommend the use of a drug like Antabuse to cure alcoholism does not relieve us of the problem of preventing people from taking to drink to dull their misery in the first place.

The context in which the whole of this discussion takes place is that of a world rapidly outrunning its resources. To speak of limiting technology, of exchanging material for non-material satisfactions, will seem irrelevant to countries where poverty is widespread and basic services, including medical care, are few or absent. Yet there is no prospect of raising the whole world to the current US standard of living or even of nutrition, and by the end of the century, with another 3,500 million people added to the population, the task will be even more hopeless. It may well be that a measure of equality will be restored by reducing the demands and the material standard of living of the richer countries to something like that of the poorer, rather than by upgrading the latter. Underdeveloped countries are perhaps the only ones still in ecological balance with the environment.

Such a reduction is unlikely to be made voluntarily, of course; it will more probably be brought about by plague or war.

As the Club of Rome has pointed out, efforts made now to feed a larger population may only ensure an even greater disaster later. The appalling choice with which we are faced is whether it is better to let tens of millions starve to death now rather than hundreds of millions later on. Equally, if exhortations and programmes of population control are successful, this may encourage people to believe that they can press on with industrialization, only to bring about a disaster from the disruption of ecosystems by pollution. As Professor J. W. Forrester has demonstrated on computers, there are many alternative outcomes, in the present situation, all disastrous and escape from Scylla may mean running on to Charybdis.

It is for such reasons that the Club of Rome advocates an immediate reduction of 75 per cent in the rate of usage of natural resources—a remarkable recommendation for an organization which includes many businessmen. They also recommend a 20 per cent *reduction* in the production of food, coupled with a 30 per cent reduction in the birth rate (which would have the effect of stabilizing the world population at the 1970 level). Possibly even more remarkable, for such an organization, is their recommendation to cut the rate of generation of capital investment by 40 per cent. The reduction of health services is also recommended. It seems improbable that any of these recommendations will be implemented.

VI. *Ultra-violence and Revolution*

If we take none of the measures I have indicated, we shall have to resign ourselves to the prospect of a steady increase in the amount of physical violence. For, as I said earlier, the origin of violence is frustration: it represents a crude, immature attempt to cope with a situation, to achieve an objective. (It frequently fails to do so, either because it evokes counter-violence or because it wrecks the system, or both.) Since society is growing increasingly frustrated, violent impulses will increase; since social controls on violence are weakening, that violence will be more often expressed; and since more and more powerful weapons and tools are being invented, the expressed violence will do more harm.

Optimists often try to brush the problem under the carpet by saying: 'We have always had violence.' They point to the Renaissance with its lawless bands of *condottieri*, or to the garotters and Jack-the-Rippers of the nineteenth century. They recall the cruel methods of execution devised by tyrants to terrify possible imitators of the rebel or criminal or heretic concerned. However, there have also been non-violent periods and societies. It is really an unhelpful response to a problem to point out that it has occurred before. We do not neglect smallpox because there were epidemics in the past. Moreover, the argument is not wholly convincing. Though there were violent episodes, especially where people were in religious or political conflict, the 'mindless' violence and vandalism we know today were comparatively rare, and the inhabitant of a small village or country town might pass his life without seeing rape or murder, or robbery with violence, as we know from diarists of many periods.

Moreover, the future cannot really be compared with the past because technology has put such powerful weapons in people's hands. Two hundred years ago, it was impossible for a teenage boy to kill twenty or thirty people in an afternoon, as happened in America not long ago, simply because the rifle had not been invented. Still less was it possible for a single man to destroy a whole building and the people in it, or to wreck a dam or bridge. A level of violent impulse which was perhaps socially tolerable in the past is intolerable today and will become even less tolerable in the future.

In addition to the violence of the street, as we may term it, there will be growing violence in political life in the sense intended by the Marxists when they talk about violence, and this will necessarily evoke increasingly repressive responses. Already kidnapping of public figures, placing bombs in aircraft and public buildings, and political assassination, have become frequent: they will soon be normal. War, too, has become more ruthless: the limitations so painfully achieved in the first half of the century have been ignored in Vietnam. At the psychological level, too, more violent verbal attacks will be made, and the discrediting of people by smear-techniques, etc., will become increasingly ruthless and more general. Fantasy life will become more violent, and the trend will penetrate marriage, the home, industrial relations and so on. Violence will also become more sophisticated, and will seek to undermine not just a class but society as a whole.

Failure to curb aggressive impulses will be accompanied by failure to curb selfish and acquisitive ones, and we shall see an increase in dishonesty, pilfering, careless work, bad driving, littering and polluting, incivility and lack of consideration for others generally. It is not an attractive prospect.

When a society is sick in this way, it either breaks up, is conquered, or looks for a dictator to restore order. Thus we are on a collision course, and it is vital that we make a titanic effort to reduce the frustrations which give rise to violence, both the situational elements in society and the built-in aggressions which derive from poor childhoods. Unfortunately, our leaders have no inkling of this.

Marxism makes the claim to be thinking of the good of the greatest number, that is, to be based on love; but what revolutionaries preach and practise is hatred. To justify this assertion let me recount an incident at a seminar on the New Left in America.

At the seminar, a radical woman detailed her plans for society after the revolution. 'A professor said to her, "I'm just a shade right of far left. I'm not prepared to go all the way with you and will stay just a shade right of far left. How would you deal with people such as me after the revolution?" She replied, "We'd re-educate you." But he persisted, "I consider myself pretty well educated already, and I prefer the position I hold now. What would you do about that?" With hate in her eyes and ice in her voice, she replied, "We'd eliminate you." '

One cannot achieve the ends of love by the means of hatred. And the sad fact is, many revolutionaries are in the game for the revolution itself.

Faced with the great difficulty of changing society, students in particular ask the question: 'Is violence justifiable?' This is a nonsense
question. One must first ask: 'What degree of violence, of what kind,
applied by whom to whom, for what end?' To approve or disapprove
of violence, in a blanket fashion, would be as absurd as to approve or
disapprove of oxygen. Too much or too little oxygen, or oxygen in the
wrong place, will kill you; yet without oxygen you cannot live. If
violence is to be used to impose on some sections of society to whom it
is repugant a life-style which others desire, then it is being used for the
wrong end. What democracy is, or should be, about, is permitting the
co-existence of alternative life-styles, and the evolution of more rewarding from less rewarding ones.

I say 'evolution' but the change I ask for constitutes a revolution in
the metaphorical sense of the word: a complete transformation of our
ideas and institutions. In this sense, at least, I am for revolution.

VII. *Is Happiness Possible?*

Kenneth Keniston, the sociologist, declares that Americans have lost
faith in the possibility of establishing Utopia or indeed any better
society. 'Americans rarely if ever now attempt to construct an imaginary
society better than that in which they live.' I doubt if this is true, bearing
in mind the wide sale of the works of Lewis Mumford, not to mention
B. F. Skinner's *Walden II*, Reich's *The Greening of America*, Roszak's *The
Making of a Counter-Culture*, and so on. It is certainly not true of
those who establish communes or even of those who support Marxism,
anarchism and other theories. It is true, however, that Americans are
more cynical than they were, and, like Europeans, no longer think that
progress will occur automatically.

However, there are some people who take a profoundly disillusioned
view, such as Malcolm Muggeridge, who, under the slogan 'Backward,
Christian Soldiers!' declared cynically: 'Deliverance from happiness
would seem to be the greatest need of mankind today and the Christian
churches are an ideal instrument for bringing it about. The New and
Old Testaments are full of the hopelessness of looking for anything but
tribulation in this world, etc., etc.' But the playwright Henri Monther-
lant observes: 'Unhappiness is often merely a false interpretation of life.'

Of course, the word happiness is an ill-defined one.

Obviously, it is not the case that human beings can continue in a
state of permanent euphoria. Nor is a policy of simple hedonism
enough. The satisfaction of higher needs usually means the frustration
of lower ones. The satisfaction of conquering a mountain implies the
enduring of cold, hunger and strain. Always to do things the easy way
is to miss out on the profounder satisfactions—a lesson many people

today have forgotten. Greater convenience does not mean greater satisfaction, despite the advertising which tells us the contrary. But if we equate happiness with fulfilment, then to assert that no greater degree of fulfilment than we have at present is possible seems to me plain folly.

My fear is that the term 'paraprimitive' will be read by some people as meaning simply 'primitive' and that the concept will be attacked as just one more romantic regression to the past. (Equally, if I had chosen the term 'meta-technological', the technologists would have been appeased but others would have seen it as technomania in disguise.) So let me say once more, very emphatically, that it is a synthesis of the two that I propose. Some people hope for a marvellous, new, hitherto unheard-of solution. But there are no miracles in store. We have to make do with the facts, which are: man's primitive, age-old needs and his new, technological skills. The change we have to make—the only change which anyone can make—is to re-order priorities, to shift the weight we attach to different values. There are grounds for cautious optimism in the fact that such a shift does seem to be occurring. The ingenious Japanese are even trying to establish an 'index of happiness'.

If what I have said seems too simple, it is precisely because I have tried to keep it simple. I recognize many of the complexities and subtleties and no doubt there are others I do not recognize. But let's get the general idea established first, or we may lose sight of the wood for the trees.

It is the mistake of sociologists and still more of economists to over-simplify man—to treat him as a complex machine which needs only to be fuelled, maintained and programmed to function satisfactorily. And perhaps I, in my efforts to avoid woolliness and deal in the concrete may have given a similar impression. But man is immeasurably more complex than that. For instance, man feels a need for mystery: it is hard to imagine a robot doing that. His psychic life can be polluted in ways we can hardly perceive, much less understand. How can we qualify the effects of a loss of naïveté, for instance? How can we give economic weight to it, or seek to gratify such a need?

We can only say that, in a paraprimitive world, removed both from the stresses of competitive economics and those of an unstable technological environment, and only in such conditions, can man find time and scope and sensitivity enough to pay heed to these profounder manifestations of his mysterious humanity.

I have tried to write this book in a calm, detached manner, since anger antagonizes and confuses. But there is good cause for anger. The grotesque inadequacy of our handling of mental disturbance, and the repeated scandals concerning mental hospitals and homes, alone, would provide fuel for as much anger as is good for anyone. When we look at the steely complacency of many public officials, the ruthlessness of many industrialists, the arrogance of many of the young, the prejudice and indifference of many of the old, and, above all, at the self-satisfied mediocrity of those cats and peacocks we call politicians, it is a mystery to me that anyone can remain calm.

But to understand all, they say, is to forgive all. Dissatisfied or content, the rock-like fact remains that we have bought for ourselves the privilege—the burdensome privilege—of choosing what way of life we shall have. The intentional society is here. So we had better exercise that privilege or we shall drift into the nightmare-world foreseen by the technomaniacs: we are already well on the way.

Dr Edrita Fried, a psychoanalyst, describes how, during a year in Nepal, she met many Buddhists. 'Their own perceptions were important to them. Exploration of anything that could be seen was a source of joy. The men and women, small of stature, did not shuffle their bodies along but moved freely through the rice-fields and along the bumpy roads. Play, song, smiles, and joyful emotions were predominant. Nearly all foreigners who lived in this region thought it was a good life. It appealed to me because it was active, not in vigorous deeds, towards which these people showed no conspicuous inclination, but in perception, emotion, play, and among the educated, thought.' Which of my readers can say the same of life in their own country?

In any situation there are likely to be three alternatives: drift, return to the past or a new synthesis. How can we make quality of life, rather than power or profit or gimmickry, the criterion of all our choices? That is the paramount question for the next half century.

Notes and Sources

Prologue

The most authoritative account is N. Cohn (1957 and 1970) which has a remarkable bibliography, and on which I have drawn heavily.

Chapter 1—The Receding Utopia

page

7. Tiselius: Tiselius (1970).
7. Christopher Mayhew: cited in 'Feedback 13', *Ecologist* (1971) *1* (10): 32.
8. Allard Lowenstein: Duchêne (1970) p. 96.
8. Shannon Dixon: Mead (1955) p. 76.
8. 'system-breaks': Boulding (1968).
9. Arnold Mitchell: *San Francisco Examiner* (2.5.71).
9. Bertrand de Jouvenel: 'Technology as a Means' in Baier and Rescher (1969) p. 218.
15. 50,000 people attempt suicide every year: *B.M.J.* (6.2.71) *1*: 310.
15. E. Stengel: *Sociological Review* (1962) cited by McCormick (1964) p. 15.
15. A. W. Stearns studying 167 attempted suicide cases: cited McCormick (1964) p. 201.
16. Howard Jones: Jones (1963).
16. 'Midtown' study: Langner and Michael (1963).
16. Dept of Justice figures: cited by *The Times* (30.12.71).
17. Robert Redfield, *Peasant Society*, Wiesner: cited by Brown (1971) p. 23.
19. American psychologists Dollard and Miller: Dollard and Miller (1944).
21. Marx and Utopianism: see Buber (1960) for a convenient summary.
22. Maslow: Maslow (1954 and 1970), particularly Ch. 11.
23. Dobu: Fortune (1932).

Chapter 2—The Sexual Swings

page

27. Le Blanc: Le Blanc (1747).
27. Zetzner: Zetzner (1905).
28. For many further details of eighteenth-century morality, see Rattray Taylor (1954), especially Ch. 9; and for the women's side of the story, see Rattray Taylor (1958), especially Ch. 14.
28. Queen Medb and Princess Findabair: Briffault (1927) *iii*: 379.
29. Smohalla: *Annual Report of Bureau of American Ethnology* (1896) *XIV*. ii: 721.
29. child's identification with parents: Storr (1960) Ch. 6.
31. Trobrianders: Malinowski (1932).
33. convictions of a Brisbane man: *Guardian* (18. Jan 72).
33. Leary: Leary (1970) p. 107.
36. Assimilation between appearance: Rattray Taylor (1954) pp. 82, 149, 289.
36. Mary Douglas on shagginess and smoothness: Douglas (1970) p. 72 ff.
36. Addison: Allen (1937).

page
37. the picturesque: Price (1794).
37. he preferred dead and decaying trees: for a much fuller treatment of this topic, see Rattray Taylor (1958) Ch. 11, where other Romantic preferences are also linked to this one.
37. Piers and Singer: Piers and Singer (1953).
40. cult of the Virgin Mary: Briffault (1927) *iii*: 182–3 and 499–501.
41. Goethe: Hitschmann (1932).
43. Anthony Storr: Storr (1960) pp. 77–9, 80.

Chapter 3—The Success Society

page
48. tough- and tender-mindedness: James (1890).
48. Eysenck on tough–tender scale: Eysenck (1954) Ch. 4.
49. Ruth Benedict's studies of three societies: Benedict (1935).
50. Mary Douglas's success society: Douglas (1970), especially Ch. 9.
51. sense of unity with all nature described by Bucke: I give this passage in the version cited by Butler in his *Western Mysticism* (1922), which differs from the version in the us edition of *Cosmic Consciousness*, available to me, in being in direct speech. The indirect form reads awkwardly today.
52. Tennyson: see *A Memoir by his Son*. Tennyson (1897) p. 320.
54. For accounts of Christopher Hopper, Jonathan Edwards, Peter Jaco and Duncan Wright, see Jackson (1865).
54. he had many depressive attacks: Cowper (1816) p. 11.
55. Schuecking on 'moral hypochondria': Schuecking (1929) p. 13.
55. Sewall: cited by Miller and Johnson (1938) p. 391.
56. Coleridge: Fausset (1926) p. 191.
56. 'But here mid-way the *Mountain* . . .': Shaftesbury (1732).
57. 'the sense of the numinous': Otto (1925).
57. 'So unusual was the effect . . .': Mr Barrington in 'On the Progress of Gardening' *Archaeologia*, Vol. v, (1728), cited by Reynolds (1909) p. 252.
58. Paul McCartney, quoted by Miss Alice Bacon: Parliamentary Debate in House of Commons on Friday, 28 July 1967, cited by Leary (1970) p. 91.
59. French students: Durandeaux (1968) p. 126.
61. early Christianity relatively pantheist and father-free: Rattray Taylor (1954) Ch. 13.
64. notably anal in their preoccupations: Rattray Taylor (1958) pp. 157 ff.
64. association of protestantism and capitalism: Tawney (1926).
64. The Kwakiutl: Benedict (1938).
64. tendency to neurosis seems to be inherited: (1952).
65. R. H. Thouless: cited by Eysenck (1954) pp. 120–1.

Chapter 4—The Value of Values

page
67. Martin Bronfenbrenner: 'Economic Consequences of Technological Change' in Baier and Rescher (1969) p. 453–71.
67. 'Values are in dissolution . . .': Morgan (1968) Ch. 3.
68. three conversations often repeated: Neidorf (1971) p. 54.
69. Crestwood Heights study: Seeley (1956).
71. all placed Freedom at the top of a list of five values: Berkley Eddins (1971) p. 15, but see Rokeach, 'The Measurement of Values and Value Systems,' n.d.
71. study of the Navaho Indians: Kluckhohn (1946).
71. Florence Kluckhohn: 'Value Orientations' in Grinker (1952) pp. 83–93.

page
72. society is not wholly individualistic: Mead (1937).
74. Americans find it hard to look more than five or ten years in either direction: Mead (1950).
77. we actually lock them up: Keniston (1965) p. 319.
77. instrumental and institutional attitudes: Ayres (1944).
78. the battle between instrumental and institutional practices: Wheelis (1959), p. 189.
78. 'The prosaic mentality': Morgan (1968) pp. 81 ff.
81. Sherpas of Tibet: Fürer-Haimendorf (1963) Ch. 7.
82. For more on the anthropology of morals, see Ladd (1957), a study of the Navaho; also see Ginsberg (1956–61) and Fürer-Haimendorf (1963).
83. products of reason tend to be converted into articles of faith: Wheelis (1959) pp. 133 ff.
83. 'It is possible for super-ego values to be lost': Wheelis (1959) p. 165.

Chapter 5—The Psychological Slum

page
89. Ribble: Ribble (1945).
90. human beings have a 'need to be held': see Hollander (1970) pp. 445–53, and also Montagu (1971) p. 311.
90. a catalogue of human needs: Malinowski (1944); the hint was not taken, though a few psychologists have touched on the subject such as David Katz in the thirties—Katz (1937)—Maslow and Ashley Montagu in the fifties—Maslow (1954/70) and Montagu (1970 revised) Ch. 7.
92. 'the worst thing you can suffer in life': Townsend 'Isolation, Loneliness and the Hold on Life' in Josephson (1962) p. 331.
97. 'I really didn't have a job to do': L. K. Taylor (1972) p. 16.
99. frustrating nature of industrial work: the topic is treated much more fully in Rattray Taylor (1950 a) pp. 15, 29, 30, 34 ff, 179.
100. a yearly strike: Rattray Taylor (1950 a) p. 134.
100. Job Enrichment: R. Cooper in *Science Journal* (Feb 1968) and L. K. Taylor (1972).
100. Wyatt and Fraser's experiment: R. Cooper (1968).
100. money not the only motive: among many references, see also Herzberg (1959).
100. Rowntree chocolate factory: Hall and Locke (1938).
100. S. N. F. Chant's study: Chant (1932).
100. Cadillac experiment: Drucker (1947).
101. Blauner's study: 'Work Satisfaction and Industrial Trends in Modern Society' in Bendix and Lipset (1967) pp. 473–87 and Table 4 on p. 477.
101. Lewis Way on frustration of basic needs in work: Way (1948) pp. 22–8.
102. Schumacher: Schumacher (1968).
102. Buddhist belief that work has three functions: Schumacher (1968).
103. 'Life in western society is a new fatalism . . .': Bertrand de Jouvenel 'The Power of Values' in Baier and Rescher (1969) p. 219.
104. Eysenck shows extroverts demand more stimulus than introverts: Eysenck (1970) p. 110.
104. 'Many of the activities of the juvenile delinquent seem to stem from boredom . . .': Eysenck (1970) p. 110.
105. attempts to categorize human needs: Maslow (1954/70), especially pp. 54, 57, 271.
106. no hope of a challenging and worthwhile role: Goodman (1961) Ch. 6.

Chapter 6—Social Suicide

page

109. Lincoln Steffens' description of Paris: Steffens (1931).

109. 'The mark of a community is that one's life may be lived wholly within it': McIver (1961) pp. 8–10.

110. 'an assessment group': Rattray Taylor (1948) p. 58.

111. onlookers fail to help: Latane and Darley (1970).

112. unconscious anxieties: Bion (1961).

113. a new hand joined a works: T. N. Whitehead (1936).

113. *The Status Seekers*: Packard (1959).

119. Gemeinschaft was being replaced by Gesellschaft: Tönnies (1955) pp. 37–9.

119. R. E. Park: cited Powell (1970).

122. frustration of cats: Masserman (1964)—this was only one of hundreds of experiments in which cats were confused or frustrated by puffs of air, electric shocks, reducing the space in which they were confined or changing the nature of the response they had to give to achieve reward or avoid punishment. Earlier hundreds of similar experiments were performed with rats, the object being to explore many aspects of learning, neurosis, etc.

123. Durkheim's studies on suicide: Durkheim (1964) Ch. 5.

124. anomic individuals: McIver (1961).

124. to be richer than other people: Merton (1957) Ch. 4.

125. Tulsa study: Powell (1970), Table 1, p. 16; see also Dublin (1963) for a modern survey.

126. Srole demonstrated that a link exists between anomia and authoritarianism: Srole (1956) p. 715.

127. L. Radzinowicz: Radzinowicz (1966).

127. H. B. M. Murphy on frequency of depressive disorders: Kantor (1965) pp. 5–29.

129. phrase our aims in certain forms: Merton (1938) pp. 672–80.

Chapter 7—Who Am I and Where?

page

131. Inburn: Keniston (1963).

132. Blake: in Marriage of Heaven and Hell in Blake (1941) p. 195.

132. 'A state of mind which can find a social order remote . . .': Nisbet (1962) preface.

133. modern man's alienation from objects produced and process of production: Fromm (1956) pp. 127–136; see also Nisbet, op. cit., Mitscherlich (1969) p. 163.

134. people become alienated from institutions: Vickers (1971) pp. 116–34.

134. Franz Neumann's examination of the process known as Caesarism in: Stein (*et al.*) (1960) pp. 269–290.

135. alienation from 'mystery of being': Winthrop (1971) p. 10.

135. 'estranged from himself . . .': Fromm (1956) p. 120, see also Winthrop (1971) p. 8.

135. man is a thing: Fromm (1956) p. 124.

136. Erikson: see especially Erikson (1971) and his contribution to Stein, Vidich and White (1960) pp. 37–87.

138. Way: Way (1948).

140. Wheelis on identity: Wheelis (1959) p. 20.

141. 'The social character now coming to prevail . . .': Wheelis (1959) p. 85.

141. 'Not knowing what he stands for, he does not know what he is': Wheelis (1959) p. 129.

141. Margaret Mead's observation that culture is becoming homogenized: Stein *et al.* (1960) pp. 96–7.

page

144. Sir Geoffrey Vickers' belief we are nearing end of period of 'free fall': Vickers (1968), especially Ch. 4.
144. personal integrity dependent on being able to will: James (1890) p. 458.
144. Wheelis on weakening of the will: Wheelis (1959) pp. 43–4.
145. Identity of an orphaned American-born girl: Erikson 'The Problem of Ego Identity' in Stein (1960) p. 61.
146. rites de passage: see Briffault (1927).
147. Frankl's study at Vienna Polyclinic: Frankl (1964) pp. 109–110.
148. 'The question which faces every man . . .' Lin (1939) p. 127.
148. 'To commit allegiance . . .' Wheelis (1959) p. 87.
149. the meaning of life: Frankl (1964) pp. 109–10.
149. 'an unbridled lucidity can destroy our understanding . . .' Polanyi (1958) Ch. 1.

Chapter 8—The Paraprimitive Society

page

154. solar power sources: see Daniels, F. (1970).
155. paraprimitive society: Rattray Taylor (1949a), p. 237.
160. trivia: see Papanek (1972).
161. a saving of at least $2,000m. a year: Lave and Seskin (1970) pp. 723–31.
162. one of Ralph Nader's staff: Jacobs (1972) p. 45.
163. Julien G.: Durandeaux (1968) p. 13 (my translation).
163. Education has three aspects: Mitscherlich (1969) Ch. 2.
164. 'the answer is that we have been miseducated . . .': Montagu (1970) p. 299.
164. James Clark Moloney: Montagu (1970) p. 246.
165. Julien G: Durandeaux (1968) p. 13 (my translation).
166. The Barns Experiment: Wills (1945).
169. W. B. Reddaway: Reddaway (1939)—he thought the population of the United Kingdom would fall 20 per cent in each successive generation!

Chapter 9—The Rat Race

page

172. 'It is progressively harder for industry . . .': Schon (1967) p. 198.
173. dangers of breathing asbestos dust: Rattray Taylor (1970) pp. 122–7.
173. short weight and U.S. Dept of Defense is overcharged: Jacobs (1972) p. 45
177. a blacksmith would refuse higher payment: Bourne (1923) Ch. 37—indeed the customary price was adhered to even when inflation had made it wholly unprofitable.
177. externalities: for a detailed review, see Goldman (1967).
179. price-mechanism: Rattray Taylor (1947) Ch. 6.
180. Canada is becoming the largest producer of sulphur: Anonymous (1972) 'Sky-rocketing sulphur stock-piles'.
181. A.T. & T.: Goulden (1970).
183. French peasants offered glasses of water: or would only sell bottled water at exorbitant prices: *War Diaries* cited by *The Sunday Times* (19 March 1972).
187. self-perpetuating nature of large concerns: Townsend (1972) pp. 27–38.
187. T. K. Quinn: cited by Townsend (1972) p. 33.
189. Boimondau: Rattray Taylor (1949b) p. 70–7.
190. W. J. C. Plumb: cited by Gillman and Woolf (1972) p. 37.
190. economic activities always take place within legal framework: Mishan (1969) Ch. 5.

Chapter 10—Citizens of Utopia

page

192. Zuñi Indians: Bunzel (1929730) p. 480.

192. the American character in 1888: Bryce (1914–15 revised) p. 293.

192. the six traits rated highest: Hunt (1935–6) pp. 222–4.

192. Marquesas Islands: Suggs (1966).

194. different upbringings may account for behavioural differences: Kardiner (1944).

194. Kardiner and some of those who took up his ideas: see, for instance, Haring (1949).

195. societies vary widely in treatment of children: Mead (1950).

196. the tendency to neurosis, no less, is inherited: Eysenck (1952).

196. absence of the father: Biller (1971).

196. father is absent in 10 per cent of all families: Herzog and India (1970).

198. tough/tender dichotomy: Eysenck (1954) Ch. 4.

198. heredity accounts for 70–80 per cent of the effect: McLeod cited by Eysenck (1954) Ch. 6.

199. societies with low father availability have higher rate of crime than average: Bacon, Child and Barry (1963) pp. 291–300, cited by Biller (1971).

200. Cambridge Somerville Youth Study: McCord (1959).

201. study of aggressive delinquent boys: Bandura and Walters (1959) Ch. 7.

201. 'conscienceless psychopath': Greenacre (1953) and also see Aichhorn (1936).

202. Neil and William Smelser's study of 253 boys: Smelser (1963) pp. 200–2.

202. article by U. Bronfenbrenner: cited by Smelser (1963) p. 353.

203. 'stimulus hunger' is hereditary: shown by McLeod and cited by Eysenck (1954).

203. lower class have less effective consciences than persons of middle class: Spinley (1953).

206. R. D. Laing: Laing (1965); see Holbrook (1968) p. 35 ff. for an excellent critique.

206. Laing quoting Henry: Cranston (1970) pp. 179 ff. and p. 182 for quotation by Henry.

207. *The Bird of Paradise*: Laing (1967).

207. The mad are sane and the sane mad: an argument put still more strongly by Szasz (1971).

209. Dorothy Burlingame and Anna Freud: *Monthly Reports, Hampstead Nurseries* (May 1944) (unpublished) cited Bowlby (1952) p. 21.

211. D. H. Stott: cited Clegg and Megson (1968) p. 19.

212. far higher incidence of such children in industrial as against rural areas: Clegg and Megson (1968) p. 49.

212. increases in abandonment of British children: Clegg and Megson (1968) p. 79.

Chapter 11—The New Anarchism

page

216. asked whether criminals ought to be flogged: Langner and Michael (1963) Table 16.8, p. 465; see also Spinley (1953).

219. accountability to Parliament: Rattray Taylor (1950b).

227. 'Corporations do subvert' . . .: Braybrooke 'Skepticism of Wants' in Hook (1967) p. 225.

231. 'Less representation and more self-government': Kropotkin (1912).

231. such communities end by acting like capitalist concerns: Buber (1960)—Buber recounts the historical development of these ideas, and their perversion by Marx and Lenin.

page
232. Lerner: 'Anarchism and the American Counter Culture' in Apter and Joll (1971) pp. 34–59, quoting part of 'Space Cowboy' by the Steve Miller Band.

Chapter 12—The Technomaniacs

page
234. 'The walls of the room were pulsating liquid crystal . . .': *Kaiser News* (c) (1971).
234. *Tomorrow Through Research*: an unsigned article in this publication produced by the S.W. Institute of Research, San Antonio, Texas (Autumn 1970).
235. Chairman of British airline: Adam Thomson cited in *The Times* (9 Feb 1971).
236. the competitive, materialistic pattern of the 'success society': McClelland (1961) Ch. 5.
237. 'want economic achievement badly enough . . .': McClelland (1961) p. 430.
238. 'Some undeniably dangerous attitudes do exist in science's present stance . . .': Blackburn (1971) p. 1004.
238. C. H. Waddington: Waddington (1972).
239. skills, institutions and ideas for the future may be rendered inept: Vickers (1968) pp. 77–78.
240. Thomas H. Homes and Richard Rahe: Toffler (1970) pp. 291–5.
240. Vickers: Vickers (1968) pp. 77–8, 80.
242. D. Gabor: Gabor (1958).
242. $40 to $50 billion: de Closets (1970).
243. Bertrand de Jouvenel: 'Technology as a Means' in Baier and Rescher (1969) p. 232.
243. conservatism in U.S. building industry: Schon (1971) pp. 245–6.
244. Margaret Mead on continuous impermanence: 'Culture Change and Character Structure' in Stein (1960) p. 95.
245. People must find their self-respect in their adaptability: Schon (1971).
246. Jerry Rubin: 'An Emergency Letter etc.' in the *New York Review of Books* (13 Feb 1969) cited Bettelheim (1969)
249. technology is not concerned merely with machines: Ellul (1965).
251. technological fixes: see Etzioni and Remp (1972).
251. Club of Rome: 'Shock evaluation of National Programs' in *International Associations* (Oct 1971) *23* (8): 478–81; see also Meadows (1972) for a report for the Club of Rome's project on the predicament of mankind.
254. 'we'd eliminate you . . .': George Morrone in a letter to *Playboy* (Jan 1972).
254. Americans have lost faith in the possibility of establishing Utopia: Keniston (1965) p. 297 ff.
254. 'Deliverance from happiness . . .': Muggeridge (1967) pp. 159–60.
256. she met many Buddhists: Fried (1970) Preface.

Bibliography

ANON. 1971. 'Crystal Set' in 'Telecommunications: One World Mind' issue of *Kaiser News* (c) (published by Kaiser Aluminium and Chemical Corp., Oakland, California).

ANON. 1972. 'Sky-rocketing Sulphur Stock-piles', *Science Dimension 4* (1): 10–16.

AICHHORN, A. 1936. *Wayward Youth*. Putnam, London.

ALLEN, B. S. 1937. *Tides in English Taste 1619–1800*. Harvard U.P., Mass.

ANNUAL REPORT OF BUREAU OF AMERICAN ETHNOLOGY. 1896. Vol XIV, ii: 721.

APTER, D. E. and JOLL, J. E. (eds) 1971. *Anarchism Today*. Macmillan, London.

ARONFREED, J. 1968. *Conduct and Conscience*. Academic Press, N.Y.

AYRES, C. 1944. *Theory of Economic Progress*. University of North Carolina, Chapel Hill, N.C.

BACON, M., CHILD, I. L. and BARRY, H. 1963. 'A Cross-cultural Study of Correlatives of Crime', *Journal of Abnormal and Social Psychology 66*: 291–300.

BAIER, K. and RESCHER, B. (eds). 1969. *Values and the Future: The Impact of Technological Change on American Values*. The Free Press, N.Y.

BANDURA A. and WALTERS, R. 1959. *Adolescent Aggression*. Ronald, N.Y.

BENDIX, R. and LIPSET, S. M. 1967. *Class Status and Power: Social Stratification in Comparative Perspective*. Routledge and Kegan Paul, London.

BENEDICT, RUTH. 1938. *Patterns of Culture*. Routledge, London.

BETTELHEIM, BRUNO. Sept 1969. 'Obsolete Youth', *Encounter XXXIII* (3): 39.

BION, W. R. 1961. *Experiences in Groups and Other Papers*. Tavistock Publications, London.

BILLER, H. B. 1971. *Father, Child and Sex Role: Paternal Determinants of Personality Development*. Heath Lexington Books, Lexington, Mass.

BLACKBURN, T. R. 4 June 1971. 'Sensuous-Intellectual Complementarity in Science', *Science 172* (3987): 1003–7.

BLAKE, W. 1932. *Poetry and Prose of William Blake*. (ed. G. KEYNES) Nonesuch Press, London.

BORSODI, R. 1938. *Prosperity and Security*. Harper and Row, N.Y.

BOULDING, K. 1968. *Beyond Economics*. University of Michigan Press, Ann Arbor, Michigan.

BOURNE, G. (i.e. STURT, G.). *The Wheelwright's Shop*. Cambridge U.P., Cambridge.

BOWLBY, JOHN. 1952. *Maternal Care and Mental Health*. W.H.O. Monograph No. 2. Geneva.

BRANSCOMB, L. W. 12 March 1971. 'Taming Technology', *Science 171*: 972–979.

BRAYBROOKE, D. 1967. 'Skepticism of Wants', in HOOK, S. (q.v.).

BRIFFAULT, ROBERT. 1927. *The Mothers*. George Allen and Unwin, London.

BRONFENBRENNER, M. 1969. 'Economic Consequences of Technological Change', in BAIER, K. and RESCHER, B. (q.v.).

BROWN, GEORGE E., JR. Oct 1971. 'Physics and Social Change' *Physics Today 24* (10): 23–7.

BRYCE, J. 1917. *The American Commonwealth*. ii: 293. Macmillan, N.Y.

BUBER, MARTIN. 1960. *Paths in Utopia*. Beacon Press, Boston.

BUCKE, P. M. 1905. *Cosmic Consciousness*. Innes and Son, Philadelphia.

BUNZEL, R. L. 1929–30. 'Introduction to Zuñi ceremonialism', *Annual Report of Bureau of American Ethnology 47*: 480.

BURLER, J. 1972. *Polluting Britain*. Penguin, London.

BUTLER, CUTHBERT. 1922. *Western Mysticism: The Teaching of Sts Augustine, Bernard Gregory on Contemplation etc*. Constable, London.

CHANT, S. N. F. 1932. 'Measuring the factors which make a job interesting', *Personnel Journal, 11*: 1.

CLEGG, A. and MEGSON, B. 1968. *Children in Distress*. Penguin Books, London.

COHN, N. 1957. *The Pursuit of the Millennium*. Secker and Warburg, London (Paladin, London, 1970).

COMFORT, A. 1950. *Authority and Delinquency in the Modern State: A Criminological Approach to the Problem of Power*. Routledge and Kegan Paul, London.

COOPER, DAVID. 1971. *The Death of the Family*. Allen and Unwin, London.

COOPER, ROBERT. Feb 1968. 'The Psychology of Boredom', *Science Journal 4*: 38–42.

CRANSTON, MAURICE (ed.) 1970. *The New Left: Six Critical Essays*. The Bodley Head, London.

COWPER, WILLIAM. 1816. *Memoir of the Early Life of William Cowper Esq. Written by Himself*. R. Edwards, London.

DANIELS, F. 1970. *Direct Use of the Sun's Energy*. Yale U.P., New Haven and London.

DE CLOSETS, FRANÇOIS. 1970. *En Danger de Progrès*. Denoël, Paris.

DE JOUVENEL, B. 1967. 'Technology as a Means', in BAIER, K. and RESCHER, B. (q.v.).

DOLLARD, J. and MILLER, N. E. *et al.* 1944. *Frustration and Aggression*. Yale U.P., Newhaven, Conn., and Routledge and Kegan Paul, London.

DOUGLAS, MARY. 1970. *Natural Symbols: Explorations in Cosmology*. Barrie and Rockliff: The Cresset Press, London.

DOWNS, ANTHONY. March 1971. 'New Directions in Urban Research', *Technology Review* pp. 27–35.

DRUCKER, PETER. 1947. *Big Business*. Heinemann, London.

DUBLIN, L. 1963. *Suicide: A Sociological and Statistical Study*. Ronald Press, N.Y.

DUCHENE, E. (ed). 1970. *The Endless Crisis: America in the 70's*. Simon and Schuster, N.Y.

DURANDEAUX, J. 1968. *Les Journées de Mai 1968*. Desclée de Brouwer, Paris.

DURKHEIM, EMILE. 1964. *Suicide: A Study in Sociology*. Routledge and Kegan Paul, London.

EDDINS, BERKLEY. Dec 1971. 'Presidential Candidates as Social Thinkers', *The Center Report* (published by the Center for the Study of Democratic Institutions, Santa Barbara, California) p. 15.

ELLUL, JACQUES. 1965. *The Technological Society*. Jonathan Cape, London.

ERIKSON, ERIK. 1946. 'Ego Deviation and Historical Change', in *Psychoanalytic Study of the Child II*, International Universities Press, N.Y.

——1960. 'The Problem of Ego Identity' in STEIN, M. *et al.* (q.v.).

——1971. *Identity: Youth and Crisis*. Faber and Faber, London.

ETZIONI, A. and REMP, R. 7 Jan 1972. 'Technological "Shortcuts" to Social Change', *Science 175*: 31–38

EYSENCK, H. J. 1952. *The Scientific Study of Personality*. Praeger, N.Y.

——1954. *The Psychology of Politics*. Routledge and Kegan Paul, London.

——1970. *Crime and Personality*. Paladin, London.

FAUSSET, H. 1926. *Samuel Taylor Coleridge*. Jonathan Cape, London.

FORRESTER, J. W. 1971. *World Dynamics*. Wright-Allen Press, Cambridge, Mass.

FORTUNE, R. F. 1932. *Sorcerers of Dobu: The Social Anthropology of the Dobu Islanders in the Western Pacific*. George Routledge and Sons, London.

FRANKL, VICTOR. 1964. *Man's Search for Meaning*. Hodder and Stoughton, London.

FRIED, EDRITA. 1970. *Active/Passive: The Crucial Psychological Dimension*. Grune and Stratton, N.Y. and London.

FROMM, ERICH. 1956. *The Sane Society*. Routledge and Kegan Paul, London.

FÜRER-HAIMENDORF, C. VON. 1963. *Morals and Merit*. Weidenfeld and Nicolson, London.

GABOR, D. 1958. Inaugural Address, Imperial College, London.

GALBRAITH, J. K. 1969. *The Affluent Society*. Hamish Hamilton, London.

GILLMAN, P. and WOOLF, A. 2nd April 1972. 'The Dangerous Dust', *The Sunday Times Magazine*, pp. 32 ff.

GINSBERG, M. 1956–61. *The Diversity of Morals: Essays on Sociology and Social Philosophy*, Vol 3. Routledge and Kegan Paul, London.

GOLDMAN, MARSHAL J. (ed.) 1967. *Controlling Pollution*. Prentice-Hall, N.Y.

GOODMAN, PAUL. 1961. *Growing Up Absurd*. Gollancz, London.

GOULDEN, JOSEPH C. 1970. *Monopoly*. Pocket Book Edn, N.Y.

GREENACRE, P. 1953. *Trauma, Growth and Personality*. Hogarth Press, London.

GRINKER, R. R. (ed). 1952. *Towards a Unified Theory of Human Behaviour*. Basic Books, London and N.Y.

HALL, P. and LOCKE, H. W. 1938. *Incentives and Contentment*. Pitman, London.

HANDLER, PHILIP. 1970. 'Can Man Shape his Future?', The 1970 W.O. Atwater Memorial Lecture. *Perspectives in Biology and Medicine 14* (2): 207–27.

HARING, DOUGLAS E. (ed.) 1949. *Personal Character and Cultural Milieu*. Syracuse, N.Y.

HERZBERG, F. (*et al.*) 1959. *The Motivation to Work*. J. Wiley and Co., N.Y.

HERZOG, E. and INDIA, C. E. 1970. *Boys in Fatherless Families*. Office of Child Development, Washington D. C.

HITSCHMANN, EDUARD. 1932. 'Psychoanalytisches zur Personlichkeit Goethes', reprinted in *Neurose und Genialität* (Johannes Cremerius ed.), 1971. S. Fischer Verlag, Frankfurt-am-Main.

HOLBROOK, DAVID. Aug 1968. 'R. D. Laing and the Death Circuit', *Encounter*, pp. 35 ff.

HOLLANDER, M. H. 1970. 'The Wish to Be Held', *Archives of General Psychiatry 22*: 445–453.

HOOK, S. 1967. *Human Values and Economic Policy*. University Press, N.Y.

HUNT, A. M. 1935–6. 'A Study of the Relative Nature of Certain Ideals', *J. Abn. and Soc. Psychol. 30*: 222–4.

JACKSON, T. (ed.). 1865. *Lives of Early Methodist Preachers*. Wesleyan Conference Office, London.

JACOBS, J. Jan/Feb 1972. 'Pollution, Consumerism, Accountability', *The Center Magazine*, p. 45.

JACQUES, E. 1956. *Measurement of Responsibility*. Tavistock Publications, London.

JAMES, WILLIAM. 1890. *The Principles of Psychology*. Macmillan, London.

JONES, HOWARD. 1963. *Alcohol Addiction*. Tavistock Publications, London.

JOSEPHSON, E. and M. (eds). 1962. *Man Alone*. Dell Publishing, N.Y.

KANTOR, M. B. (ed.). 1965. *Mobility and Mental Health*. C. C. Thomas, Springfield, Ill.

KAPLAN, B. (ed.). 1961. *Studying Personality Cross-culturally*. Row, Peterson, and Co., N.Y.

KARDINER, ABRAM. 1939. *The Individual and his Society*. Columbia U.P., N.Y.

——1945. *The Psychological Frontiers of Society*. Columbia U.P. N.Y.

KATZ, DAVID. 1937. *Animals and Men*. Longmans, London.

KENISTON, KENNETH. 1965. *The Uncommitted*. Harcourt Brace and World, N.Y.

——1963. 'Inburn: An American Ishmael', in WHITE, R. W. (q.v.).

KLUCKHOHN, C. and LEIGHTON, D. C. 1946. *The Navaho*. Harvard U.P., Cambridge, Mass. (1962 Doubleday, Garden City).

KLUCKHOHN, F. 1952. 'Value Orientations', in *Towards a United Theory of Human Behaviour* (ed. BRINKER, R. R.). Basic Books, N.Y.

KROPOTKIN, P. A. 1912. *Fields, Factories and Workshops*. Nelson, London.

LADD, JOHN. 1957. *The Structure of a Moral Code*. Harvard U.P., Cambridge, Mass.

LAING, R. D. 1965. *The Divided Self: An Existential Study in Sanity and Madness*. Pelican Books, London.

——1967. *The Politics of Experience and the Bird of Paradise*. Penguin Books, London.

LANGNER, T. S. and MICHAEL, S. T. 1963. *Life Stress and Mental Health*. Free Press, Glencoe, Ill.

LATANE, B. and DARLEY, J. M. 1970. *The Unresponsive Bystander*. Appleton-Century-Crofts, N.Y.

LAVE, L. B. and SESKIN, E. P. 1970. 'Air Pollution and Human Health', *Science 169* (3947), pp. 723–31.

LEARY, TIMOTHY. 1970. *The Politics of Ecstasy*. MacGibbon and Kee, London.

LE BLANC, J. B. 1747. *Letters on the English and French Nations*. J. Brindley *et al.*, London.

LIN YUTANG. 1939. *The Importance of Living*. Heinemann, London.

LINDBECK, A. 1972. *The Political Economy of the New Left—An Outsider's View*. Harper and Row, N.Y.

MCCLELLAND, D. 1961. *The Achieving Society*. Van Nostrand, Princeton.

MCCORMICK, D. 1964. *The Unseen Killer*. Muller, London.

MCCORD, W. and J. 1959. *Origins of Crime*. Columbia U.P., N.Y.

MCIVER, R. M. 1961. *Society: An Introductory Analysis*. Macmillan, N.Y.

MALINOWSKI, B. 1932. *The Sexual Life of Savages in North-Western Melanesia*. Routledge and Sons, London.

——1944. *A Scientific Theory of Culture*. Univ. of N. Carolina Press, Chapel Hill, N.C.

MASLOW, A. 1954/70. *Motivation and Personality*. Harper and Row, N.Y.

MASSERMAN, J. H. 1964. *Behaviour and Neurosis: An Experimental Psychoanalytical Approach to Psychobiological Principles*. Hafner, N.Y.

MEAD, MARGARET. 1937. *Co-operation and Competition in Primitive Societies*. McGraw-Hill, N.Y. and London.

——1950. *Male and Female: A Study of the Sexes in a Changing World*. Gollancz, London.

——1955. *Cultural Patterns and Technical Change*. Man and Nature. Lectures for American Museum of Natural History.

——1960. 'Culture Change and Character Structure' in STEIN, M. *et al.* (q.v.).

MEADOWS, D. L. *et al.* 1972. *The Limits to Growth*. Earth Island, London.

MERTON, ROBERT K. 1938. 'Social Structure and Anomie', *American Sociological Review 3*: 672–80.

——1957. *Social Theory and Social Structure*. Free Press, Glencoe, Ill.

MILLER, P. and JOHNSON, J. H. 1938. *The Puritans*. The American Book Co., N.Y.

MISHAN, E. J. 1969. *Growth: The Price We Pay*. Staples Press, London.

MITSCHERLICH, V. A. 1969. *Society Without The Father*. Tavistock Publications, London.

MONTAGU, ASHLEY. 1970. *The Direction of Human Development*. Hawthorn Books Inc., N.Y. (revised).

——1971. *Touching*. Columbia U.P., London.

MORGAN, GEORGE W. 1968. *The Human Predicament*. Dell Publishing, N.Y.

MUGGERIDGE, MALCOLM. 1967. *Tread Softly*. Collins, London.

NEIDORF, ROBERT. 1971. 'The Missing Sense of the Past', *The Center Magazine* Vol. *IV*(1): 54–5.

NEUMANN, F. 1960. 'Anxiety and Politics' in STEIN, M. *et al.* (q.v.).

NISBET, ROBERT. 1962. *Community and Power*. Oxford U.P., London.

OSTERGAARD, G. and CURRELL, M. 1971. *The Gentle Anarchists*. The Clarendon Press, Oxford.

OTTO, RUDOLPH. 1925. *The Idea of the Holy*. Humphrey Mitford, London.

PACKARD, VANCE. 1959. *The Status Seekers*. David McKay, N.Y.

PAPANEK, V. 1972. *Design for the Real World: Making to Measure*. Thames and Hudson, London.

PARK, R. E. 1952. *Human Communities*. Free Press, Glencoe, Ill.

PIERS, G. and SINGER, M. B. 1953. *Shame and Guilt*. C. C. Thomas, Springfield, Ill.

PLATT, JOHN. 28 Nov 1969. 'What We Must Do', *Science 166*: 1115.

POLANYI, MICHAEL. 1958. *Personal Knowledge—Towards a Post-Critical Philosophy*. Routledge and Kegan Paul, London.

POWELL, E. H. 1970. *The Design of Discord*. Oxford U.P., London.

PRICE, UVEDALE. 1794. *On the Picturesque*. Edinburgh and London.

RADZINOWICZ, L. 1966. *Authority and Crime*. Columbia U.P., N.Y.

READ, HERBERT. 1954. *Anarchy and Order*. Faber and Faber, London.

REDDAWAY, W. B. 1939. *The Economics of a Declining Population*. Allen and Unwin, London.

REICH, CHARLES. 1970. *The Greening of America*. Random House, N.Y.

REYNOLDS, M. 1909. *The Treatment of Nature in English Poetry between Pope and Wordsworth*. Chicago U.P.

RIBBLE, MARGARET. 1945. *The Rights of Infants*. Columbia U.P., N.Y.

RIESMAN, DAVID. 1961. *The Lonely Crowd*. Yale U.P., New Haven, Conn.

ROKEACH, M. 'The Measurement of Values and Value Systems.' Michigan State University, n.d.

ROSZAK, T. 1969. *The Making of a Counter-Culture*. Anchor Books, N.Y; Faber and Faber, London.

SCHON, DONALD. 1967. *Technology and Change: The New Heraclitus*. Pergamon, London.

———1971. *Beyond the Stable State*. Temple Smith, London.

SCHUECKING, L. L. 1929. *Die Familie in Puritanismus*. B. G. Teubner, Leipzig and Berlin.

SCHUMACHER, E. F. 1968. 'Buddhist economics', *Resurgence 1*: (11).

SEARS, R. R., MCCOBY, E. and LEVIN, M. 1957. *Patterns of Child Rearing*. Row, Peterson, N.Y.

SEELEY, J. R. (*et al.*). 1956. *Crestwood Heights: A Study of the Culture of Suburban Life*. Basic Books, N.Y., and Constable, London.

SHAFTESBURY (3RD EARL). 1732. *The Characteristicks*. London.

SKINNER, B. F. 1962. *Walden II*. Macmillan Paperbacks, N.Y.

———1972. *Beyond Freedom and Dignity*. Jonathan Cape, London.

SMELSER, NEIL and WILLIAM. 1963. *Personality and Social System*. Wiley, N.Y.

SPINLEY, B. M. 1953. *The Deprived and the Privileged*. Routledge and Kegan Paul, London.

SROLE, LEO. 1956. 'Social Integration and Certain Corollaries: An Exploratory Study', *American Sociological Review 21* (6): 709–16.

STEFFENS, LINCOLN. 1931. *Autobiography*. Harcourt Brace, N.Y.

STEIN, M., VIDICH, A. J. and WHITE, D. M. (eds). 1960. *Identity and Anxiety*. The Free Press, N.Y.

STEPHENSON, G. M. 1966. *The Development of Conscience*. Routledge and Kegan Paul, London.

STORR, ANTHONY. 1970. *Integration of the Personality*. Pelican Books, London.

STOTT, D. H. 1956. *Unsettled Children and their Families*. Univ. of London Press.

SUGGS, R. C. 1966. *Marquesan Sexual Behaviour*. Constable, London.

SZASZ, THOMAS S. 1971. *The Manufacture of Madness*. Routledge and Kegan Paul, London.

TAWNEY, R. H. 1926. *Religion and the Rise of Capitalism*. Murray, London and N.Y.

TAYLOR, G. RATTRAY. 1947. *Economics for the Exasperated*. The Bodley Head, London.

———1948. 'The Nature of an Organic Society', *The Sociological Review XL*: 57–65.

TAYLOR, RATTRAY G. 1949a. *Conditions of Happiness.* The Bodley Head, London.

——1949b. 'Total Partnership: a French social experiment', in *Future IV* (5): 70–7.

——1950a. *Are Workers Human?* The Falcon Press, London.

——1950b. *Accountability to Parliament.* Acton Society Trust, London.

——1954. *Sex in History.* Thames and Hudson, London.

——1958. *The Angel Makers.* William Heinemann, London.

——1968. *The Biological Time-Bomb.* Thames and Hudson, London.

——1970. *The Doomsday Book.* Thames and Hudson, London.

TAYLOR, LYNDA KING. 1972. *Not for Bread Alone: An Appreciation of Job Enrichment.* Business Books, London.

TENNYSON, ALFRED LORD. 1897. *A Memoir by his Son.* Macmillan, London.

TISELIUS, A. 1970. 'The Place of Values in a World of Facts', in *Nobel Symposium 14.* Almqvist and Wiksell, Stockholm; Wiley, New York.

TOFFLER, ALVIN. 1970. *Future Shock.* Random House, N.Y.

TÖNNIES, FERDINAND. 1955. *Community and Association.* Routledge and Kegan Paul, London.

TOWNSEND, P. 1962. 'Isolation, Loneliness and the Hold on Life', in JOSEPHSON, E. and M. (q.v.).

TOWNSEND, ROBERT. Jan/Feb 1972. 'The Ups and Downs of Working Life', *The Center Magazine V* (1): 27–38.

VICKERS, G. 1968. *Value Systems and Social Process.* Tavistock Publications, London.

——1970. *Freedom in a Rocking Boat: Changing Values in an Unstable Society.* Allen Lane, The Penguin Press, London.

——1971. 'Changing Ethics of Distribution', *Futures 3* (2).

WADDINGTON, C. H. 28 Jan 1972. *Nature 235:233*

WAY, LEWIS. 1948. *Man's Quest for Significance.* Allen and Unwin, London.

WEDGWOOD BENN, ANTHONY. 1970. *The New Politics: A Socialist Reconaissance.* Fabian Society Tract No. 402, London.

WHEELIS, ALLEN. 1959. *The Quest for Identity.* Gollancz, London.

WHITE, R. W. (ed.) 1963. *The Study of Lives.* Atherton Press, N.Y.

WHITEHEAD, ALFRED NORTH. 1925. *Science and the Modern World.* MacMillan, N.Y.

WHITEHEAD, T. N. 1936. *Leadership in a Free Society.* Cambridge U.P.

WILLS, W. D. 1945. *The Barns Experiment.* Allen and Unwin, London.

WINTHROP, HENRY. 1968. *Ventures in Social Interpretation.* Appleton-Century-Crofts, N.Y.

——1971. *Psychological Aspects of Community: Alienation Identity and Social Behaviour.* MSS Educ. Publ., N.Y.

ZETZNER, J. E. 1905. *Londres et l'Angleterre A.D. 1700* (ed. R. Reuss). Librairie Noiviel, Strasbourg.

Index